Book 7: Financial Planning Case Studies

Financial Education

KAPLAN UNIVERSITY SCHOOL OF PROFESSIONAL AND CONTINUING EDUCATION

At press time, this edition contains the most complete and accurate information currently available. Due to the nature of advanced designation examinations, however, information may have been added recently to the actual test that does not appear in this edition. Please contact the publisher to verify that you have the most current edition.

This publication is designed to provide accurate and authoritative information in regard to the subject matter covered. It is sold with the understanding that the publisher is not engaged in rendering legal, accounting, or other professional services. If legal advice or other expert assistance is required, the services of a competent professional should be sought.

KAPLAN UNIVERSITY SCHOOL OF PROFESSIONAL AND CONTINUING EDUCATION
FINANCIAL EDUCATION REVIEW FOR THE CFP® CERTIFICATION EXAMINATION BOOK 7:
FINANCIAL PLANNING CASE STUDIES 2017
©2017 Kaplan, Inc. All rights reserved.

CLU®, ChFC®, Registered Health Underwriter®, RHU®, REBC® Chartered Life Underwriter®, Chartered Financial Consultant®, Registered Employee Benefits Consultant®, Chartered Advisor for Senior Living™, and CASL™ are registered trademarks of The American College.

CPCU®, ARM®, and AIC® are registered trademarks of the American Institute for CPCU and the Insurance Institute of America.

CFP®, CERTIFIED FINANCIAL PLANNER™, and CFP® are certification marks or registered certification marks of Certified Financial Planner Board of Standards, Inc.

Published by Kaplan Financial Education

Printed in the United States of America.

ISBN: 978-1-4754-4486-5

Preface

KAPLAN FINANCIAL EDUCATION REVIEW COURSES FOR THE CFP® EXAM

Kaplan Financial Education offers several options to meet the diverse needs of candidates.

THE LIVE REVIEW COURSE

Instruction in both the traditional and virtual classroom programs consists mainly of teaching substantive material and helping students master both the knowledge and application of topics that they will likely encounter on the exam. Material is also presented integrating CFP Board's Job Task Domains with exam topics. The course includes working through various types of problems to ensure that the substantive materials taught can be applied to exam-like questions. Students also receive instruction in actual exam-management techniques.

Many videos are available to Live Review students. These videos help students study important CFP® Exam topics prior to the Live Review. In preparation for the Live Review, students also have access to videos that help them with case studies and the Kaplan Financial Education mock exam.

Traditional Classroom Program

Kaplan Financial Education offers the Traditional Classroom Program in major metropolitan areas across the country. The Four-Day Review is an intensive program consisting of over 30 hours of instruction conducted, in most cases, Thursday through Sunday.

The Virtual Classroom Program

Kaplan Financial Education's Virtual Review is an instructor-led, web-based program that provides all the benefits of a classroom review from the convenience of the student's home or office. This program format is a great option for those who have access to the web and prefer not to incur the expense of travel. This course is an intensive program consisting of 33 hours of instruction in 11 three-hour classes. Students receive real-time interaction with their instructor and have access to a recorded playback option. Playbacks are available for review until the first day of the CFP® Exam.

LIVE REVIEW STUDY TOOLS

In-Class Guide

The In-Class Guide is an easy-to-use Live Review class companion with study notes to help keep students organized during and after class.

Diagnostic Exam

Available only to Live Review students, the Diagnostic Exam allows students to identify areas of strength and weakness prior to studying for the CFP® Exam. This study aid allows students to tailor their study plans to the areas identified on a report provided once the Diagnostic Exam is completed.

Pre-Review Videos

Available on demand, pre-review videos provide additional instruction for those taking the CFP® Exam. Viewing these videos early in the study process helps students understand how CFP Board may test topics.

Case Videos

A considerable number of points for the CFP® Exam are case-related, so case preparation is critical. Students can develop important case analysis skills with this on-demand study tool.

Mock Exam Videos

Students learn how to approach the CFP® Exam with this video that provides exam strategies to be used as they take the online mock exam and the national CFP® Exam.

BOOKS 1–6

Books 1–6 contain complete reference outlines that give detailed coverage of each of the six tested areas of the CFP® Exam. Each book contains examples, illustrations, and an index. Each book has been updated to reflect 2017 law and inflation adjustments available at date of printing.

BOOK 7—FINANCIAL PLANNING CASE STUDIES

Book 7—Financial Planning Case Studies is designed to prepare students for the comprehensive cases included on the exam. This valuable study tool provides the exam candidate with 12 comprehensive cases, item sets, and mini-cases that test students' knowledge and application of the exam topics. The answers and explanations for each multiple-choice question are provided, and the text has been updated to reflect 2017 law and inflation adjustments available at the date of printing. Students who have used the *Financial Planning Case Studies* have said that this book is a must to be prepared for the exam.

MOCK EXAM AND SOLUTIONS

Mock Exam and Solutions simulates the six-hour comprehensive CFP® Exam. Much like the actual exam, this online exam is divided into two sessions with a three-hour time limit for each session. Each session contains multiple-choice questions, item sets, and comprehensive cases. This mock exam serves as a diagnostic tool useful in identifying a student's areas of strength and weakness and can be used to help them focus on topics that they find more difficult. The mock exam is also updated to reflect 2017 law and inflation adjustments.

UNDERSTANDING YOUR FINANCIAL CALCULATOR

Understanding Your Financial Calculator is a book designed to assist students in gaining proficiency in using a financial calculator to work through problems they may encounter on the exam. In addition to helping master the keystrokes for the financial calculator, it is also designed to assist students with the underlying financial theory of these problems. All calculations are worked out step by step, showing keystrokes and displays for several of the most popular financial calculators. For more information, contact a Kaplan academic advisor at 1-877-446-9034 or advisor@kaplan.com.

EXAM PREP/REVIEW (EPR) ONLINE REVIEW QBANK

Designed to be used in conjunction with Books 1–7 and the mock exam, the EPR online review QBank is an interactive software product of high cognitive level questions designed to give students practice in answering questions relating to content most likely tested on the CFP® Exam. There are two cognitive levels of questions in the EPR QBank:

- Analyze & Apply QBank: higher cognitive exam-type level questions that challenge students studying for the CFP® Exam.
- Recall & Review QBank: questions that reinforce knowledge that CFP® Exam candidates should have at a base level. It is intended to be used for the review of concepts learned in CFP® Exam base courses or as a refresher for those students challenging the exam.

Students can create customized, timed practice quizzes from the six topics tested on the CFP® Exam. All practice quizzes are scored and allow students to analyze their competencies by topical areas. Customized quizzes may be saved for future reference.

CORE LECTURE VIDEOS

Students can reinforce their knowledge and application of the core concepts of the CFP® Exam with online videos. Explanations and examples of these concepts are presented in an easy-to-understand manner by subject matter experts.

EXAM TIPS VIDEOS

Students have the opportunity to watch innovative videos that provide strategies and tips for CFP® Exam preparation. Video topics include CFP Board domains and topics, the CFP® Exam format, how to approach multiple-choice questions and case studies, Kaplan Financial Education tools available for exam success, and what to expect on exam day.

FROM THE PUBLISHER

This text is intended as the basis for preparation for the CFP® Exam, either as self-study or as part of a review course. The material is organized according to the six functional areas tested on the exam and is presented in an outline format that includes examples and illustrations that help candidates quickly comprehend the material.

The material is organized into six manageable study books and a comprehensive case book:

- *Book 1—General Financial Planning Principles, Professional Conduct, and Regulation*
- *Book 2—Risk Management, Insurance, and Employee Benefits Planning*
- *Book 3—Investment Planning*
- *Book 4—Tax Planning*
- *Book 5—Retirement Savings and Income Planning*
- *Book 6—Estate Planning*
- *Book 7—Financial Planning Case Studies*

We are indebted to Certified Financial Planner Board of Standards, Inc. for permission to reproduce and adapt their publications and other materials.

Wishing you success on the exam,

Kaplan Financial Education

CONTRIBUTING AUTHORS

- Kathy L. Berlin
    - —Senior Content Specialist, Kaplan Financial Education
    - —Successfully passed CFP® Certification Examination
    - —Certified Public Accountant (Inactive)
    - —BA from Loyola University of New Orleans, Louisiana
    - —Former CFO of a large nonprofit organization
    - —Co-author of Kaplan Financial Education's *Personal Financial Planning Cases and Applications, 5th–8th Editions* textbook and instructor manual
    - —Co-author of Kaplan University/Financial Education's *Personal Financial Planning Cases and Applications, 9th Edition* textbook and instructor manual
    - —Co-author of Kaplan Financial Education's *Personal Financial Planning Theory and Practice, 4th–7th Editions* textbook and instructor manual
    - —Co-author of Kaplan University/Financial Education's *Personal Financial Planning Theory and Practice, 8th–9th Editions* textbook and instructor manual
    - —Co-author of the *Kaplan Schweser Review for the CFP® Certification Examination, 9th–14th Editions*
    - —Co-author of the *Kaplan Schweser Review for the CFP® Certification Examination, July–November 2010, March–November 2011, and 2012–2013 Exams*
    - —Co-author of Kaplan University/Financial Education's *CFP® Exam Prep Review Books 1–7, 2014–2017*
    - —Co-author of the *Kaplan University/Kaplan Schweser Certification Examination Education Program, 4th–11th Editions* materials
    - —Co-author of Kaplan University/Financial Education's *CFP® Exam Required Education Course Materials 2014–2017*
- Glen Kramer, MSF, CRPC®, GCPM, PMP®, CFP®
    - —Senior Content Specialist, Kaplan Financial Education
    - —BS in Economics from University of Wisconsin–Stevens Point
    - —MSF from Kaplan University
    - —Over 12 years of experience in the insurance and securities business
    - —Former General Securities Representative
    - —Former Life and Health Insurance Licensed Sales Representative in Arizona, Nevada, and Wisconsin
    - —Co-author of Kaplan Financial Education's *Personal Financial Planning Cases and Applications, 7th and 8th Editions* textbook and instructor manual
    - —Co-author of Kaplan University/Financial Education's *Personal Financial Planning Cases and Applications, 9th Edition* textbook and instructor manual

—Co-author of Kaplan Financial Education's *Personal Financial Planning Theory and Practice, 7th Edition* textbook and instructor manual

—Co-author of Kaplan University/Financial Education's *Personal Financial Planning Theory and Practice, 8th–9th Editions* textbook and instructor manual

—Co-author of the *Kaplan Schweser Review for the CFP® Certification Examination, March–November 2011, and 2012–2013 Exams*

—Co-author of Kaplan University/Financial Education's *CFP® Exam Prep Review Books 1–7, 2014–2017*

—Co-author of the *Kaplan University/Kaplan Schweser Certification Examination Education Program, 8th–11th Editions* materials

—Co-author of Kaplan University/Financial Education's *CFP® Exam Required Education Course Materials 2014–2017*

■ Michael Long, CLU®, ChFC®, CFP®

—Senior Content Specialist, Kaplan Financial Education

—Over 25 years' experience in insurance and securities as a sales manager, classroom instructor, product manager, and advanced underwriting consultant

—BS in Business Administration, Indiana State University

—Co-author of Kaplan Financial Education's *Personal Financial Planning Cases and Applications, 6th–8th Editions* textbook and instructor manual

—Co-author of Kaplan University/Financial Education's *Personal Financial Planning Cases and Applications, 9th Edition* textbook and instructor manual

—Co-author of Kaplan Financial Education's *Personal Financial Planning Theory and Practice, 6th–7th Editions* textbook and instructor manual

—Co-author of Kaplan University/Financial Education's *Personal Financial Planning Theory and Practice, 8th–9th Editions* textbook and instructor manual

—Co-author of the *Schweser Review for the CFP® Certification Examination, 13th–14th Editions*

—Co-author of the *Kaplan Schweser Review for the CFP® Certification Examination, July–November 2010 Exams, and 2012–2013 Exams*

—Co-author of Kaplan University/Financial Education's *CFP® Exam Prep Review Books 1–7, 2014–2017*

—Co-author of the *Kaplan University/Kaplan Schweser Certification Examination Education Program, 8th–11th Editions* materials

—Co-author of Kaplan University/Financial Education's *CFP® Exam Required Education Course Materials 2014–2017*

■ James Maher, MBA, CLU®, ChFC®, CFP®

—Senior Content Specialist, Kaplan Financial Education

—Former securities and insurance instructor, Kaplan Financial

—Former Insurance Representative – General Securities

—BBA from Florida International University

—MBA from Kaplan University

—Co-author of Kaplan Financial Education's *Personal Financial Planning Cases and Applications, 6th–8th Editions* textbook and instructor manual

—Co-author of Kaplan University/Financial Education's *Personal Financial Planning Cases and Applications, 9th Edition* textbook and instructor manual

—Co-author of Kaplan Financial Education's *Personal Financial Planning Theory and Practice, 5th–7th Editions* textbook and instructor manual

—Co-author of Kaplan University/Financial Education's *Personal Financial Planning Theory and Practice, 8th–9th Editions* textbook and instructor manual

—Co-author of the *Kaplan Schweser Review for the CFP® Certification Examination, 12th–14th Editions*

—Co-author of the *Kaplan Schweser Review for the CFP® Certification Examination, July–November 2010, March–November 2011, and 2012–2013 Exams*

—Co-author of Kaplan University/Financial Education's *CFP® Exam Prep Review Books 1–7, 2014–2017*

—Co-author of the *Kaplan University/Kaplan Schweser Certification Examination Education Program, 6th–11th Editions* materials

—Co-author of Kaplan University/Financial Education's *CFP® Exam Required Education Course Materials 2014–2017*

■ Cindy R. Riecke, MSF, CLU®, ChFC®, CFP®

—Senior Director, Kaplan Financial Education

—BS in Business Administration from Louisiana State University in Baton Rouge, Louisiana

—MSF from Kaplan University

—Member of the Financial Planning Association

—Former Director of Marketing Development for an international insurance and financial services company

—Co-author of Kaplan Financial Education's *Personal Financial Planning Cases and Applications, 5th–8th Editions* textbook and instructor manual

—Co-author of Kaplan University/Financial Education's *Personal Financial Planning Cases and Applications, 9th Edition* textbook and instructor manual

—Co-author of Kaplan Financial Education's *Personal Financial Planning Theory and Practice, 4th–7th Editions* textbook and instructor manual

—Co-author of Kaplan University/Financial Education's *Personal Financial Planning Theory and Practice, 8th–9th Editions* textbook and instructor manual

—Co-author of the *Kaplan Schweser Review for the CFP® Certification Examination, 9th–14th Editions*

—Co-author of the *Kaplan Schweser Review for the CFP® Certification Examination, July–November 2010, March–November 2011, and 2012–2013 Exams*

—Co-author of Kaplan University/Financial Education's *CFP® Exam Prep Review Books 1–7, 2014–2017*

—Co-author of the *Kaplan University/Kaplan Schweser Certification Examination Education Program, 4th–11th Editions* materials

—Co-author of Kaplan University/Financial Education's *CFP® Exam Required Education Course Materials 2014–2017*

- Stephan E. Wolter, JD, MBA, ChFC®

  —Senior Content Specialist, Kaplan Financial Education

  —Successfully passed July 2008 CFP® Certification Examination

  —JD from Indiana University, Indianapolis

  —MBA from University of Colorado at Colorado Springs

  —Co-author of Kaplan Financial Education's *Personal Financial Planning Cases and Applications, 6th–8th Editions* textbook and instructor manual

  —Co-author of Kaplan University/Financial Education's *Personal Financial Planning Cases and Applications, 9th Edition* textbook and instructor manual

  —Co-author of Kaplan Financial Education's *Personal Financial Planning Theory and Practice, 6th–7th Editions* textbook and instructor manual

  —Co-author of Kaplan University/Financial Education's *Personal Financial Planning Theory and Practice, 8th–9th Editions* textbook and instructor manual

  —Co-author of the *Kaplan Schweser Review for the CFP® Certification Examination, 13th–14th Editions*

  —Co-author of the *Kaplan Schweser Review for the CFP® Certification Examination, July–November 2010, March–November 2011, and 2012–2013 Exams*

  —Co-author of Kaplan University/Financial Education's *CFP® Exam Prep Review Books 1–7, 2014–2017*

  —Co-author of the *Kaplan University/Kaplan Schweser Certification Examination Education Program, 7th–11th Editions* materials

  —Co-author of Kaplan University/Financial Education's *CFP® Exam Required Education Course Materials 2014–2017*

ACKNOWLEDGMENTS AND SPECIAL THANKS

We are most appreciative of the tremendous support and encouragement we have received from everyone throughout this project, and are extremely grateful to the users of our texts who were gracious enough to provide us with valuable comments.

We very much appreciate the continued support of the many registered programs who have adopted our review materials. We understand that our success is a direct result of that support.

We greatly appreciate the assistance of Marguerite Merritt, who reviewed the front matter and appendices for technical accuracy and assisted the subject-matter expert team with invaluable support.

We deeply appreciate the cooperation of CFP Board for granting us permission to reproduce and adapt their publications and other materials. CFP Board's Standards of Professional Conduct, copyrighted by CFP Board, is reprinted (or adapted) with permission.

Thanks to John J. Dardis for granting us permission to use material from "Estate & Benefit Planning Symposium" in *Book 6—Estate Planning*.

Introduction

PURPOSE OF BOOKS 1–6

Books 1–6 serve as the basis for preparation for the CFP® Exam either as self-study materials or as part of a review course. These books are organized by the six topic areas tested on the exam. Each book presents its core content in outline format using examples, illustrations, and exhibits to help candidates quickly comprehend the material.

Books 1–6 cover the following topics, and *Book 7* is a comprehensive case book, which integrates all six topics covered in *Books 1–6*:

- *Book 1—General Financial Planning Principles, Professional Conduct, and Regulation*
- *Book 2—Risk Management, Insurance, and Employee Benefits Planning*
- *Book 3—Investment Planning*
- *Book 4—Tax Planning*
- *Book 5—Retirement Savings and Income Planning*
- *Book 6—Estate Planning*
- *Book 7—Financial Planning Case Studies*

ABOUT THE CFP® EXAM

EXAMINATION PROCEDURES

Read carefully the procedures outlined in the *Guide to CFP® Certification*, available at www.cfp.net. The section entitled "CFP® Certification Examination" covers:

- dates of examinations;
- alternate test dates and test facilities;
- fees for the examination;
- scheduling confirmations;
- withdrawal from the exam;
- medical emergencies;
- items to bring to the examination;
- examination misconduct;
- examination scoring;
- score reports;
- pass score;
- reexamination procedures; and
- review and appeals.

A copy of the *Guide to CFP® Certification* also may be obtained from CFP Board, at the following address:

Certified Financial Planner Board of Standards, Inc.
1425 K Street, NW, Suite 500
Washington, DC 20005
Telephone: 1-800-487-1497
Fax: 1-202-379-2299
Website: www.cfp.net
Email: mail@CFPBoard.org

DATE GIVEN

The exam is administered at Prometric locations three times a year in March, July, and November over a five-day window in each month.

It is the student's responsibility to verify the exam and registration dates, as well as register for the exam.

For updates and information regarding the CFP® Exam, your exam registration, exam application deadlines, and so forth, please refer to CFP Board's website at www.cfp.net.

For updates to Kaplan Financial Education study materials (e.g., errata, legislative changes, and inflation-adjusted tax rate summaries), please refer to the EPR Updates/Errata folder on the Exam Prep Review dashboard.

QUESTION TYPES

The examination consists of approximately 170 multiple-choice questions. The majority of these are stand-alone questions that contain all relevant information within the body of the question. Also included are item set and mini-case questions where one fact pattern will be used to answer multiple questions. A portion of the exam is in the form of case analysis. There will be one case in either or both of the two exam sessions; each case will have approximately 10–15 questions. The information needed to answer these questions is generally found within the body of the case. These cases can be several pages long, making it somewhat difficult to efficiently organize the information to answer the questions.

The stand-alone questions, item sets, mini-cases, and case questions may test only one particular area of financial planning, such as investments. Many of the questions, however, are integrated questions, meaning that more than one topic is covered in the question. For example, a question might integrate investments and taxation. These integrated questions are designed to test your ability to analyze fact situations involving many planning considerations.

TIME AND TIME ANALYSIS

There are six hours of examination time:

- Two 3-hour sessions separated by a 40-minute break
- Approximately 170 questions overall
- Case questions, average 10–15 per case

PASS RATES

Student pass rates have ranged from 51% to 70% on recent exams. This exam is a pass/fail professional exam with no partial credit. Therefore, it is vitally important that you be thoroughly prepared for all the topics—and the application of the topics—covered on this examination.

CFP® CERTIFICATION EXAMINATION JOB TASK DOMAINS AND PRINCIPAL TOPICS

CFP BOARD

CERTIFIED FINANCIAL PLANNER BOARD OF STANDARDS, INC.

2015 Financial Planning Job Task Domains

The following Financial Planning Job Task Domains are based on the results of CFP Board's 2015 Job Analysis Study. The Job Tasks are used to provide guidance for developing content for the CFP® Certification Examination and other case-based scenarios.

Eight Major Domains

1. **Establishing and Defining the Client-Planner Relationship**
2. **Gathering Information Necessary to Fulfill the Engagement**
3. **Analyzing and Evaluating the Client's Current Financial Status**
4. **Developing the Recommendation(s)**
5. **Communicating the Recommendation(s)**
6. **Implementing the Recommendation(s)**
7. **Monitoring the Recommendation(s)**
8. **Practicing within Professional and Regulatory Standards**

1. Establishing and Defining the Client-Planner Relationship

A) Identify the client (e.g., individual, family, business, organization)
B) Discuss the financial planning process
C) Explain scope of services offered
D) Assess and communicate ability to meet the client's needs and expectations
E) Identify and disclose conflicts of interest in client relationships
F) Discuss responsibilities of parties involved
G) Define and document the scope of the engagement
H) Provide client disclosures
    1) Regulatory disclosure
    2) Compensation arrangements and associated potential conflicts of interest

2. Gathering Information Necessary to Fulfill the Engagement

A) Explore with the client their personal and financial needs, priorities and goals
B) Assess the client's level of knowledge, experience and risk tolerance
C) Evaluate the client's risk exposures (e.g., longevity, economic, liability, healthcare)
D) Gather relevant data including:
    1) Summary of assets (e.g., cost basis information, beneficiary designations and titling)
    2) Summary of liabilities (e.g., balances, terms, interest rates)
    3) Summary of income and expenses
    4) Estate planning documents
    5) Education plan and resources
    6) Retirement plan information
    7) Employee benefits

8) Government benefits (e.g., Social Security, Medicare)
9) Special circumstances (e.g., legal documents and agreements, family situations)
10) Tax documents
11) Investment statements
12) Insurance policies and documents (e.g., life, health, disability, liability)
13) Closely held business documents (e.g., shareholder agreements)
14) Inheritances, windfalls, and other large lump sums

3. Analyzing and Evaluating the Client's Current Financial Status

A) Evaluate and document the strengths and vulnerabilities of the client's current financial situation including:
   1) Statement of financial position/balance sheet
   2) Cash flow statement
   3) Capital needs analysis (e.g., insurance, retirement, major purchases)
   4) Asset protection (e.g., titling, trusts, etc.)
   5) Asset allocation
   6) Client liquidity (e.g., emergency fund)
   7) Government benefits (e.g., Social Security, Medicare)
   8) Employee benefits
   9) Investment strategies
   10) Current, deferred and future tax liabilities
   11) Estate tax liabilities
   12) Tax considerations
   13) Income types
   14) Retirement plans and strategies (e.g., qualified plans, IRAs)
   15) Accumulation planning
   16) Distribution planning
   17) Estate documents
   18) Ownership of assets
   19) Beneficiary designations
   20) Gifting strategies
   21) Executive compensation (e.g., deferred compensation, stock options, RSUs)
   22) Succession planning and exit strategy
   23) Risk management (e.g., retained risk and insurance coverage)
   24) Educational financial aid
   25) General sources of financing
   26) Special circumstances (e.g., divorce, disabilities, family dynamics, etc.)
   27) Inheritances, windfalls, and other large lump sums
   28) Charitable planning
   29) Aging and eldercare
   30) Mental capability and capacity issues
B) Identify and use appropriate tools and techniques to conduct analyses including:
   1) Financial calculator
   2) Computer spreadsheet
   3) Financial planning software

4. Developing the Recommendation(s)

A) Evaluate alternatives to meet the client's goals and objectives
    1) Sensitivity analysis (e.g., factors outside of client control)
B) Consult with other professionals as appropriate
C) Develop recommendations considering:
    1) Client attitudes, values and beliefs
    2) Behavioral finance issues (e.g., anchoring, overconfidence, recency)
    3) Their interdependence
D) Document recommendations

5. Communicating the Recommendation(s)

A) Present financial plan and provide guidance
    1) Goals
    2) Assumptions
    3) Observations and findings
    4) Alternatives
    5) Recommendations
B) Obtain feedback from the client and revise the recommendations as appropriate
C) Provide documentation of plan recommendations and any additional disclosures
D) Verify client acceptance of recommendations

6. Implementing the Recommendation(s)

A) Create a prioritized implementation plan with timeline
B) Directly or indirectly implement the recommendations
C) Coordinate and share information, as authorized, with others
D) Define monitoring responsibilities with the client (e.g., explain what will be monitored, frequency of monitoring, communication method(s))

7. Monitoring the Recommendation(s)

A) Discuss and evaluate changes in the client's personal circumstances (e.g., aging issues, change in employment)
B) Review the performance and progress of the plan
C) Review and evaluate changes in the legal, tax and economic environments
D) Make recommendations to accommodate changed circumstances
E) Review scope of work and redefine engagement as appropriate
F) Provide ongoing client support (e.g., guidance, education)

8. Practicing within Professional and Regulatory Standards

A) Adhere to CFP Board's *Standards of Professional Conduct*
B) Manage practice risk (e.g., documentation, monitor client noncompliance with recommendations)
C) Maintain awareness of and comply with regulatory and legal guidelines

CONTEXTUAL VARIABLES

In addition to the Principal Knowledge Topics, other important variables are to be considered when dealing with specific financial planning situations. These are referred to as "Contextual Variables" and are used as part of content development for the CFP® Certification Examination or other case-based scenarios.

More specifically, financial planning situations require the application of financial planning knowledge for different types of clients. Important client details to consider as part of financial planning situations are:

- **Family Status** (traditional family, single parent, same-sex couples, blended families, widowhood)
- **Net Worth** (ultra-high net worth, high net worth, mass affluent, emerging affluent, mass market)
- **Income Level** (high, medium, low)
- **Life or Professional Stage** (student, starting a career, career transition, pre-retirement, retirement)
- **Other Circumstances** (health issues, divorce, change of employment status, aging parents, special needs children)

CFP BOARD
2015 JOB TASK ANALYSIS
EXAMINATION AND EDUCATION REQUIREMENTS

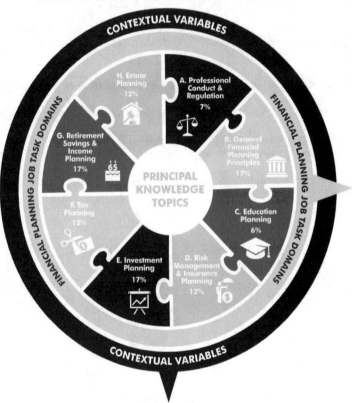

FINANCIAL PLANNING JOB TASK DOMAINS

1 Establishing & Defining the Client-Planner Relationship

2 Gathering Information Necessary to Fulfill the Engagement

3 Analyzing & Evaluating the Client's Current Financial Status

4 Developing the Recommendation(s)

5 Communicating the Recommendation(s)

6 Implementing the Recommendation(s)

7 Monitoring the Recommendation(s)

8 Practicing Within Professional & Regulatory Standards

CONTEXTUAL VARIABLES

FAMILY STATUS	NET WORTH	INCOME LEVEL	LIFE OR PROFESSIONAL STAGE	OTHER CIRCUMSTANCES
Traditional family	Ultra-high net worth	High	Student	Health issues
Single parent	High net worth	Medium	Starting a career	Divorce
Same-sex couples	Mass affluent	Low	Career transition	Change of employment status
Blended families	Emerging affluent		Pre-retirement	Aging parents
Widowhood	Mass market		Retirement	Special needs children

CERTIFIED FINANCIAL PLANNER BOARD OF STANDARDS, INC.

2015 Principal Knowledge Topics (72 Topics)

The following Principal Knowledge Topics are based on the results of CFP Board's 2015 Job Analysis Study.

The Principal Knowledge Topics serve as the blueprint for the March 2016 and later administrations of the CFP® Certification Examination. Each exam question will be linked to one of the following Principal Knowledge Topics, in the approximate percentages indicated following the general category headings.

The Principal Knowledge Topics serve as a curricular framework and also represent subject topics that CFP Board accepts for continuing education credit, effective January 2016.

Eight Principal Knowledge Topic Categories

A. Professional Conduct and Regulation (7%)

B. General Financial Planning Principles (17%)

C. Education Planning (6%)

D. Risk Management and Insurance Planning (12%)

E. Investment Planning (17%)

F. Tax Planning (12%)

G. Retirement Savings and Income Planning (17%)

H. Estate Planning (12%)

A. Professional Conduct and Regulation

A.1.   CFP Board's Code of Ethics and Professional Responsibility and Rules of Conduct

A.2.   CFP Board's Financial Planning Practice Standards

A.3.   CFP Board's Disciplinary Rules and Procedures

A.4.   Function, purpose, and regulation of financial institutions

A.5.   Financial services regulations and requirements

A.6.   Consumer protection laws

A.7.   Fiduciary

Professional Conduct & Regulation

B. General Principles of Financial Planning

General Financial Planning Principles

B.8.	Financial planning process
B.9.	Financial statements
B.10.	Cash flow management
B.11.	Financing strategies
B.12.	Economic concepts
B.13.	Time value of money concepts and calculations
B.14.	Client and planner attitudes, values, biases and behavioral finance
B.15.	Principles of communication and counseling
B.16.	Debt management

C. Education Planning

Education Planning

C.17.	Education needs analysis
C.18.	Education savings vehicles
C.19.	Financial aid
C.20.	Gift/income tax strategies
C.21.	Education financing

D. Risk Management and Insurance Planning

Risk Management & Insurance Planning

D.22.	Principles of risk and insurance
D.23.	Analysis and evaluation of risk exposures
D.24.	Health insurance and health care cost management (individual)
D.25.	Disability income insurance (individual)
D.26.	Long-term care insurance (individual)
D.27.	Annuities
D.28.	Life insurance (individual)
D.29.	Business uses of insurance
D.30.	Insurance needs analysis
D.31.	Insurance policy and company selection
D.32.	Property and casualty insurance

E. Investment Planning

E.33.	Characteristics, uses and taxation of investment vehicles
E.34.	Types of investment risk
E.35.	Quantitative investment concepts
E.36.	Measures of investment returns
E.37.	Asset allocation and portfolio diversification
E.38.	Bond and stock valuation concepts
E.39.	Portfolio development and analysis
E.40.	Investment strategies
E.41.	Alternative investments

F. Tax Planning

F.42.	Fundamental tax law
F.43.	Income tax fundamentals and calculations
F.44.	Characteristics and income taxation of business entities
F.45.	Income taxation of trusts and estates
F.46.	Alternative minimum tax (AMT)
F.47.	Tax reduction/management techniques
F.48.	Tax consequences of property transactions
F.49.	Passive activity and at-risk rules
F.50.	Tax implications of special circumstances
F.51.	Charitable/philanthropic contributions and deductions

G. Retirement Savings and Income Planning

G.52.	Retirement needs analysis
G.53.	Social Security and Medicare
G.54.	Medicaid
G.55.	Types of retirement plans
G.56.	Qualified plan rules and options
G.57.	Other tax-advantaged retirement plans
G.58.	Regulatory considerations
G.59.	Key factors affecting plan selection for businesses

Investment Planning

Tax Planning

Retirement Savings & Income Planning

G.60.   Distribution rules and taxation

G.61.   Retirement income and distribution strategies

G.62.   Business succession planning

H. Estate Planning

H.63.   Characteristics and consequences of property titling

H.64.   Strategies to transfer property

H.65.   Estate planning documents

H.66.   Gift and estate tax compliance and tax calculation

H.67.   Sources for estate liquidity

H.68.   Types, features, and taxation of trusts

H.69.   Marital deduction

H.70.   Intra-family and other business transfer techniques

H.71.   Postmortem estate planning techniques

H.72.   Estate planning for non-traditional relationships

Contextual Variables

In addition to the Principal Knowledge Topics, other important variables are to be considered when dealing with specific financial planning situations. These are referred to as "Contextual Variables" and are used as part of content development for the CFP® Certification Examination or other case-based scenarios.

More specifically, financial planning situations require the application of financial planning knowledge for different types of clients. Important client details to consider as part of financial planning situations are:

- **Family Status** (traditional family, single parent, same-sex couples, blended families, widowhood)
- **Net Worth** (ultra-high net worth, high net worth, mass affluent, emerging affluent, mass market)
- **Income Level** (high, medium, low)
- **Life or Professional Stage** (student, starting a career, career transition, pre-retirement, retirement)
- **Other Circumstances** (health issues, divorce, change of employment status, aging parents, special needs children)

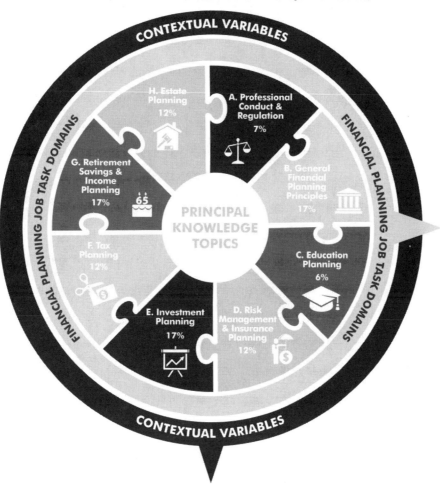

CFP BOARD

2015 JOB TASK ANALYSIS
EXAMINATION AND EDUCATION REQUIREMENTS

CONTEXTUAL VARIABLES

FINANCIAL PLANNING JOB TASK DOMAINS

FINANCIAL PLANNING JOB TASK DOMAINS

H. Estate Planning 12%

A. Professional Conduct & Regulation 7%

G. Retirement Savings & Income Planning 17%

B. General Financial Planning Principles 17%

PRINCIPAL KNOWLEDGE TOPICS

F. Tax Planning 12%

C. Education Planning 6%

E. Investment Planning 17%

D. Risk Management & Insurance Planning 12%

CONTEXTUAL VARIABLES

CONTEXTUAL VARIABLES

FINANCIAL PLANNING JOB TASK DOMAINS

1
Establishing & Defining the Client-Planner Relationship

2
Gathering Information Necessary to Fulfill the Engagement

3
Analyzing & Evaluating the Client's Current Financial Status

4
Developing the Recommendation(s)

5
Communicating the Recommendation(s)

6
Implementing the Recommendation(s)

7
Monitoring the Recommendation(s)

8
Practicing Within Professional & Regulatory Standards

CONTEXTUAL VARIABLES

FAMILY STATUS	NET WORTH	INCOME LEVEL	LIFE OR PROFESSIONAL STAGE	OTHER CIRCUMSTANCES
Traditional family	Ultra-high net worth	High	Student	Health issues
Single parent	High net worth	Medium	Starting a career	Divorce
Same-sex couples	Mass affluent	Low	Career transition	Change of employment status
Blended families	Emerging affluent		Pre-retirement	Aging parents
Widowhood	Mass market		Retirement	Special needs children

Table of Contents

Case Study 1: Chris and Faith Nicholson

Case Study Facts

Today is December 31, 2017. Chris and Faith Nicholson have come to you, a CFP® professional, for help in developing a plan to accomplish their financial goals. From your initial meeting together, you have gathered the following information.

PERSONAL BACKGROUND AND INFORMATION

Chris Nicholson (Age 27)

Chris is a correctional officer with a privately owned minimum security prison. He has a bachelor's degree in criminal justice and a master's degree in social work.

Faith Nicholson (Age 24)

Faith is an assistant manager for a clothing store.

The Children

Chris and Faith have no children from their marriage. Chris has two children, Jeremy (age 4) and Joshua (age 3), from a former marriage. Jeremy and Joshua live with their mother, Alice.

The Nicholsons

Chris and Faith have been married for two years.

Chris must pay $325 per month in child support until both Joshua and Jeremy attain age 18. In addition, the divorce decree required Chris to create a life insurance trust for the support of the children and contribute $175 per month to the trust. The trustee is Alice's father. The beneficiaries do not have withdrawal powers. The trust is to be used for the education and/or maintenance of the children in the event of Chris's death. The trustee has the power to invade the trust principal for the beneficiaries at the earlier of Chris's death or Joshua attaining age 18.

During the current year, Chris paid his former spouse, Alice, $3,000 in cash. This payment was not part of the original divorce agreement. Alice used some of the money to fix the roof on her house, and the remainder of the money was applied to her mortgage on her house. Both Chris and Alice occupied the house when they were married, and the house was transferred solely into Alice's name upon their divorce.

PERSONAL AND FINANCIAL OBJECTIVES

- Save for an emergency fund
- Eliminate debt
- Save for a 20% down payment on a new home. The current value of the house is $150,000. Property taxes and insurance would be $2,500 and $750, respectively. Both taxes and insurance are expected to increase at the rate of inflation.
- Contribute to tax-advantaged savings vehicles

ECONOMIC INFORMATION

- Inflation is expected to be 4% annually.
- Salaries should increase 5% per year for the next 5 to 10 years.
- No state income tax.
- Stocks are expected to grow 9.5% annually.

Bank lending rates are as follows:

—15-year mortgages: 7.5%

—30-year mortgages: 8%

—Secured personal loans: 10%

—Prime rate: 6%

INSURANCE INFORMATION

Life Insurance

	Policy A	Policy B	Policy C
Insured	Chris	Chris	Faith
Face amount	$250,000	$78,000[2]	$20,000
Policy Type	Whole life	Group term	Group term
Cash value	$2,000	$0	$0
Annual premium	$2,100	$156	$50
Premium payer	Trustee	Employer	Employer
Beneficiary	Trustee[1]	Alice	Chris
Policyowner	Trust	Chris	Faith

[1] Joshua and Jeremy are beneficiaries of the trust.
[2] This figure increased from $50,000 to $78,000 on January 1, 2017.

Health Insurance

Chris and Faith are covered under Chris's employer group plan, which is a major medical plan with a $200 per person per year deductible, an 80/20 coinsurance clause, and a $1,500 family annual stop-loss limit.

Long-Term Disability Insurance

Chris is covered by an own-occupation definition of disability group policy with premiums paid fully by his employer. The benefits equal 60% of gross pay after a 180-day elimination period and can be paid until Chris attains full retirement age. The policy covers both sickness and accidents.

Faith is not covered by disability insurance.

Renters Insurance

The Nicholsons have an HO-4 renter's policy without endorsements.

Content coverage $25,000; liability coverage $100,000.

Automobile Insurance

Both car and truck are covered under this policy.

Coverage	PAP
Bodily injury	$25,000/$50,000
Property damage	$10,000
Medical payments	$1,000 per person
Physical damage	Actual cash value
Uninsured motorists	$25,000/$50,000
Comprehensive deductible	$500
Collision deductible	$500
Premium (annual)	$3,300

INVESTMENT INFORMATION

The Nicholsons think they need six months of cash flow, net of all taxes, savings, vacation, and discretionary cash flow, in an emergency fund. They are willing to include in the emergency fund the savings account and Chris's Section 401(k) plan vested balance because of the loan provision.

Chris has Q-Mart stock, which was a gift from his Uncle Carter. On the date of the gift (July 1, 2009), the fair market value of the stock was $3,500. Uncle Carter's tax basis was $2,500, and he paid gift tax of $1,400 on the gift. Uncle Carter had already used both his applicable credit amount and annual exclusion for gifts to Chris before the date of the gift.

The 100 shares of Macro stock was a Christmas gift to Faith from her Aunt Beatrice. On the date of the gift (December 25, 2017), the fair market value was $8,000. Beatrice paid $10,000 for the stock in 2008 (her cost basis).

Growth Mutual Fund Current value: $13,900 All distributions have been reinvested.		
Year	Deposit	Dividends & Gains
2012	$1,000	$0
2013	$1,000	$200
2014	$2,000	$400
2015	$2,000	$400
2016	$2,500	$650
2017	$3,000	$750

INCOME TAX INFORMATION (FEDERAL)

The Nicholsons' filing status is married filing jointly. The children (Jeremy and Joshua) are claimed as dependents on the Nicholsons' tax return as part of the divorce agreement.

The Nicholsons live in a state without an income tax.

Table 1 Uniform Premiums for $1,000 of Group Term Life Insurance Protection	
Under 25	.05 per month/per $1,000
25 to 29	.06 per month/per $1,000

RETIREMENT INFORMATION

Chris's employer allows employees to contribute up to 25% of their compensation each year to the Section 401(k) plan, not to exceed Internal Revenue Code maximums. Chris's employer matches contributions dollar-for-dollar up to the first 6% of compensation. Chris is currently contributing 3% of his compensation to the Section 401(k) plan.

The Section 401(k) plan allows employees to take loans from the plan at any time. The plan document imposes the following requirements on plan loans:

"If you had no loan balance within the immediate preceding 12 months, the maximum amount of the loan is the lesser of $50,000 or 50% of the vested account balance. All loans must be paid in full within five years from the date of the original loan. Loan payments can be made only through payroll deductions."

"The interest rate will be established at the beginning of each month at 1% above the prime rate as published on the last business day of the previous month. Once an interest rate is established and assigned to a loan, it will remain unchanged for the term of that loan."

Chris has never borrowed from his Section 401(k) plan. He estimates that his average rate of return on the plan's investments is 8% per year.

GIFTS, ESTATES, TRUSTS, AND WILL INFORMATION

Chris has a will leaving all of his probate estate to his children. Faith does not have a will. The Nicholsons live in a common-law state that has adopted the Uniform Probate Code.

Statement of Cash Flows
Chris and Faith Nicholson
For 2017
(Expected to be similar in 2018)

CASH INFLOWS

Salaries

Chris—salary	$26,000	
Faith—salary	20,000	
Investment income*	1,090	
Total inflows		**$47,090**

CASH OUTFLOWS

Savings—house down payment	$1,200
Reinvestment of investment income	1,090
Section 401(k) plan contribution	780
Total savings	$3,070

FIXED OUTFLOWS

Child support	$3,900
Life insurance payment (to trustee)	2,100
Rent	6,600
Renters insurance	480
Utilities	720
Telephone	360
Auto insurance	3,300
Gas, oil, maintenance	2,400
Student loans	3,600
Credit card debt	1,800
Furniture payments	1,302
Total fixed outflows	$26,562

VARIABLE OUTFLOWS

Taxes—Federal income tax and FICA	$6,319	
Food	2,910	
Clothing	1,000	
Entertainment and vacation	1,500	
Payment to former spouse (nonrecurring)	3,000	
Total variable outflows	$14,729	
Total cash outflows		**$44,361**
Net cash flow (surplus)		**$2,729**

* $340 from dividends are from Q-Mart stock and $750 are from distributions from the Growth Mutual Fund

Statement of Financial Position
Chris and Faith Nicholson
Year ending December 31, 2017

ASSETS[1]		LIABILITIES AND NET WORTH	
Cash and equivalents		**Liabilities[3]**	
Cash	$500	Credit card balance	$9,000
Savings account	1,000	Student loan—Chris[4]	45,061
Total cash and equivalents	$1,500	Auto loan—Faith	14,796
		Furniture loan	1,533
Invested assets		Total liabilities	$70,390
Q-Mart stock (100 shares)[2]	$5,000		
Macro stock (100 shares)	7,200		
Growth Mutual Fund	13,900		
Section 401(k) plan	1,500	**Net worth**	$(46)
Total invested assets	$27,600		
Personal use assets			
Auto—Faith	$18,494		
Truck—Chris	4,000		
Motorcycle—Faith	1,000		
Furniture and personal property	17,750		
Total personal use assets	$41,244		
Total assets	$70,344	**Total liabilities and net worth**	$70,344

[1] Assets are stated at fair market value.

[2] Q-Mart's current dividend is $3.40 per share.

[3] Liabilities are stated at principal only as of December 31 before January payments.

[4] Chris took out the loans to pay for qualified education costs. He paid $2,732 in interest in the current year.

INFORMATION REGARDING ASSETS AND LIABILITIES

Home Furnishings

The furniture was purchased with 20% down and 18% interest financing over 36 months. The monthly payment is $108.46.

Automobile

The automobile was purchased December 31 of this year for $18,494 with 20% down and 8% interest financing over 60 months with monthly payments of $300.

Stereo System

The Nicholsons have a state-of-the-art stereo system (fair market value $10,000). They asked and received permission to alter the apartment to install built-in speakers into every room. The agreement with the landlord requires them to leave the speakers if they move because they are permanently installed and affixed to the property. The replacement value of the installed speakers is $4,500, and the noninstalled components are valued at $5,500. The system was originally purchased in late 2015 for $10,000 cash.

Questions

1. Which of the following statements accurately describes the Nicholsons' current financial condition?

    1. The child support payment to Alice is fully tax deductible.
    2. They are technically insolvent.
    3. They have inadequate life insurance.
    4. They have inadequate liability insurance.

    A. 1, 2, and 4
    B. 1 and 3
    C. 2, 3, and 4
    D. 3 and 4

2. If Chris and Faith sell the Macro stock at its current fair market value, what are the tax consequences?

    A. $2,800 long-term capital loss
    B. $2,800 short-term capital loss
    C. $800 long-term capital loss
    D. $800 short-term capital loss

3. Assuming that Chris and Faith decide to sell the Q-Mart stock next year for a total price of $5,500, what are the tax consequences?

    A. $2,600 long-term capital gain
    B. $2,000 long-term capital gain
    C. $3,000 long-term capital gain
    D. $1,600 long-term capital gain

4. As of today, how many payments have been made on the furniture?

    A. 14
    B. 16
    C. 18
    D. 20

5. Calculate the original purchase price of the furniture.

    A. $3,000
    B. $3,250
    C. $3,500
    D. $3,750

6. If the Nicholsons' apartment was burglarized and their movable stereo system components were stolen, would the components be covered under the HO-4 policy, and if so, for what value?

    A. No. They would not be covered.

    B. Yes. They would be covered, but only up to $1,000 because they are a listed item.

    C. Yes. They would be covered, but only up to the actual cash value (cost minus depreciation) less the deductible.

    D. Yes. They would be covered for full replacement value less the deductible.

7. If a fire occurred in the Nicholsons' apartment building and their built-in speaker system was destroyed, would it be covered under the HO-4 policy, and if so, to what extent?

    A. No. The system is part of the building, not personal property.

    B. Yes. The system is listed property, $1,000 less the deductible.

    C. Yes. Coverage would be limited to $2,500 (10% of personal property) under building additions.

    D. Yes. The system would be covered at full replacement value less the deductible.

8. If a fire forced them to move out of their apartment for a month, would the HO-4 policy provide coverage?

    A. No

    B. Yes, up to $25,000

    C. Yes, for loss of use up to $2,500

    D. Yes, for loss of use up to $7,500

9. Is Faith covered for liability on her motorcycle under the PAP?

    A. Yes. She is covered, but only up to $10,000.

    B. No. Motorcycles are excluded under the PAP.

    C. Yes. She is covered if the motorcycle is less than 80ccs.

    D. Yes. She is covered for liability but not for uninsured motorists.

10. The Nicholsons have asked you for advice on lowering their income tax liability. Which of the following recommendations can you make to help Chris and Faith achieve this objective?

    A. Contribute to a traditional IRA

    B. Purchase Series EE savings bonds

    C. Create a SEP for Chris and contribute by the extended due date of the joint income tax return

    D. Contribute to a Coverdell Education Savings Account for the children

11. If the Nicholsons sell the Growth Mutual Fund for the current market value, what will be the tax consequence?

    A. $2,400 long-term capital gain

    B. $2,400 short-term capital gain

    C. $2,400 ordinary income

    D. No recognized gain or loss

12. After a comprehensive review of the Nicholsons' current financial planning status, you have come to several conclusions. Which of the following may be appropriate recommendations for the Nicholsons?

    1. Draft a will for Faith
    2. Create advance medical directives for both Chris and Faith
    3. Purchase a personal liability umbrella policy (PLUP)
    4. Transfer their residence to a qualified personal residence trust (QPRT)

    A. 1 only
    B. 1, 2, and 3
    C. 1, 2, and 4
    D. 1, 2, 3, and 4

13. Do the payments of $175 per month to the insurance trust for the children constitute a taxable gift from Chris?

    A. No. The total payments are less than the annual exclusion amount.
    B. Yes. The trust does not contain a Crummey provision.
    C. Yes. The payments are a gift of a future interest.
    D. No. The payments are a legal support obligation.

14. Who will actually collect the proceeds of Chris's term life insurance if he were to die today, given that the Nicholsons live in a Uniform Probate Code state?

    A. Alice would receive the entire insurance proceeds.
    B. Faith would receive the entire insurance proceeds.
    C. Faith would receive half, and the children would receive the other half split equally.
    D. Alice would receive half, and Faith would receive half.

15. Chris is considering borrowing from his Section 401(k) plan for a vacation. Which of the following statements is CORRECT regarding this scenario?

    A. The maximum loan Chris can take from the Section 401(k) plan at this time is $50,000.
    B. Interest paid on the loan will be deductible as a miscellaneous itemized deduction on Chris's federal income tax return.
    C. Chris would be better off taking a secured personal loan for the vacation.
    D. The loan will be repaid by Chris with after-tax dollars.

16. How much must Chris's employer include in his W-2 for the group term life insurance? (Round to the nearest dollar.)

    A. $0
    B. $17
    C. $20
    D. $156

17. Chris and Faith are contemplating contributing to IRAs. Which of the following statements regarding IRAs is(are) CORRECT?

    1. Chris can roll over his employer's Section 401(k) plan into a traditional IRA while still employed at his current job.

    2. If Faith establishes a traditional IRA, she can take a lump-sum distribution and elect 10-year averaging when she retires.

    3. Chris is considered an active participant in an employer-sponsored retirement plan.

    A. 1 and 3
    B. 2 and 3
    C. 3 only
    D. 1, 2, and 3

18. What is the implied dividend growth rate of Q-Mart's stock based on the constant growth dividend discount model? (Round to the nearest percentage. Assume that the Nicholsons' required rate of return is 10%.)

    A. 0%
    B. 1%
    C. 2%
    D. 3%

19. If the IRS audits Chris and Faith next year and disputes the charitable contribution deductions they have taken in the past, which of the following can be cited as having the highest source of authority next to the Internal Revenue Code and as carrying the full force and effect of the law?

    A. Treasury Regulation
    B. Revenue Ruling
    C. Private Letter Ruling
    D. Revenue Procedure

20. The Nicholsons have asked you for advice about using their net cash surplus. Which of the following planning recommendations would allow the Nicholsons to use their net cash surplus in a manner that will make the most sense from a savings and net worth perspective?

    A. Apply the net cash surplus toward their outstanding student loan debt
    B. Contribute an additional 3% of Chris's salary to his Section 401(k) plan
    C. Set money aside in an S&P 500 Index mutual fund to help fund a down payment on their dream home
    D. Purchase a flexible premium deferred variable annuity to help provide an income stream for their retirement

21. Which of the following statements regarding the $3,000 cash payment made to Alice by Chris this year is(are) CORRECT?

    1. The payment will be excluded from Alice's gross income for federal income tax purposes.

    2. The payment to Alice is a gift for gift tax purposes.

    3. Only the portion of the $3,000 that was used to pay Alice's mortgage will be considered alimony for federal income tax purposes.

    4. The entire payment will be considered alimony because the payment was made in cash and the home is solely in Alice's name.

    A. 1 only

    B. 1 and 2

    C. 1 and 4

    D. 3 only

ANSWER SUMMARY

1. C	6. C	11. D	16. C	21. B
2. D	7. C	12. B	17. C	
3. A	8. D	13. D	18. D	
4. D	9. B	14. A	19. A	
5. D	10. A	15. D	20. B	

SUMMARY OF TOPICS

1. Fundamentals—Financial Analysis
2. Tax—Basis of Gift
3. Tax—Basis of Gift
4. Fundamentals—Time Value of Money
5. Fundamentals—Time Value of Money
6. Insurance—Homeowners (HO-4)
7. Insurance—Homeowners (HO-4)
8. Insurance—Homeowners (Loss of Use)
9. Insurance—PAP Exclusions
10. Tax—Tax Liability
11. Investments—Tax Basis of Investment
12. Fundamentals—Financial Recommendations
13. Estates—Gifts
14. Insurance—Contract
15. Retirement—Section 401(k) Plan Loan Provisions
16. Tax—Group Term Life Insurance
17. Retirement—IRAs
18. Investments—Constant Growth Dividend Discount Model
19. Tax—Sources of Law
20. Fundamentals—Budgeting
21. Tax—Alimony

Solutions

Fundamentals—Financial Analysis

1. **C**

    The child support payment is for support of the children and is not tax deductible.

    The Nicholsons are technically insolvent because of a small negative net worth (–$46). The debt ratios are especially revealing. The addition of the automobile payments of $300 per month beginning in 2018 reduces their net cash flow for 2018 by $600. (Projected 2018 net cash flow: $2,729 in 2018, plus $3,000 one-time payment to the ex-spouse less $3,600 car payment outflows in 2018 equals $2,129.) They have both inadequate life insurance and liability insurance.

Tax—Basis of Gift

2. **D**

Sale price	$7,200
Faith's basis	(8,000)*
Gain or (loss)	($800)

    This is a short-term capital loss because the holding period begins on the date of the gift and is less than one year and one day.

    *The basis of a gift to a donee for an asset that has a fair market value less than the donor's basis is the fair market value (FMV) on the date of the gift for losses and the donor's basis for gains (double-basis rule). Because the stock was sold at a loss, the loss basis of $8,000 (FMV on date of gift) is used.

Tax—Basis of Gift

3. **A**

    Proportion attributed to appreciation: ($1,000 ÷ $3,500) × $1,400 = $400.

    Because appreciated property was gifted, a portion of the gift tax paid by the donor is added to the donee's basis. Add $400 to the donor's basis. Chris's adjusted basis is $2,900.

Sale price	$5,500	Donor's basis	$2,500
Adjusted basis	(2,900)	Pro rata share of gift tax paid	400
Long-term capital gain	$2,600	Chris's adjusted basis	$2,900

FMV @ date of gift	$3,500
Donor's basis	(2,500)
Appreciation	$1,000

Gift tax paid	$1,400

Fundamentals—Time Value of Money

4. **D**

The loan has a 36-month term and is 80% of the original value.

The annual interest rate is 18%.

The payment is $108.46 per month.

$$
\begin{aligned}
n &= 36 \\
i &= 1.5 \,(18 \div 12) \\
PMT_{OA} &= 108.46 \\
PV &= (3,000.08), \text{ or } \$3,000.08
\end{aligned}
$$

The current balance on the statement of financial position under liabilities is $1,533.

$$
\begin{aligned}
FV &= (1,533) \\
PV &= 3,000 \\
PMT_{OA} &= (108.46) \\
i &= 1.5 \,(18 \div 12) \\
n &= 20
\end{aligned}
$$

Fundamentals—Time Value of Money

5. **D**

Use the result from the first half of the solution to Question 4.

$$
\begin{aligned}
\$3,000 &= .80x \\
x &= \$3,000 \div .80 \\
x &= \$3,750
\end{aligned}
$$

Insurance—Homeowners (HO-4)

6. **C**

Yes. The components would be covered, but only at the actual cash value (cost minus depreciation) less the deductible because the policy is without endorsement.

Insurance—Homeowners (HO-4)

7. **C**

Yes. The system would be covered, but only to $2,500 (10% of personal property coverage under the building additions section).

Insurance—Homeowners (Loss of Use)

8. **D**

Yes. The policy would provide coverage for loss of use up to 30% of the $25,000 on the basis of their incremental loss (.30 × $25,000 = $7,500).

Insurance—PAP Exclusions

9. **B**

No. Section B of the PAP specifically excludes liability for motorcycles even if not owned.

Tax—Tax Liability

10. A

Because their income is below the MAGI limits, they can each contribute to traditional IRAs and take full deductions.

No tax deductions are available for purchasing EE bonds.

Chris is an employee; he cannot establish a personal SEP.

Contributions to a Coverdell Education Savings Account are not tax deductible.

Investments—Tax Basis of Investment

11. D

The question requires the determination of the adjusted tax basis of the Growth Mutual Fund.

Basis determination:

Contributions (deposits)	$11,500
Taxable income (earnings)	2,400 (2012–2017)
Adjusted tax basis	$13,900

Sales price	$13,900
Adjusted tax basis	(13,900)
No gain or loss	$0

Fundamentals—Financial Recommendations

12. B

Statement 4 is incorrect because the Nicholsons do not own a home.

Estates—Gifts

13. D

No. This is legal support required by a divorce decree and is not subject to gift tax.

Insurance—Contract

14. A

Alice would collect because she is the named beneficiary even though she and Chris are divorced. Because there is a valid beneficiary designation, the proceeds are not subject to probate.

Retirement—Section 401(k) Plan Loan Provisions

15. **D**

Because Chris will repay the loan through payroll deductions, he essentially will be paying back the loan with after-tax dollars.

Chris's vested Section 401(k) plan balance is only $1,500. Therefore, his maximum loan would be $1,500. The maximum amount a participant may borrow from the plan is 50% of the participant's vested account balance or $50,000, whichever is less. An exception to this limit is if 50% of the vested account balance is less than $10,000; in such a case, a participant may borrow up to $10,000. Plans are not required to include this exception. A participant can never borrow more than the vested balance in the account.

Interest paid on Section 401(k) plan loans is nondeductible personal interest for federal income tax purposes.

The Section 401(k) plan interest rate is prime plus one, or 7% (6% prime rate plus 1%). The personal loan rate is 10%, and neither type of interest expense is tax deductible. Therefore, a Section 401(k) plan loan would be more appropriate than a personal loan.

Tax—Group Term Life Insurance

16. **C**

This figure is calculated by multiplying the number of thousands over $50,000 by the Table 1 IRS Uniform Premiums for $1,000 of Group Term Life Insurance Protection schedule per month by 12 months ($78,000 − $50,000 = $28,000). Then, (0.06 × 28 × 12) = $20.16.

Retirement—IRAs

17. **C**

Chris could not roll his Section 401(k) plan balance over to an IRA while still employed. Rollovers are not the same as contributions; contributions are new funds. Ten-year forward averaging does not apply to distributions from an IRA, and Faith would not qualify because she was born after January 1, 1936. Chris is considered an active participant in a retirement plan.

Investments—Constant Growth Dividend Discount Model

18. **D**

Using the constant growth dividend discount model, solve for the implied dividend growth rate (g):

$$V = \frac{D_1}{r - g}$$

$$\frac{\$3.40\,(1 + g)}{0.10 - g} = \$50\ (\$5,000 \div 100\ \text{shares})$$

$$
\begin{aligned}
3.40\,(1 + g) &= 50\,(0.10 - g) \\
3.40 + 3.40g &= 5.00 - 50g \\
50g + 3.4g &= 5.00 - 3.40 \\
53.4g &= 1.60 \\
g &= 1.60 \div 53.4 \\
g &= 0.02996,\ \text{or}\ 3\%
\end{aligned}
$$

Tax—Sources of Law

19. **A**

Treasury Regulations have the highest source of authority next to the Code and have the full force and effect of the law. Revenue Rulings and Procedures can be relied on, but they do not have the same authority of the IRC or Treasury Regulations. Private Letter Rulings (PLRs) cannot be relied on by taxpayers. However, PLRs may give insight into the IRS's approach on certain transactions.

Fundamentals—Budgeting

20. **B**

Chris's employer offers a dollar-for-dollar match of employee contributions, up to 6% of salary. Because Chris is contributing only 3% of his salary to the Section 401(k) plan, he is missing out on some matching contributions. By contributing an additional 3% to the Section 401(k) plan, he is essentially doubling his money.

Although paying off the student loan debt is generally a good idea, the Nicholsons would be better served by paying off their credit card debt.

Although investing in an indexed mutual fund is not a bad planning idea, the Nicholsons should be more concerned with taking advantage of the employer match in the Section 401(k) plan and paying off debt.

An annuity is probably not a better choice than the Section 401(k) plan at this time. The annuity would be funded with after-tax dollars, whereas the additional Section 401(k) contribution is funded with before-tax dollars and includes an employer match.

Tax—Alimony

21. **B**

Because the payment was not made pursuant to a written divorce agreement, the payment will not be considered alimony. Chris will not receive an income tax deduction for the payment, and the payment will be excluded from Alice's gross income.

The payment is considered a gift for gift tax purposes; however, the $3,000 cash payment is below the gift tax annual exclusion amount of $14,000 in 2017

Case Study 2: Derek and Olga Berger

Case Study Facts

Derek and Olga Berger have come to you, a CFP® professional, for help in developing a plan to accomplish their financial goals. From your initial meeting together, you have gathered the following information. Today is December 31, 2017.

PERSONAL BACKGROUND AND INFORMATION

Derek Berger (Age 26)

Derek Berger is employed as a salesperson and trainer at a computer retailer. He has been employed with this company for five years.

Olga Berger (Age 26)

Olga Berger is a German citizen and is employed as a floral designer for a local florist.

The Bergers

Derek and Olga have been married for two years.

Children

The Bergers have one child, Ursula (age 1).

Derek's Parents

Derek's parents, Adriana and Leonard, are wealthy and live in Idaho. They own all of their property as community property. They have known Olga for a long time, and any gifts that they make will be to both Derek and Olga. Adriana and Leonard have made no previous taxable gifts.

The Bergers expect Derek's parents either to lend interest free or to give them a $30,000 down payment (approximately 27% of the purchase price) to purchase a house.

PERSONAL AND FINANCIAL INFORMATION AND OBJECTIVES

- Derek wants to start his own business in 10 years. In the meantime, he plans to advance in his current job. He wants to open a business similar to his current employment and expects he will need $100,000 in today's dollars to start the company.
- They want to buy a house in the $110,000 price range. They expect taxes and insurance to average $200 per month.
- They like to take vacations (twice a year) with an average cost of $2,250 per vacation. Derek and Olga also like to go out with friends or entertain weekly.
- They plan to retire in 30 years and believe $50,000 per year (in today's dollars) would be sufficient during retirement.
- They expect compensation increases to average 3.5% over their remaining work life expectancy.
- They both expect to live until age 90.

ECONOMIC INFORMATION

- Expected inflation (CPI) will average 3.5% annually.
- Expected return for the S&P 500 Index is 11% annually.
- T-bills are currently yielding 5%. Treasury bonds are currently yielding 7%.
- Current mortgage rates are:
    - —Fixed 15-year mortgage: 7.5%
    - —Fixed 30-year mortgage: 8.0%
- Home closing costs are expected to be 3% of any mortgage.
- Savings accounts currently yield 1.5% annually, compounded monthly.
- One-year certificates of deposit are currently yielding 5%.
- Unemployment is currently 6%.

INSURANCE INFORMATION

Life Insurance	
Insured	Derek
Owner	Derek
Beneficiary	Olga
Face amount	$50,000
Policy type	Group term
Settlement option	Lump sum
Premium	Employer-paid

Health Insurance	
Premium	Derek's premium is fully paid by employer; Olga and Ursula are dependents under Derek's policy.
Coverage	Major medical, 80/20 coinsurance; dental coverage is not provided.
Deductible	$250 per person (three-person maximum)
Family out-of-pocket limit	$2,500

Disability Insurance	
Neither Derek nor Olga has disability insurance	

Automobile Insurance	
Premium	$1,000 total annual premium for both vehicles
Bodily damage and property damage	$10,000/$25,000/$5,000 for each vehicle
Comprehensive	$250 deductible
Collision	$500 deductible

Renters Insurance	
Type	HO-4
Contents coverage	$35,000
Premium	$180 per year
Deductible	$250
Liability	$100,000
Medical payments	$1,000 per person
Endorsements	None

INVESTMENT INFORMATION

Both Derek and Olga have a high risk tolerance. They have a balance of $3,840 in Derek's Section 401(k) plan. He is currently deferring 4% of his salary, and the plan allows him to defer up to 10%. The plan offers a variety of mutual funds ranging from aggressive growth stock funds to money market funds. Derek currently has 100% invested in the Growth Fund.

Several years ago, Derek's grandfather gave him URS stock. The fair market value at the date of the gift was $6,000. Derek's grandfather originally paid $2,000 for the stock. He had already used his annual exclusion for gifts to Derek, and he paid gift tax of $2,400 on the gift.

The Bergers' required rate of return for investments is 1% below the forecasted S&P 500 Index return.

INCOME TAX INFORMATION

Their federal income tax rate is 10% and state is 2%.

RETIREMENT INFORMATION

Derek is a participant in his employer's Section 401(k) plan. The Section 401(k) plan has a two-to six-year graduated vesting schedule. The company has made matching contributions of $1,500, which is included in Derek's Section 401(k) plan balance. The balance also includes $1,500 of contributions by Derek and prorated earnings of $840. Derek has not designated a beneficiary for the account.

Olga and Derek each contributed $2,000 to an IRA for the current tax year.

GIFTS, ESTATES, TRUSTS, AND WILL INFORMATION

Derek and Olga have simple handwritten wills leaving all probate assets to each other.

Statement of Cash Flows
Derek and Olga Berger
For 2017 (Monthly)
(Expected to be similar in 2018)

CASH INFLOWS

Salary—Derek[1]	$2,000	
Salary—Olga[2]	2,000	
Interest income	1	
Total inflows[3]		$4,001

CASH OUTFLOWS

IRA contributions	$333	
Section 401(k) plan contribution	80	
Rent	650	
Groceries	348	
Utilities	80	
Water	25	
Telephone	40	
Auto fuel	100	
Auto repair	50	
Cable TV	35	
Child care	200	
Entertainment	100	
Vacations[4]	375	
Auto insurance	84	
Renters (HO-4) insurance	15	
State withholding	80	
Federal withholding and FICA	806	
Student loan—Derek 1	144	
Student loan—Derek 2	111	
Student loans—Olga	45	
Credit card 1—Derek	51	
Gas card—Derek	9	
Credit card 2—Olga	42	
Credit card 3—Olga	165	
Credit card 4—Olga	33	
Total outflows		$4,001
Net cash flow		$0

Notes to financial statements:

[1] $2,000/month salary = $24,000 per year.

[2] $2,000/month salary = $24,000 per year.

[3] Reinvested dividend income is not included.

[4] Vacations = two vacations totaling $4,500 per year; $4,500 ÷ 12 months = $375.

Statement of Financial Position
Derek and Olga Berger
As of December 31, 2017

ASSETS[1]		LIABILITIES[7] AND NET WORTH	
Cash/cash equivalents		**Current liabilities**[8,9]	
Checking[2]	$750	Credit card 1 (Derek)	$1,500
Savings[3]	1,000	Credit card 2 (Olga)	1,200
Certificate of deposit[4]	3,000	Credit card 3 (Olga)	4,800
EE savings bonds[5]	500	Credit card 4 (Olga)	950
Total cash/cash equivalents	$5,250	Gas card 1 (Derek)	200
		Total current liabilities	$8,650
Invested assets			
URS stock	$10,000	**Long-term liabilities**	
Stock portfolio[6]	22,000	Student loans	
Derek's Section 401(k) plan	3,840	Derek 1	$20,000
Total invested assets	$35,840	Derek 2	15,000
		Olga 1	6,000
		Total long-term liabilities	$41,000
Personal use assets			
Auto 1	$7,500	**Total liabilities**	**$49,650**
Auto 2	4,500		
Furniture	6,000		
Personal property	7,000	**Net worth**	**$16,440**
Total personal-use assets	$25,000		
Total assets	**$66,090**	**Total liabilities and net worth**	**$66,090**

Notes to financial statements:

[1] All assets are stated at fair market value.

[2] Checking is a non-interest bearing account.

[3] Current annual interest rate is 1.5%.

[4] Certificate of deposit maturing December 1, 2018.

[5] Series EE savings bonds; five bonds with present value of $100 each; 6% annual interest, final maturity date of 2041.

[6] Stock portfolio in brokerage account managed by Derek.

[7] Liabilities are stated at principal only.

[8] All liability payments are as indicated on monthly cash flow statement.

[9] The average interest rate for all credit cards is 15% and for student loans is 10%.

INFORMATION REGARDING ASSETS AND LIABILITIES

Detailed Investment Portfolio

Derek's Section 401(k) Plan					
Description	Shares	Price/Share	Total Value	2016 Return	2017 Return
Growth Fund	93	$41.29	$3,840	13%	7%

Stock Portfolio						
Stock	Date acquired	Cost basis	Fair market value as of 12/31/17	Beta	Current dividend	Dividend growth rate
A	1/09	$300	$2,800	1.3	$200	3.50%
B	3/10	3,000	700	1.6	33	5.00%
C	6/16	5,000	7,000	1.0	400	4.00%
D	7/16	12,000	2,500	1.1	197	2.00%
E	7/16	9,000	9,000	1.2	500	4.25%
Total		$29,300	$22,000	N/A	$1,330	N/A

Questions

1. Assuming the Bergers have no savings set aside for the acquisition of Derek's future business, how much should be saved at the end of each month, beginning this month, to be able to acquire Derek's business? Assume they will invest in a no-load S&P 500 Index fund and will pay taxes on current earnings out of their regular budget. They will reinvest all earnings in this account.

    A. $460.83
    B. $566.55
    C. $569.97
    D. $650.05

2. Which of the following insurance products would be most appropriate for Derek to purchase at this time?

    A. Tax qualified long-term care policy with an inflation-adjusted benefit
    B. Fixed annuity with life and 20-year term certain payout options
    C. Personal liability umbrella policy
    D. Long-term disability insurance policy

3. Which of the following statements regarding the planned contribution to Derek and Olga's IRA for 2017 is(are) CORRECT?

    1. Derek is an active participant in a qualified plan.
    2. Olga's contribution is fully deductible.
    3. Derek's contribution is nondeductible because he is covered by a qualified plan.
    4. Olga's contribution is partially deductible.

    A. 1 and 2
    B. 1 and 3
    C. 1 and 4
    D. 1, 2, and 3

4. If Derek were to sell the URS stock today, what would be the current tax consequences to the Bergers?

    A. Long-term capital gain of $4,000
    B. Long-term capital gain of $6,400
    C. Short-term capital gain of $4,000
    D. Long-term capital gain of $8,000

5. Assume Derek had the following sale transactions in his stock trading account during 2017:

Sold stock	Date	Sales price, net of commissions
A	August 15	$2,750
B	August 15	$600
C	April 1	$8,000
D	April 1	$3,000
		$14,350 total proceeds

What are the net gains or losses from the above stock transactions during 2017?

A. Long-term capital loss of $2,400

B. Long-term capital gain of $2,450

C. Short-term capital loss of $5,950

D. Short-term capital loss of $9,000

6. If the stock market returns 17%, what is the expected return for the Bergers' stock portfolio under the capital asset pricing model (CAPM), based on today's value?

A. 19.0%

B. 18.8%

C. 18.5%

D. 18.2%

7. Assume that the Bergers purchased the stocks in their stock portfolio based on your recommendations and that they have retained you to monitor the performance of the portfolio. Their objective is to sell any stock that appears to be overvalued. Which stocks would you recommend that they sell to meet their objective? (Assume that the dividends for all the stocks are growing at a constant rate.)

A. Stocks A and E

B. Stocks B and C

C. Stocks A, D, and E

D. Stocks B, C, D, and E

8. If Derek's parents donate the down payment on the house ($30,000), which of the following statements is(are) CORRECT?

1. The gift qualifies for the annual exclusion.

2. The parents, Leonard and Adriana, must file a gift tax return.

3. The parents are liable for a small amount of gift tax.

4. This donation is a taxable gift.

A. 1 only

B. 1 and 2

C. 1 and 3

D. 1, 2, 3, and 4

9. Assume Adriana and Leonard decide to make an interest-free loan for the house down payment to Olga and Derek instead of giving it to them. Which of the following statements regarding the tax consequences is(are) CORRECT? (The federal rate for imputed interest is 9%.)

    A. Adriana and Leonard have made a taxable gift of $2,700 to Derek and Olga.

    B. Olga and Derek must impute $2,700 of taxable income.

    C. Adriana and Leonard must impute $2,700 of taxable income.

    D. This loan has no adverse tax consequences to Olga and Derek.

10. Which of the following statements regarding Derek's options for his Section 401(k) plan is CORRECT, assuming he left his current job?

    A. Derek could have the distribution transferred directly from the Section 401(k) plan to an IRA account, but only 80% of the balance would transfer because the 20% withholding rule would apply.

    B. Derek could transfer the distribution to an IRA account but would receive only 60% of the employer contributions and earnings in his account because he is only partially vested.

    C. Derek could have the distribution rolled over (converted) directly into a Roth IRA account.

    D. Derek must transfer the distribution directly to a trustee for a traditional IRA and then have the trustee convert the traditional IRA to a Roth IRA.

11. Reviewing Derek's retirement accounts and assuming Derek terminated employment when the account balances are as stated after 5 years of employment, how much could Derek take with him, plan permitting?

    A. $3,072

    B. $3,456

    C. $3,540

    D. $3,840

12. Derek and Olga want to make sure that he is able to start his own business in 10 years and do not want to leave it to chance. You should do all of the following at the first meeting with Derek and Olga EXCEPT

    A. explain the scope of the services you can offer Derek and Olga

    B. provide a detailed financial plan with a timeline to Derek and Olga

    C. identify and resolve apparent conflicts of interest you may have with Derek and Olga

    D. discuss the financial planning process with Derek and Olga

13. After consulting with the Bergers, you recommend that they begin addressing their estate planning deficiencies. The Bergers accept your recommendation and ask you to put together a plan for achieving this objective. Which of the following would be appropriate steps to include in the couple's implementation plan?

    1. Have an attorney draft a durable power of attorney for health care for both Derek and Olga
    2. Designate Olga as beneficiary of Derek's Section 401(k) plan
    3. Begin an annual gifting program to take advantage of the annual exclusion afforded to Derek and Olga
    4. Gift the Series EE savings bonds to Ursula so she can take advantage of the tax benefits of these bonds when she redeems them for college

    A. 1 and 2
    B. 1, 3, and 4
    C. 1 and 4
    D. 2 and 3

14. What is the best course of action for the Bergers regarding their debt situation?

    A. They should not adjust their debt situation in any way at this time because it would reduce their emergency fund (liquid assets).
    B. They should sell their stock portfolio and pay off Derek's $20,000 student loan.
    C. They should not liquidate their stock portfolio but should sell the URS stock and use the proceeds to pay off their credit card debt.
    D. They should liquidate all or a portion of their stock portfolio and use the proceeds to pay off the credit card debt.

15. Which of the following statements regarding deficiencies in the Bergers' current estate planning is(are) CORRECT?

    1. They are subject to probate.
    2. Their handwritten wills are legally invalid.
    3. They have made no provision for guardianship of their children.
    4. They have made no provision for an advance medical directive.

    A. 1 and 2
    B. 1, 2, and 3
    C. 1, 3, and 4
    D. 2, 3, and 4

USE THE FOLLOWING INFORMATION FOR QUESTIONS 16 THROUGH 21

While on a vacation in Montana, the Bergers experienced several unfortunate incidents.

- A deer collided with their car, causing $800 worth of damage to the front of the car.
- Soon after Derek rented a motorcycle, his wallet was stolen. He thought he had lost the wallet on the mountain during a fall, so he did not report the loss to his credit card companies until he returned home.
- Derek, not experienced in driving in the mountains, drove the motorcycle into another motorcycle on the road, causing damage to both motorcycles and to Derek. The driver of the other motorcycle, Oscar Applebaum, had minor medical injuries.
- Upon returning home, they discovered their apartment building had been destroyed by fire.

16. How much will the insurance company pay to have the front of the car repaired due to the collision with the deer?

    A. $250

    B. $300

    C. $550

    D. $800

17. When Derek and Olga received their credit card statements, they discovered that the thief charged the following amounts:

Credit card 1	$200
Credit card 2	$450
Credit card 3	$35
Credit card 4	$60

    How much of the above charges will they be responsible for?

    A. $50

    B. $185

    C. $200

    D. $745

18. The fire that destroyed the apartment building also destroyed all of their personal property. Although the depreciated or actual cash value of all their property was $5,000, it would cost the Bergers about $37,000 to replace all of the items. How much will the insurance company pay for this loss?

    A. $4,750

    B. $5,000

    C. $35,750

    D. $36,750

19. Derek's collision with the motorcycle caused $1,200 of damage to the motorcycle owned by Oscar Applebaum. Which of the following statements is CORRECT?

    A. The HO-4 will cover the entire loss if Derek is found to be responsible.
    B. The HO-4 will cover the $1,200 loss less the $250 deductible.
    C. The HO-4 will pay nothing because this situation is excluded under all homeowners policies.
    D. The HO-4 will pay nothing because this is property damage and the liability coverage extends only to bodily injury.

20. Oscar Applebaum, the motorcycle owner, suffered $200 in emergency medical expense to reset his broken arm caused by the incident. Which of the following statements is CORRECT?

    A. The liability section of the HO-4 will pay the full $200.
    B. The medical payments section of the HO-4 will pay the full $200.
    C. The automobile policy will pay these medical expenses.
    D. Neither the HO-4 nor the automobile policy will pay these medical expenses.

21. In the motorcycle accident, Derek suffered medical expenses of $1,450. Which of the following statements is(are) CORRECT?

    1. The automobile policy will cover the expenses, but only up to $1,000.
    2. The HO-4 will not cover these expenses.
    3. The major medical policy will cover 80% after the $250 deductible.
    4. The major medical policy will not cover this situation because the motorcycle is rented.

    A. 1 and 3
    B. 1 and 4
    C. 2 only
    D. 2 and 3

22. Which of the following is the best reason for the Bergers to defer purchasing a house?

    A. Do not want to pay property tax
    B. Expect to relocate within 1–3 years
    C. Do not want to tie themselves to doing yard work
    D. Do not want to purchase homeowners insurance

23. Derek's company sponsors a death benefit only (DBO) plan, which is not part of its group term life insurance plan. Under the plan, the company will pay a $30,000 death benefit to Derek's wife in the event of his death. How much of the death benefit will be taxable to his wife if Derek dies?

    A. $0
    B. $15,000
    C. $25,000
    D. $30,000

24. Olga is interested in purchasing a bond for the Bergers' investment portfolio. Which of the following bonds would have the least volatility from changing interest rates, assuming all of the bonds listed below have a 20-year maturity?

    A. Zero-coupon bond with a 6% yield
    B. Zero-coupon bond with a 4% yield
    C. Corporate bond priced at par with a 6% yield
    D. Corporate bond priced at par with a 4% yield

25. Derek will undergo gallbladder surgery in March. If the hospital costs for the surgery are $8,000, how much will Derek be responsible for paying out of pocket?

    A. $8,000
    B. $6,200
    C. $1,800
    D. $1,550

26. You recommend that the Bergers develop an investment policy statement. Which of the following is NOT included in this statement?

    A. Investment selection
    B. Time horizon
    C. Risk tolerance
    D. Portfolio objectives

27. The Bergers are trying to decide what education funding vehicle they should use to reach their goal to pay for college education. Which of the following would best suit their needs for the monthly investment, assuming the Bergers will try to increase the amount of each deposit in the future?

    A. Section 529 plan
    B. Coverdell Education Savings Account
    C. Series EE bonds
    D. Roth IRA

28. The Bergers are concerned about funding Ursula's education. They are planning to develop an asset allocation for the funds and need some assistance. Based on the Bergers' risk tolerance and objectives, what is the most appropriate asset allocation?

    A. 10% Growth Fund, 15% Value Fund, 25% Balanced Fund, 30% Bond Fund, 10% Small-Cap Fund, 10% Money Markets
    B. 20% Growth Fund, 20% Value Fund, 35% Balanced Fund, 10% Small-Cap Fund, 15% Money Markets
    C. 25% Growth Fund, 30% Value Fund, 20% Bond Fund, 15% Small-Cap Fund, 10% International Fund
    D. 20% Growth Fund, 25% Value Fund, 10% Balanced Fund, 25% Small-Cap Fund, 20% International Fund

29. Although the Bergers have Series EE savings bonds, they do not understand all of the rules and features available with these bonds. They have come to you for assistance. Which of the following statements is CORRECT?

    A. The taxation of interest on a Series EE savings bond is always deferred until redeemed or until the bond reaches maturity.

    B. The interest accrued on Series EE savings bonds can continue to be deferred by exchanging the bonds for I bonds; the interest deferral continues until the I bonds are sold or mature.

    C. Both Series I savings bonds and Series EE savings bonds have the same advantages regarding the exclusion from income for qualifying higher education costs.

    D. Like I bonds, Series EE savings bonds are always issued at 50% of their face value.

30. Assume Derek's uncle died in 2017 and left Derek $100,000. Derek gave a gift of $20,000 cash to Olga. What are the gift tax ramifications of this gift, assuming Derek did not make any other gifts to Olga?

    A. $14,000 of the gift is eligible for the annual exclusion (for 2017), and the remaining $6,000 is a taxable gift.

    B. No gift tax is owed because of the unlimited marital deduction.

    C. Olga does not qualify for the unlimited marital deduction, so the entire gift is subject to gift tax.

    D. Up to $149,000 (for 2017) of present interest gifts from Derek to Olga per year are not subject to gift tax.

31. Assume Derek dies while Olga has a dependent at home. Will Olga qualify for Social Security benefits?

    A. No; she must reside in the United States to receive Social Security.

    B. No; only citizen spouses qualify for Social Security.

    C. Yes; a survivor benefit can be paid to noncitizen spouses outside the United States.

    D. Yes; she can receive a benefit if the child remains a U.S. citizen.

ANSWER SUMMARY

1.	D	6.	B	11.	B	16.	C	21.	D	26.	A	31. C
2.	D	7.	B	12.	B	17.	B	22.	B	27.	A	
3.	A	8.	A	13.	A	18.	A	23.	D	28.	C	
4.	B	9.	D	14.	D	19.	C	24.	C	29.	C	
5.	C	10.	C	15.	C	20.	D	25.	C	30.	D	

SUMMARY OF TOPICS

1. Fundamentals—Time Value of Money
2. Insurance—Needs Analysis
3. Retirement—Traditional IRA
4. Tax—Sale Capital Assets
5. Investments—Tax on Sale of Stock
6. Investments—Capital Asset Pricing Model
7. Investments—Constant Growth Dividend Discount Model
8. Estates—Gift Tax
9. Tax—Below-Market Loans
10. Retirement—Section 401(k) Plan Distributions
11. Retirement—Vesting
12. Fundamentals—Financial Planning Process
13. Estates—Estate Planning
14. Fundamentals—Debt Management
15. Estates—Estate Planning
16. Insurance—Auto Insurance
17. Fundamentals—Consumer Protection Laws
18. Insurance—Homeowners Insurance
19. Insurance—Liability Insurance
20. Insurance—Medical Expenses
21. Insurance—Medical Expenses
22. Fundamentals—Financing Strategies
23. Insurance—Life Insurance Taxation
24. Investments—Volatility of Bonds
25. Insurance—Medical Insurance
26. Investments—Investment Policy Statement
27. Fundamentals—Education Funding
28. Investments—Asset Allocation
29. Investments—Series EE Bonds
30. Estates—Alien Spouse
31. Retirement—Social Security Benefits

Solutions

Fundamentals—Time Value of Money

1. **D**

   For Derek to start his own business in 10 years with an estimated cost of $100,000 in today's dollars, the Bergers would have to save $650.05 at the end of each month because they have no savings set aside.

   First, calculate the future value of $100,000 over a 10-year period with an interest rate (inflation) of 3.5% per year.

   Second, calculate the monthly payment of the future value of $141,060 calculated in Step 1.

Step 1:		Step 2:	
PV	= −100,000	FV	= 141,060
n	= 10	n	= 120 (10 × 12)
i	= 3.5	i	= .9167 (11 ÷ 12)
FV	= 141,060	PMT_{OA}	= −650.05, or $650.05

Insurance—Needs Analysis

2. **D**

   Because Derek is young, and the fact pattern does not indicate a family history of long-term care needs, a long-term care policy is not a priority.

   Derek should take advantage of a traditional or Roth IRA before considering an annuity.

   Although Derek may need an umbrella policy, the question asks for the most appropriate product, which would be a disability policy.

Retirement—Traditional IRA

3. **A**

   Statement 1 is correct. Derek is an active participant in a qualified plan. Statement 2 is also correct.

   Any contribution made by Olga will be fully deductible. The beginning of the traditional IRA deduction phaseout is $99,000 in 2017 for married couples filing jointly, and a spouse who is an active participant will not preclude deduction of the entire amount of the other spouse until the MAGI reaches the phaseout limits for 2017 of $186,000–$196,000, when the deduction is phased out completely.

Tax—Sale Capital Assets

4. **B**

The Bergers would have a long-term capital gain of $6,400. Calculate Derek's basis in the stock and then the gain or loss.

Step 1: Establish Derek's basis.		Step 2: Determine gain.	
Carryover basis of donor	$2,000	Proceeds	$10,000
Pro rata share of gift tax paid by donor*	1,600	Basis	(3,600)
Derek's basis	$3,600	Gain	$6,400

$$* \quad \frac{\text{Appreciation}}{\text{FMV}} \times \text{gift tax paid} = \frac{\$4,000}{\$6,000} \times \$2,400 = \$1,600$$

Investments—Tax on Sale of Stock

5. **C**

The net result of the sale transactions is a short-term capital loss of $5,950.

Property held longer than 12 months qualifies for long-term capital gain/loss treatment. Property held for 1 year or less is treated as a short-term gain/loss. The day of disposition is included in the holding period. Consequently, the sale of Stock A results in a long-term capital gain of $2,450, and the sale of Stock B results in a long-term capital loss of $2,400. The net long-term capital gain is $50. The sale of Stock C results in a short-term capital gain of $3,000. The sale of Stock D results in a short-term capital loss of $9,000. The net short-term capital loss is $6,000. The net of all gains and losses is a $5,950 net short-term capital loss.

STCG	$3,000	C	LTCG	$2,450	A
STCL	(9,000)	D	LTCL	(2,400)	B
Net STCL	($6,000)		Net LTCG	$50	

Net STCL	($6,000)
Net LTCG	50
Net STCL	($5,950)

Investments—Capital Asset Pricing Model

6. **B**

The expected return for the Bergers' stock portfolio under the capital asset pricing model (CAPM) based on a stock market return of 17% is 18.8%.

The first step in calculating the expected return is to find the beta for the portfolio. Using this calculated beta of 1.15, the second step is to determine the expected return of 18.8%.

Step 1: Calculate the portfolio's beta.

$2,800	×	1.3	=	$3,640
700	×	1.6	=	1,120
7,000	×	1.0	=	7,000
2,500	×	1.1	=	2,750
9,000	×	1.2	=	10,800
$22,000				$25,310

$25,310 ÷ $22,000 = 1.1505

Step 2: Determine expected return.

$$r_i = r_f + (r_m - r_f)\beta_i$$

$$r_i = .05 + (.17 - .05)1.15$$

$$r_i = 18.8\%$$

Note: The T-bill rate of 5% is used to estimate r_f.

Investments—Constant Growth Dividend Discount Model

7. **B**

Stocks B and C are overvalued.

The constant growth dividend discount model is used to determine the price for a security that pays dividends that are growing at a constant rate. The formula for this model is:

$$V = D_1 \div (r - g)$$

Problems will often provide D_0, which is the dividend today. D_1 can be determined by multiplying D_0 by $(1 + g)$.

Stock	Current dividend	D_1	Required return (r)	Growth rate (g)	Diff. (r – g)	D_1/diff.	FMV	Valued
A	$200	$207.00	10%	3.50%	6.50%	$3,185	$2,800	Undervalued
B	$33	$34.65	10%	5.00%	5.00%	$693	$700	Overvalued
C	$400	$416.00	10%	4.00%	6.00%	$6,933	$7,000	Overvalued
D	$197	$200.94	10%	2.00%	8.00%	$2,512	$2,500	Undervalued
E	$500	$521.25	10%	4.25%	5.75%	$9,065	$9,000	Undervalued

Estates—Gift Tax

8. **A**

The gift qualifies for the annual exclusion. The gift is from community property and is a joint gift, not a split gift. A gift tax return is not required for gifts of community property that do not exceed a total of $28,000 (2017). Adriana is gifting $7,500 to Derek and $7,500 to Olga. Leonard is also giving $7,500 to Derek and $7,500 to Olga. These gifts qualify for the annual exclusion because they are gifts of a present interest. There is no taxable gift because each individual gift is less than the annual exclusion.

Tax—Below-Market Loans

9. **D**

Derek and Olga will have no adverse tax consequences because of the loan. Adriana and Leonard will have to recognize $1,345 of imputed interest income. The loan is more than $10,000 but less than $100,000. The borrowers' net investment income is $1,345, which is less than the imputed interest of $2,700; therefore, Adriana and Leonard will report $1,345 of imputed interest income on their tax return.

Savings interest	$15	Investment income	$1,345
Dividends	1,330	Deductible investment expenses	0
	$1,345		$1,345

Retirement—Section 401(k) Plan Distributions

10. **C**

Direct transfers are not subject to 20% withholding.

Derek is 100% vested in his own contributions and 80% vested in the contributions and earnings of his employer.

A transfer can be made directly from a qualified plan into a Roth IRA.

A plan participant is not required to transfer a distribution from a qualified plan to a traditional IRA before moving the distribution to a Roth IRA.

Retirement—Vesting

11. **B**

The Section 401(k) matching contribution must vest over 2–6 years. Derek has a vested interest of 80% in the employer's contribution and the earnings on those contributions. Derek's own contributions and the earnings on those contributions are immediately 100% vested.

Section 401(k) plan (employer match): ($1,500 + $420) × 0.80 = $1,536

Vested total: $1,500 + $420 + $1,536 = $3,456

Fundamentals—Financial Planning Process

12. **B**

You are not ready to provide Derek and Olga with a detailed financial plan. That is something that would not occur until the implementation phase of the financial planning process and would not occur at the first meeting.

Estates—Estate Planning

13. **A**

Statement 1 is correct. A durable power of attorney for health care would be an appropriate document in any estate plan.

Statement 2 is correct. Designating Olga as beneficiary of Derek's Section 401(k) plan will provide Olga with greater flexibility in taking distributions if Derek should die.

Statement 3 is incorrect. Derek and Olga's estate is not large enough to benefit from an annual gifting program.

Statement 4 is incorrect. To take advantage of the income exclusion for Series EE savings bonds, the bonds must be redeemed by the original purchaser.

Fundamentals—Debt Management

14. D

The credit card debt has an interest rate of 15% and the student loans carry a rate of 10%. Because the Bergers' required return is 10% (1% less than the S&P 500) and their after-tax return is certainly lower, they should eliminate the higher interest rate debt. In addition, the stock portfolio has several loss positions that could generate a capital loss to reduce their current income tax.

Estates—Estate Planning

15. C

Statement 2 is incorrect. Handwritten wills are not necessarily invalid. Statements 1, 3, and 4 are deficiencies that the Bergers should correct.

Insurance—Auto Insurance

16. C

Derek's insurance company will pay $800 for the damage to the car less the comprehensive deductible for a net payment of $550.

Damage	$800
Less: comprehensive deductible	(250)
Insurance company payment	$550

Fundamentals—Consumer Protection Laws

17. B

According to the Fair Credit Billing Act, the Bergers will not be liable for more than $50 per card because the use of the cards was unauthorized and notices were given to each card issuer. As a result, their total liability is $185.

Credit card 1	$50
Credit card 2	50
Credit card 3	35
Credit card 4	50
Total liability	$185

Insurance—Homeowners Insurance

18. A

Under the HO-4 policy (renters insurance), the insurance company will pay $4,750 (actual cash value less deductible) for the loss of the Bergers' personal property that resulted from the fire in the apartment building. Even though the contents coverage under this policy is $35,000 and the replacement cost of the lost items is $37,000, the insurance company is obligated to pay the lesser of the actual cash value and the replacement cost because the policy was issued without an endorsement for replacement cost on personal property.

$5,000	Actual cash value
250	Deductible
$4,750	Insurance company payment

Insurance—Liability Insurance

19. C

The HO-4 policy will pay nothing because liability resulting from the operation of a motor vehicle is excluded under all homeowners and renters policies.

Insurance—Medical Expenses

20. D

The HO-4 policy will not pay for these medical expenses because coverage for medical expenses resulting from the operation of a motor vehicle is excluded under all homeowners and renters policies. The automobile policy also excludes 2-wheeled vehicles. Derek may have to personally pay for any liability.

Insurance—Medical Expenses

21. D

The major medical policy will pay 80% of the medical expenses after the $250 deductible. The HO-4 policy will not cover the medical expenses because they were the result of an excluded activity.

Fundamentals—Financing Strategies

22. B

If the Bergers expect to relocate within 1–3 years, they should not buy the house.

Although renters do not pay property taxes, this is not the best reason to rent as opposed to purchasing a home. Note that property taxes are tax deductible.

Not wanting to do yard work it is not the best reason to rent. Landscaping services may be available at a reasonable cost. In addition, some homeowners have this service covered by their homeowners association.

Renters should purchase an HO-4 (renters) policy to protect their contents and provide liability protection.

Insurance—Life Insurance Taxation

23. D

The entire $30,000 will be taxable to Olga if Derek dies because the death benefit is not part of a group term life insurance policy.

Investments—Volatility of Bonds

24. C

The corporate bond priced at par with a 6% yield would have the shortest duration.

The zero-coupon bonds and the 4% corporate bond are incorrect because there is an inverse relationship between coupon rate and duration.

Insurance—Medical Insurance

25. C

Total hospital cost	$8,000
Less deductible	(250)
Net cost	$7,750
Coinsurance percentage	× 20%
Derek's responsibility	$1,550
Derek's deductible amount	+ $250
Derek's total liability	$1,800

Investments—Investment Policy Statement

26. A

Investment selection is not included in an investment policy statement.

Fundamentals—Education Funding

27. A

A Section 529 plan would allow for the largest contributions and tax-free distributions. A Coverdell ESA has annual contribution limits that do not adjust with inflation so it is not the best answer. The Series EE savings bonds would not provide the return close enough to the S&P 500 Index. A Roth IRA is not the best choice because of its low annual contribution limits and because a portion of the distribution may be subject to income taxation.

Investments—Asset Allocation

28. C

Important issues:

■ The Bergers' risk tolerance is high, and they expect to earn a return equal to 1% less than the S&P 500.

■ Their child is age 1. They have a 17-year time horizon.

■ Conclusion: They should have a large allocation to equities.

Investments—Series EE Bonds

29. C

Both Series I savings bonds and Series EE savings bonds have the same advantages regarding the exclusion from income for qualifying higher educational costs. The Series EE purchaser has the option to recognize interest for tax purposes when earned. Series EE savings bonds cannot be exchanged for I bonds. Both Series EE and Series I savings bonds are issued at face value.

Estates—Alien Spouse

30. D

Olga is a German citizen and does not qualify for the unlimited marital deduction. However, a noncitizen spouse can receive up to $149,000 (in 2017) per year free of gift tax. This noncitizen spouse annual exclusion is subject to the same rules as the $14,000 (for 2017) annual exclusion applicable to all gifts (i.e., must be a present interest).

Retirement—Social Security Benefits

31. C

A survivor's benefit can be paid to noncitizen spouses.

Case Study 3: William and Paula Savage

Case Study Facts

William and Paula Savage have come to you, a CFP® professional, for help in developing a plan to accomplish their financial goals. From your initial meeting, you have gathered the following information. Today is December 31, 2017.

PERSONAL BACKGROUND AND INFORMATION

William Savage (Age 37)

William is the owner/manager of a bar named The Tack Room. The Tack Room is a small, neighborhood bar open only at nights and has five part-time employees (< 1,000 hours each). He inherited the bar six years ago from his Uncle Wesley. Five years ago, he left General Construction Services, Inc., and now dedicates all of his efforts to The Tack Room.

Paula Savage (Age 37)

Paula is a loan officer at Bank of Texas. She has been employed by the bank for eight years. She has a BBA in finance and also attended State University where she earned her MBA.

The Savages

William and Paula have been married for 11 years. They both plan to retire in 25 years. They own a three-bedroom house with a pool, two cars, and the bar in Dallas, Texas. They have three children and do not plan to have any more.

Shane Savage (Age 10)

Shane attends Sunshine Grammar School (the local public school) and is in the fourth grade.

Lorraine Savage (Age 5)

Lorraine also attends Sunshine Grammar School and is in kindergarten. Lorraine spends the afternoon at Discovery Day Care Center.

Gretchen Savage (Age 2)

Gretchen attends Discovery Day Care Center for nine hours a day, Monday through Friday.

Dionne Savage (Age 62)

William's mother, Dionne, was widowed four years ago when her husband was age 60. Her income is $600 a month from Social Security and $500 a month from William and Paula. She does not spend the $600 from Social Security; she saves it in her money market account. She lives 100 miles from William and Paula.

Benita St. Martin (Age 70)

Paula's mother, Benita, is a lifelong resident and citizen of Peru and is fully supported by William and Paula. Her support costs them $300 per month.

PERSONAL AND FINANCIAL GOALS

The Savages have the following financial objectives in order of priority:

1. Provide a standard of living after retirement equal to that provided by 80% of their preretirement income.
2. Accumulate sufficient assets to send the children to a state university away from home, but in the state of Texas.
3. Minimize their current tax liabilities.
4. Expand The Tack Room to include a daytime grill within the next five years.
5. Be mortgage debt free at retirement.

ECONOMIC INFORMATION

- The Savages expect inflation to average 3% annually, both currently and long term.
- The Savages expect Paula's salary to increase 5% annually, both currently and long term.
- Current mortgage rates are 7.5% for 15 years and 8.0% for 30 years. Closing costs of 3% will be paid separately at the time of closing.
- William's after-tax savings rate is 6%.

INSURANCE INFORMATION

Life Insurance

	Policy 1	Policy 2
Insured	Paula	William
Policy through	Employer	All Farm
Face amount	$50,000	$150,000
Policy type	Group Term	Whole Life
Cash value	$0	$21,250*
Annual premium	$102 (Employer-paid)	$2,361
Beneficiary	William	Paula
Contingent beneficiary	3 children	None
Policyowner	Paula**	William**
Settlement option chosen	None	Life Annuity

*Cash value on December 31, 2017, was $20,900 and the 2017 dividend was $100.

**Community property.

Paula also has a $100,000 accidental death and dismemberment policy through her employer. She pays a premium of $68 per year for this coverage.

Health Insurance

All family members are covered by Paula's employer under a group health plan with an annual family deductible of $400. After the deductible is met, the plan pays 100% of the first $2,000 of covered medical expenses, and 80% thereafter. The policy contains a maximum out-of-pocket limit of $2,000 (includes the deductible). The plan will then pay 100% of any other covered expenses, as long as they are reasonable and customary.

Dental Insurance

The Savages have dental insurance with an annual premium of $216.

Disability Insurance

William has a personal disability income policy with an *own occupation* definition of disability that provides a monthly benefit of $2,000 and has a 30-day elimination period. The policy was purchased from a local insurance company. This policy covers both accidents and sickness and has a benefit period of five years. The annual premium is $608. Paula has a group disability plan with an *own occupation* definition of disability that provides a monthly benefit of 65% of gross pay and has a 90-day elimination period. The policy covers both accidents and sickness to age 65. The annual premium is $460, and the employer pays half of the premiums and Paula pays half of the premiums.

Homeowners Insurance

The Savages have an HO-3 policy with a $250 deductible and dwelling coverage of $97,000 purchased through All Home Insurance Company (premium is $739 per year). The policy offers $100,000 liability per person.

Automobile Insurance

Both Cars	
Policy type	Personal Auto Policy (PAP)
Liability	$100,000/300,000
Medical payments	$5,000 per person
Physical damage, own car	Actual cash value
Uninsured motorist	$25,000/$50,000
Collision deductible	$1,000
Comprehensive deductible	$500
Premium (per year)	$1,080

INVESTMENT DATA

The Savages' risk tolerance on a scale of "1 to 10" ("1" being most risk averse) is considered to be a "7". They expect to be more conservative as they get closer to retirement.

INCOME TAX INFORMATION

Their federal marginal income tax rate is currently 25%. There is no state income tax in Texas.

RETIREMENT INFORMATION

The Savages plan to retire in 25 years when they are both 62 years old. They would like to have a standard of living equal to that provided by 80% of their preretirement income. At or before retirement, the Savages plan to sell the bar and travel. They expect to be in retirement for 28 years.

Paula has a Section 401(k) plan through Bank of Texas. The Bank of Texas matches $1 for every $4 contributed by Paula up to an employer maximum contribution of 2% of her salary. She has been contributing 5% of her salary since she began working for the bank. Her Section 401(k) plan has averaged an annual return of 7% over the past eight years. Her estate is named as the beneficiary.

William has an IRA through his bank. He opened the account 10 years ago and has been contributing $2,000 each year. He is hoping to contribute $3,000 for 2017. He has averaged a 6% annual return over the past 10 years. His estate is named as the beneficiary.

William expects to collect $13,500 in Social Security benefits at full retirement age or 70% ($9,450) at age 62 (in today's dollars). Paula expects to collect $9,000 in Social Security benefits at full retirement age or 70% ($6,300) at age 62 (in today's dollars). They expect to receive Social Security benefits as soon as they retire.

GIFTS, ESTATES, TRUSTS, AND WILL INFORMATION

The Savages have simple wills leaving all assets to one another.

Statement of Cash Flows
William and Paula Savage
For the Year Ended December 31, 2017 (Annual Basis)

INFLOWS

William's net earnings from the bar (Schedule C)	$64,000	
Paula's salary	57,200	
Dividend income	777	
Checking interest income	130	
Savings interest income	400	
Certificate of deposit interest income	275	
Total Inflows		**$122,782**

OUTFLOWS

Planned Savings

Section 401(k) plan deferrals of 5% for Paula	$2,860	
IRA for William	2,000	
Total Planned Savings	**$4,860**	

Other Cash Outflows

Mortgage (P&I)	$10,267	
Homeowners insurance premium	739	
Church donations—cash	5,200	
Lease on Honda	3,588	
P&I on Cherokee	7,800	
Gas/oil/maintenance	2,000	
Auto insurance payments (both cars)	1,080	
Credit card payments	6,200	
Taxes on income*	41,019	
Property taxes on residence	2,657	
Utilities	1,200	
Telephone	600	
Life insurance premiums (William)	2,361	
Accidental death & dismemberment (Paula)	68	
Support for Dionne and Benita	9,600	
Health	2,592	
Dental insurance	216	
Child care (paid to Discovery Day Care)	4,500	
Disability premium (both)	838	
Vacation expense	4,000	
Entertainment expense	3,250	
Food	3,250	
Clothing	3,000	
Total Other Cash Outflows	116,025	
Total Outflows		**$120,885**
Net Cash Flow (surplus)		**$1,897**

*Notes on taxes:

Self-employment tax—William (on $64,000)	$9,043	($64,000 × 0.9235 × 0.153)
FICA—Paula (7.65% on $57,200)	4,376	
Estimated payments—William	12,600	
Federal withholding—Paula	15,000	
Total income taxes withheld	$41,019	

Statement of Financial Position
William and Paula Savage
December 31, 2017

ASSETS[1]			LIABILITIES[3] & NET WORTH	
Cash/Cash equivalents			**Current liabilities**	
Checking account (2.5%)	CP	$5,200	Credit card balances (14.7%)	$8,200
Savings account (3.25%)[2]	CP	12,300	Car loan (Jeep Cherokee)	11,000
Total Cash/Cash Equivalents		$17,500	Total Current Liabilities	$19,200
Invested assets			**Long-term liabilities**	
Certificate of deposit	CP	$5,000	Home mortgage (9.25%, 30 yrs.)	$98,836
(5.5%, 2 yrs., mat. January 1, 2018)			Total Long-Term Liabilities	$98,836
Savings bonds (EE bonds)	CP	4,000		
Mutual funds (see detail)	CP	18,800		
Stocks	CP	13,600		
Section 401(k) plan (Paula's vested balance)	CP	31,331	**TOTAL LIABILITIES**	$118,036
IRA (William)	CP	27,942		
The Tack Room	CP	138,000		
Rental property	Paula	84,000		
Cash value life insurance	CP	21,250		
Total Investments		$343,923		
			NET WORTH	$402,787
Personal-use assets				
Personal residence	CP	$125,000		
Jewelry (1 Diamond)	CP	8,000		
Jeep Grand Cherokee	CP	24,000		
Baseball card collection	William	2,400		
Total Personal Use		$159,400		
Total assets		**$520,823**	**Total liabilities and net worth**	**$520,823**

Client name = Separate property

CP   = Community property

Notes to Financial Statements:

[1] Assets are stated at fair market value.

[2] The savings account is currently serving as their emergency fund.

[3] Liabilities are stated at principal only and are all community obligations.

GENERAL NOTE: The bracketed percentages indicate the current interest rate.

INFORMATION REGARDING ASSETS AND LIABILITIES

The Tack Room

Wesley had a tax basis in the bar of $10,000 at his death. The fair market value at the time of Wesley's death was $40,000. Two years ago, William executed a legal document making The Tack Room community property with Paula.

William completely refurbished the bar in 2011 at a cost of $30,000. The building and property are currently valued at $78,000. Property taxes are high in this district; they are currently $2,278. The bar could be sold at a fair market value of $138,000 and is increasing in value at 3.5% per year. The bar's net income for the last three years was $64,000 (this year), $59,600 (last year), and $57,500 (2 years ago).

They also expect William's net income and cash flows from The Tack Room to increase at 3.5% annually, both currently and over the long term.

William is considering implementing some or all of the following benefit plans for The Tack Room:

- A group term life insurance arrangement in which William and all of the employees of The Tack Room would receive $25,000 of insurance coverage. Premiums would be paid exclusively by The Tack Room.

- A cafeteria plan that includes benefits for long-term care insurance, disability income insurance, dental insurance, and up to two weeks of additional vacation time

- $50 of free parking at the local garage provided each month only to William and two selected employees of The Tack Room

- Membership for all employees at the local health club

All costs of these benefits would be paid solely by The Tack Room.

Personal Residence

The Savages purchased their house and financed the mortgage over 30 years at 9.25%. The house, which is a two-story, three-bedroom, brick house, has a pool in the backyard and a monitored security system.

Rental Property

The rental property, which is valued at $84,000, is located in Tallahassee, Florida, and consists of a small strip shopping center. The property is in a poor location and is currently a break-even proposition with income equaling expenses. The property was a gift to Paula from her Aunt Olivia. Olivia had a basis in the property of $20,000 and paid gift tax on the transfer of $24,000. The annual exclusion was unavailable. At the time of the gift, the property had a fair market value of $60,000. Olivia died recently, and at the time of her death the property was valued at $84,000.

Prior to Olivia's death, Paula and William would never dispose of the rental property for fear of offending Olivia. Now, however, they want to buy a strip shopping center in Dallas at a cost of $100,000, assuming a small mortgage of $16,000. There is a tenant in the Tallahassee property that would buy the rental property for the fair market value of $84,000. Straight-line depreciation of $5,130 has been taken by the Savages, and there have been no improvements made to the property.

Mutual Funds

	FMV	Beta	Expected Return	R^2	Sharpe Ratio
Balanced Fund	$5,600	0.65	8.5%	0.56	0.70
Growth Fund	2,400	1.24	12.4%	0.85	0.49
Bond Fund	10,800	0.55	6.5%	0.92	0.51
Total	$18,800				

Questions

1. How much interest income could Gretchen receive in 2017 without being subject to income tax (assuming she has no other sources of income)?

    A. $0
    B. $900
    C. $1,050
    D. $6,350

2. Which of the following statements accurately reflect the dependency status of Dionne and Benita relative to the Savages for income tax purposes?

    1. Dionne is a dependent.
    2. Dionne is not a dependent.
    3. Benita is a dependent.
    4. Benita is not a dependent.

    A. 1 and 3
    B. 1 and 4
    C. 2 and 3
    D. 2 and 4

3. How much of a dependent care credit can the Savages take for 2017?

    A. $0
    B. $480
    C. $900
    D. $960

4. Which of the following retirement plans would William be permitted to adopt for The Tack Room?

    1. SEP
    2. Profit-sharing plan
    3. SIMPLE
    4. Defined benefit pension plan

    A. 1 only
    B. 1, 2, and 3
    C. 2, 3, and 4
    D. 1, 2, 3, and 4

5. Which type of retirement plan should William adopt if he wishes to both maximize his contribution potential and minimize his cash flow commitment?

   A. SEP

   B. Money purchase pension plan

   C. Profit-sharing plan

   D. SIMPLE

6. What is the maximum contribution William can make to a profit-sharing plan as a self-employed participant-owner in the current year without a cash or deferred arrangement?

   A. $10,500

   B. $11,896

   C. $14,870

   D. $15,500

7. If Paula were to become disabled on March 1, 2018, and receive benefits beginning June 30, 2018, for the remainder of 2018, how much of her disability benefits would be included in the Savages' gross income for federal income tax purposes, assuming each monthly benefit is electronically deposited on the 30th day of each month and the 30th day of each month is a business day? (For the purpose of this problem, use Paula's 2017 salary.)

   A. $0

   B. $9,295

   C. $10,844

   D. $18,590

8. Which of the following potential qualifying events that could affect Paula would allow extended coverage to her dependents (the children) under COBRA for a maximum of 18 months?

   1. Paula reduces her hours from full time to part time.

   2. Paula meets the Social Security definition of disability.

   3. Paula is fired because the company is downsizing (considered a normal termination).

   4. Paula dies in the current year.

   A. 1, 2, and 3

   B. 1 and 3

   C. 2, 3, and 4

   D. 1, 2, 3, and 4

9. Which chart best describes the strengths and weaknesses of the disability insurance coverage for William and Paula?

<table>
<tr><td colspan="2" align="center">1</td></tr>
<tr><td colspan="2">

Strengths
- Own occupation—both
- Benefit period—both
- Paula's benefit

Weaknesses
- Taxable benefits—both
- William's benefit

</td></tr>
</table>

<table>
<tr><td colspan="2" align="center">2</td></tr>
<tr><td colspan="2">

Strengths
- Own occupation—both
- Benefit period—both

Weaknesses
- Elimination period—both
- Benefit amount—both

</td></tr>
</table>

1

Strengths
- Own occupation—both
- Benefit period—both
- Paula's benefit

Weaknesses
- Taxable benefits—both
- William's benefit

2

Strengths
- Own occupation—both
- Benefit period—both

Weaknesses
- Elimination period—both
- Benefit amount—both

3

Strengths
- Own occupation—both
- Benefit period—Paula
- Nontaxable benefits—William

Weaknesses
- Benefit period—William
- Benefit amount—William
- Partially taxable benefits—Paula

4

Strengths
- Own occupation—both
- Benefits—both
- Elimination period—both

Weaknesses
- Payer of premiums—Paula
- Benefit period—William

A. 1
B. 2
C. 3
D. 4

10. Which of the following assets would be included in William's probate estate if he died today?

A. Individual retirement account (IRA)
B. Proceeds from the life insurance policy on William's life
C. Rental property
D. Proceeds from the life insurance policy on Paula's life

11. Dionne is concerned that she may become incapacitated and not be able to manage her own financial affairs. She would like to give William the power to handle her financial affairs if she becomes incapacitated, but she does not want the power to become effective until an incapacity occurs. Which of the following estate planning documents would best meet Dionne's needs?

A. Side letter (personal instruction letter)
B. Living will
C. Nonspringing durable power of attorney for property
D. Springing durable power of attorney for property

12. What are the tax consequences for selling the Tallahassee rental property?

    A. No gain or loss

    B. $48,000 long-term capital gain; $5,130 Section 1250 recapture

    C. $48,000 long-term capital gain

    D. $58,870 long-term capital gain; $5,130 Section 1250 recapture

13. If, instead of selling the Tallahassee property, Paula uses a tax-free Section 1031 exchange to acquire the Dallas property, what is her recognized gain or loss from the Tallahassee property and her basis in the new property?

	Tallahassee gain or loss	Dallas basis in new property
A.	$0	$36,000
B.	$0	$46,870
C.	$24,000 LTCG	$76,000
D.	$48,000 LTCG	$48,000

14. William and Paula would like to begin making gifts to benefit their 3 children. They want the children to receive the income from any gifted amounts beginning immediately, but they do not want the children to obtain access to the principal until age 25. Which of the following estate planning techniques will meet the Savages' needs?

    1. Uniform Gift to Minors Act (UGMA)

    2. Guardianship

    3. Section 2503(b) trust

    4. Section 2503(c) trust

    A. 1, 2, and 3

    B. 2 and 3

    C. 3 only

    D. 4 only

15. William and Paula are concerned that they do not have enough money saved for Shane, Lorraine, and Gretchen for college. After discussing their concerns with them, you recommend that they begin putting away funds to help meet these expenses. The Savages accept the recommendation but state that they want to take advantage of any tax benefits that may be available. Assuming each child begins college at age 18 and is in college for 4 years, what steps can they take to implement their plan? (Assume contribution limits for 2017.)

     1. Set up a Coverdell Education Savings Account for the children and make the maximum deposit of $1,500 per year in the account

     2. Set up three separate Coverdell Education Savings Accounts, one for each child, and deposit $2,000 in each annually

     3. Fund their own traditional IRAs each year because penalty-free withdrawals can be taken to pay qualified education expenses at an eligible educational institution

     4. Fund a Roth IRA because they can withdraw funds tax free after age 59½ to pay college costs

     5. Each year fund Roth IRAs for $11,000, traditional IRAs for $11,000, and Coverdell Education Savings Accounts for $6,000 ($2,000 for each child's account)

     A. 1, 3, and 5
     B. 1 and 4
     C. 2 only
     D. 2 and 3

16. After hearing William's objectives and evaluating his current financial situation, you recommend that William adopt a SIMPLE IRA for The Tack Room. William accepts the recommendation and asks you to help him implement it. Which of the following actions would be suitable steps in the implementation phase of the engagement?

     1. William must ensure that the plan meets ADP testing requirements.

     2. William can contribute 2% on behalf of all eligible participants and be in compliance with IRS rules.

     3. William can choose to make matching contributions only to participants who make elective contributions.

     4. William can roll over his existing traditional IRA balance into his SIMPLE IRA.

     A. 1, 2, and 3
     B. 1, 2, and 4
     C. 2 and 3
     D. 3 and 4

17. William is reviewing his current life insurance policy. He understands that there is an economic model to determine whether he should keep his existing policy or replace it with a new policy. Which of the following models would you use to determine whether he should replace his policy?

     A. Jensen's alpha
     B. Sharpe ratio
     C. Treynor ratio
     D. Belth model

18. William had an accident at the bar and was hospitalized. The cost of the surgery was $10,245. The hospital stay cost was $16,000. As a result of an infection, William needed continued physician's care after going home. The additional cost for the doctor was $585. How much did William have to pay? (All costs were considered reasonable and customary.)

    A. $3,200
    B. $2,000
    C. $2,585
    D. $2,400

19. The Savages have identified their nonretirement mutual funds as funds available for college costs for the children. Which of the following recommendations would be most appropriate?

    A. With the time frame for college funding and the risk tolerance level, the current portfolio is appropriate.
    B. With the time frame for college funding and the risk tolerance level, the current portfolio should be reallocated, placing more in the Balanced Fund.
    C. With the time frame for college funding and the risk tolerance level, the current portfolio should be reallocated to shift more to the Growth fund.
    D. With the time frame for college funding and the risk tolerance level, the current portfolio should be reallocated to increase the Bond Fund weighting.

20. What is the weighted beta and weighted expected return for the mutual fund portfolio?

	Weighted beta	Weighted expected return
A.	0.70	9.13%
B.	0.67	7.85%
C.	0.81	9.11%
D.	0.60	7.87%

21. In the current year, William's uncle died. He bequeathed the Asset Allocation Mutual Fund to William. This fund happens to have the exact same standard deviation and expected return as the Savages' current mutual fund portfolio. What can the Savages expect to happen to the standard deviation (SD) and expected return (ER) of their current mutual fund portfolio once the Asset Allocation Mutual Fund is added to the portfolio?

    A. SD goes down; ER goes down.
    B. SD remains the same; ER remains the same.
    C. SD goes down; ER remains the same.
    D. There is not enough information to solve the problem.

22. William and Paula have 3 mutual funds in their portfolio. They have been trying to learn more about investments and now understand some basics regarding risk and return. Of the funds in the portfolio, which one historically has had the highest risk-adjusted return?

    A. Balanced Fund
    B. Growth Fund
    C. Bond Fund
    D. The Bond Fund and the Balanced Fund have the same risk-adjusted return

23. Assume that as part of your financial planning engagement with the Savages, William asks you to analyze the implications of their ownership of The Tack Room. Based on your evaluation, which of the following weaknesses would you identify in connection with their ownership of the business?

    1. The Savages' ownership of the business creates the need for personal liability insurance.
    2. The Savages do not have an adequate exit strategy or succession plan in place for the business.
    3. The earnings from the business are subject to double taxation.

    A. 1 only
    B. 1 and 2
    C. 1 and 3
    D. 2 only

24. After analyzing the Savages' homeowners insurance coverage on their personal residence, you have questions regarding whether the replacement value is adequate for their style of home and the area in which they are living. What should you do next?

    A. You should do preliminary research on building costs in the area the Savages reside to determine if your concerns merit further action with the Savages.
    B. You should call the Savages' insurance agent and discuss your concerns on the adequacy of the HO-3 coverage.
    C. You should do nothing because the insurance agent is responsible for the adequacy of the HO-3 coverage.
    D. You should call the Savages and tell them to increase their coverage by at least 30%, to be safe.

ANSWER SUMMARY

1.	C	6.	B	11.	D	16.	C	21.	D
2.	B	7.	C	12.	B	17.	D	22.	A
3.	C	8.	B	13.	B	18.	B	23.	B
4.	D	9.	C	14.	C	19.	C	24.	A
5.	C	10.	A	15.	D	20.	B		

SUMMARY OF TOPICS

1. Tax—Standard Deduction
2. Tax—Dependency Exemption
3. Tax—Dependent Care Credit
4. Retirement—Plan Options
5. Retirement—Plan Selection
6. Retirement—Self-Employed Plan for Participant-Owner
7. Insurance—Taxation of Disability Benefits
8. Insurance—COBRA
9. Insurance—Adequacy of Disability Benefits
10. Estates—Probate Estate
11. Estates—Estate Planning Documents
12. Estates—Basis of Gift
13. Tax—Tax-Free Exchanges
14. Estates—Gifts to Minors
15. Retirement—Education Funding with Various Savings Vehicles
16. Retirement—SIMPLE IRA
17. Insurance—Life Insurance Replacement
18. Insurance—Health Insurance Coverage
19. Investments—Recommendations
20. Investments—Weighted Beta/Weighted Expected Return
21. Investments—Portfolio Diversification
22. Investments—Sharpe Ratio
23. Tax—Characteristics of Business Entities
24. Fundamentals—Domain 3 - Analyzing and Evaluating the Client's Current Financial Status

Solutions

Tax—Standard Deduction

1. **C**

    $1,050. Gretchen is age 2 and claimed as a dependent by her parents. Therefore, she will not receive a personal exemption, and her standard deduction will be limited to the greater of:

    ■ $1,050; or

    ■ earned income + $350.

    Because she has no earned income, her standard deduction will be $1,050, allowing her to receive up to $1,050 of interest income tax free.

Tax—Dependency Exemption

2. **B**

    Statements 1 and 4 are correct. The Savages contribute more than half of Dionne's support. Unspent Social Security is not counted as support. Benita is a citizen and lifelong resident of Peru. The exception for the citizenship and residency test extends only to those in Mexico and Canada.

Tax—Dependent Care Credit

3. **C**

    They can take a credit of $900 ($4,500 × 20%).

    The employment-related expenses eligible for the credit are limited to $3,000 if there is one qualifying individual, or $6,000 if there are two or more qualifying individuals, and are further limited to 20% for taxpayers whose AGI exceeds $43,000. The $4,500 is the actual child care expense per the Statement of Cash Flows for the two children.

Retirement—Plan Options

4. **D**

    All of the following retirement plans are permissible for The Tack Room:

    ■ SEP

    ■ Profit-sharing plan

    ■ SIMPLE

    ■ Defined benefit pension plan

Retirement—Plan Selection

5. **C**

He should adopt a profit-sharing plan (the maximum deductible employer contribution to a profit-sharing plan is 25% of compensation). Because he is self-employed, he will be limited to 20% of his net income after a reduction for the deductible portion of paid Social Security taxes. A profit-sharing plan is a qualified plan, so he could exclude his part-time employees who are working fewer than 1,000 hours annually. Although a SIMPLE may seem attractive, any employee who has earned $5,000 in any 2 preceding years and who can be reasonably expected to earn $5,000 in the current year is considered a participant in the SIMPLE and thus eligible for both deferrals and matching contributions. As long as his employees work fewer than 1,000 hours each year, they would not be considered participants in a profit-sharing plan, limiting contributions to himself.

Retirement—Self-Employed Plan for Participant-Owner

6. **B**

Schedule C income	$64,000
Less deductible self-employment tax	(4,521) ($64,000 × .9235 × .0765)
Net	$59,479
Contribution percentage	× 20% (Self-employed)
Maximum contribution	$11,896 (Rounded)

Because he is self-employed, the contribution percentage is calculated by using the formula [(%) ÷ (1 + %)], or (0.25 ÷ 1.25) = 20%.

Insurance—Taxation of Disability Benefits

7. **C**

Paula would have to wait 90 days for her elimination period, plus 30 days, because benefits are paid in arrears (at the end of each month). Paula would not receive her first payment until June 30, but would still end up receiving 7 payments (June 30, July 30, August 30, September 30, October 30, November 30, and December 30). Paula's 90-day elimination period would be satisfied with March, April, and May because she was disabled on March 1. Any disability benefits received by Paula will be 50% taxable as income in lieu of wages because her employer pays one-half of the premiums. She will receive 7 months of benefits at 65% of $57,200.
One-half will be taxable = [($57,200 × 0.65) × 0.5833] × 0.5 = $10,844.

Insurance—COBRA

8. **B**

The term of coverage is 18 months for both a reduction in hours and a normal termination from the job. If the employee meets the Social Security definition of disability, the term of coverage is 29 months. If the employee dies, the term of coverage is 36 months.

Insurance—Adequacy of Disability Benefits

9. C

Strengths	Weaknesses
William ■ Own occupation ■ Nontaxable benefit ■ 30-day elimination period ■ Coverage for sickness and accidents	William ■ Amount is only $2,000/month* (37.5% of compensation) * Makes chart #4 incorrect ■ 5-year benefit period** ** Makes charts #1 and #2 incorrect
Paula ■ ½ premium paid by employer ■ Own occupation ■ 65% gross pay ■ 90-day elimination period ■ Coverage for sickness and accidents ■ Coverage to age 65	Paula ■ ½ premium paid by Paula ■ ½ benefit is taxable

Estates—Probate Estate

10. A

The IRA will be included because William's estate is the named beneficiary. The beneficiary of William's life insurance is not his estate, so it will not pass through probate. Paula owns the rental property. The life insurance on Paula's life will not pay out at William's death.

Estates—Estate Planning Documents

11. D

A springing durable power of attorney for property will best meet Dionne's needs because it will become effective only if Dionne becomes incapacitated. A nonspringing durable power of attorney becomes effective immediately. A living will is an advance medical directive, and a side letter (personal instruction letter) is a nonbinding statement of the writer's wishes concerning funeral and other arrangements after death.

Estates—Basis of Gift

12. B

The adjusted tax basis of the gift to a donee is generally the carryover basis of the donor; however, an adjustment is made for the gift tax paid on the portion of the asset that has appreciated.

Donor's (Aunt Olivia's) adjusted basis	$20,000
Adjustment for gift tax paid [($40,000 ÷ $60,000) × $24,000]	16,000
Donee's (Paula's) basis in the gifted property at the time of the gift	$36,000
Sales price	$84,000
Adjusted basis (at time of gift minus depreciation taken after gift)	(30,870)
Gain on sale	$53,130
Less: unrecaptured Section 1250 capital gain taxed at 25%	(5,130)
Long-term capital gain	$48,000

Tax—Tax-Free Exchanges

13. B

	Old property	New property
FMV	$84,000	
Adjusted basis	(30,870)	
Realized gain	$53,130	
No gain recognized		

Boot given
Assumed mortgage adds $16,000 to basis.

FMV of new property		$100,000
Boot given	$16,000	
Old property basis	30,870	
New basis		(46,870)
Remaining potential gain		$53,130

There is no gain or loss recognized, and the basis of the new property is $46,870 ($30,870 + $16,000).

Estates—Gifts to Minors

14. C

The method that will meet the Savages' needs is a Section 2503(b) trust. With a guardianship or UGMA account, the children would receive the principal when they reach the age of majority. Under a Section 2503(c) trust, they would receive access to the principal at age 21.

Retirement—Education Funding with Various Savings Vehicles

15. D

Statement 1 is incorrect because a Coverdell Education Savings Account has a maximum contribution per account of $2,000 per year.

Statements 2 and 3 are correct.

Statement 4 is incorrect because Shane and Lorraine will be out of college and Gretchen will be finishing college when William and Paula turn age 59½.

Statement 5 is incorrect because total IRA contributions cannot exceed $11,000 for 2017 ($5,500 each for William and Paula).

Retirement—SIMPLE IRA

16. C

Statement 1 is incorrect. ADP testing does not apply to SIMPLEs because the employer is required to make mandatory matching contributions. ADP testing does apply to Section 401(k) plans and existing SARSEP plans.

Statement 2 is correct. The employer can choose to make a 2% nonelective contribution for each eligible employee.

Statement 3 is correct. The employer can match employee elective contributions dollar for dollar up to 3% of compensation; however, the employer can match as little as 1% in no more than 2 out of 5 years.

Statement 4 is incorrect. Individuals cannot transfer or roll over traditional IRA assets or qualified plan assets into a SIMPLE IRA.

Insurance—Life Insurance Replacement

17. D

The Belth model is used to determine whether someone should keep or replace an existing life insurance policy. This model compares an estimated cost per thousand dollars of coverage to an age-based table approximating pure mortality costs. A cost per thousand of up to twice the table number is considered acceptable.

Insurance—Health Insurance Coverage

18. B

William's plan features a maximum out-of-pocket limit of $2,000, including the deductible. The plan will then pay 100% of any other covered expenses as long as they are reasonable and customary.

Investments—Recommendations

19. C

Given the ages of the children and the risk tolerance level of the Savages (7 on a scale of 1–10), they can accept the additional risk of the growth fund to have an opportunity to increase the return of their mutual fund portfolio.

Investments—Weighted Beta/Weighted Expected Return

20. B

	FMV	Beta	Product
Balanced Fund	$5,600	0.65	$3,640
Growth Fund	$2,400	1.24	$2,976
Bond Fund	$10,800	0.55	$5,940
Total	$18,800		$12,556

Weighted beta = ($12,556 ÷ $18,800) = 0.6679

	FMV	Expected return	Expected earnings
Balanced Fund	$5,600	8.5%	$476.00
Growth Fund	$2,400	12.4%	$297.60
Bond Fund	$10,800	6.5%	$702.00
Total	$18,800		$1,475.60

Weighted expected return = ($1,475.60 ÷ $18,800.00) = 7.85%

Investments—Portfolio Diversification

21. D

Because the correlation coefficient between the Asset Allocation Mutual Fund and the existing portfolio was not given, there is not enough information to solve the problem, as the covariance cannot be determined.

Investments—Sharpe Ratio

22. A

The Balanced Mutual Fund has the highest Sharpe ratio. The Sharpe ratio is a measure of incremental return divided by standard deviation and provides a measure of the risk-adjusted return. The relatively low R^2 of the Balanced Fund necessitates the use of the Sharpe ratio.

Tax—Characteristics of Business Entities

23. B

Statement 1 is correct because the owner of a sole proprietorship is personally liable for any liabilities incurred by the business. The case facts do not indicate that the Savages have any personal liability insurance.

Statement 2 is correct. Although the case facts indicate that the Savages want to sell the business at or before retirement, they have not identified a potential buyer or made financing arrangements.

Statement 3 is incorrect. The earnings from a sole proprietorship are taxed directly to the owner, unlike the earnings from a corporation, which are taxed once at the corporate level and again to the owners when paid as dividends.

Fundamentals—Domain 3 - Analyzing and Evaluating the Client's Current Financial Status

24. **A**

You should do preliminary research on building costs in the area the Savages reside to determine if your concerns merit further action with the Savages. Unless you are authorized to do so, you may not discuss your concerns with the Savages' insurance agent because this will violate confidentiality. You owe a fiduciary responsibility to your client to discuss with the client any concerns you have on their financial situation, whether or not you would be the person to correct any deficiency. You should not make a recommendation to the Savages based on a guess.

Case Study 4: Eddie and Tina Topplemeir

Case Study Facts

Today is December 31, 2017. Eddie and Tina Topplemeir have come to you, a CFP® professional, for help in developing a plan to accomplish their financial goals. From your initial meeting together, you have gathered the following information.

PERSONAL BACKGROUND AND INFORMATION

Eddie Topplemeir (Age 47)

Eddie Topplemeir is an executive in the Amadeus Company, a closely held corporation. His salary is $100,000, and he expects increases of 5% per year.

Tina Topplemeir (Age 50)

Tina Topplemeir is Eddie's secretary. Her present salary is $24,000. She expects raises of 5% each year.

This is Tina's second marriage. Her first husband, Reggie, was killed several years ago. Tina was the beneficiary of his $250,000 life insurance policy, with which she created her investment portfolio.

The Topplemeirs

Eddie and Tina have been married for three years. They do not reside in a community property state.

The Children

Tina has two children from her first marriage, Brooks, age 16, and Hunter, age 12. Eddie and Tina have a daughter, Emily, who is now 2 years old. All of the children live with them. The children are cared for during the day by their grandmother who lives next door.

When they were first married, Eddie wanted to adopt Brooks and Hunter, but the children did not agree. Since then, Eddie and the two boys have been in continual conflict. As a result, Tina intends to use her investment portfolio to pay for the boys' education without asking for assistance from Eddie.

PERSONAL AND FINANCIAL GOALS

- The Topplemeirs want to start planning for their children's college educations. They plan for each child to attend a private institution for five years beginning at age 18 at a cost of $25,000 per year per child (today's cost). The expected education inflation rate is 6%.
- Eddie and Tina want to retire with 80% of their preretirement income. Both Tina and Eddie would like to retire at age 65. They expect the retirement period to be 30 years.
- Eddie wants to review both his and Tina's life insurance needs.
- During retirement, Eddie and Tina plan to travel extensively.
- They want to be debt free by the time they retire.
- They want to have wills drafted for both of them.

ECONOMIC INFORMATION

- Inflation has averaged 4% over the last 20 years.
- Inflation is expected to be 3.5% for the foreseeable future.

Current Yields for Treasury Securities

3 months	6 months	9 months	1 year	3 years	5 years	10 years	20 years	25 years	30 years
4.0%	4.5%	4.7%	5.0%	6.0%	7.5%	8.5%	9.0%	9.0%	8.8%

Current Mortgage Rates

- 8.75% for 30-year loans
- 8.25% for 15-year loans

Refinancing will cost 3% of any mortgage as closing costs but will not be included in the new mortgage. The couple will pay the closing costs from separate funds.

Economic Outlook—Investments

	Expected returns (pre-tax)	Expected standard deviation
Aggressive stocks	18%	15%
Growth stocks	14%	10%
S&P 500	11%	8%
Bonds	8%	3%
Money markets	5%	1%
T-bills	4%	1%

INSURANCE INFORMATION

Life Insurance

	Policy A	Policy B	Policy C	Policy D
Insured	Eddie	Eddie	Tina	Tina
Owner	Eddie	Eddie	Tina	Eddie
Beneficiary	Eddie's mother	Eddie's estate	Brooks and Hunter	Brooks and Hunter
Original face amount	$200,000	$100,000	$72,000	$50,000
Policy type	Group term	30-year decreasing term	Group term	Whole life
Cash value*	$0	$0	$0	$5,000
Annual premium	$250	$100	$60	$420
Premium payer	Employer	Eddie	Employer	Eddie
Date purchased	Renewed annually	2003	Renewed annually	2014
Current death benefit	$200,000	$75,000	$72,000	$50,000

*Equal to interpolated terminal reserve

Health Insurance

The entire family is covered under the Amadeus group major medical health plan. The Topplemeirs currently pay $200 per month for the employer-provided plan. The deductible is $200 per person up to a maximum of three persons. The policy contains a $2,000 stop-loss limit per year and an 80/20 coinsurance provision.

Disability Insurance

Eddie has a personally owned disability insurance policy covering accident and sickness with an own occupation definition of disability and a 180-day elimination period. The policy pays a monthly benefit of $5,000 (payable to full retirement age).

Homeowners Insurance

HO-2 Policy*	Coverage Limit
Dwelling	$150,000
Other structure	$15,000
Personal property	$75,000
Loss of use	$30,000 (20% of dwelling)

*The policy does not contain an endorsement for replacement value on personal property.

The policy has an endorsement for furs and jewelry (annual premium of $30).

SPECIAL LIMITS ON PERSONAL PROPERTY

Property description	Special limits
Money, bank notes, bullion, gold other than goldware, silver other than silverware, platinum, coins, and medals	$200
Securities, accounts, deeds, evidences of debt, letters of credit, notes other than bank notes, manuscripts, personal records, passports, tickets, and stamps	$1,000 regardless of whether printed on paper or stored on computer disks
Watercraft—including outboard motors, furnishings, equipment, and trailers	$1,000
Any trailer not used with watercraft, such as a utility or camping trailer	$1,000
Jewelry, watches, furs, and precious and semiprecious stones	$1,000 for loss by theft
Firearms of any type	$2,000 for loss by theft
Silver and silver-plated ware, gold and gold-plated ware, and pewter ware	$2,500 for loss by theft
Property used at any time, in any manner, for any business purpose	$2,500 on premises $250 off premises
Electronic apparatus while it is in, on or away from a motor vehicle (such as a car phone or portable CD player) provided the apparatus can be operated by both the vehicle's power and other power sources	$1,500

INVESTMENT INFORMATION

During Tina's marriage to Reggie, a college education fund was established for Brooks and Hunter. When Reggie died, Tina no longer contributed to this fund. At the present time, the balance is $22,747. The money was invested in short-term CDs at 6%, and the Topplemeirs have the option of renewing the short-term CDs in April at an interest rate of 4%.

When Tina received the life insurance proceeds of $250,000 upon Reggie's death, she asked a broker to help her manage the money. Her broker, Randall, has her in a wrap account with a 1% annual fee. Randall has full discretion over the account and determines both security selection and timing of trades. Randall's record regarding Tina's investment portfolio over the last five years has been as follows:

	2013	2014	2015	2016	2017
Load-adjusted return	(10.0)	?	(8.5)	12.0	3.0

Tina does not have information for 2014 and has been unable to acquire it from Randall.

Tina considers herself to be a conservative-to-moderate investor and has both limited experience and education in the area of investments. Eddie believes that he is a more moderate investor. He has more experience with investments than Tina.

INCOME TAX INFORMATION

The Topplemeirs are in the 25% marginal tax bracket for federal income tax and 8% for state income tax.

GIFTS, ESTATES, TRUSTS, AND WILL INFORMATION

The Topplemeirs have done no estate planning and neither has a will.

RETIREMENT INFORMATION

They both plan to retire when Tina reaches age 65. They expect the retirement period to be 30 years. They expect their retirement portfolio to average a 10% pretax rate of return. Social Security annual benefits for Eddie today would be $28,500 at age 67. The annual benefit for Tina at full retirement age based on her earnings would be $12,000.

Amadeus provides a profit-sharing plan with Section 401(k) provisions. The Section 401(k) plan has a 50% employer match on the first 6% the employee defers (3% maximum employer contribution). Neither Eddie nor Tina has ever participated in the Section 401(k) plan, but both have fully vested balances in the profit-sharing plan as follows:

	Vested balance
Eddie	$80,000
Tina	$12,000

The profit-sharing plan and Section 401(k) plan maintains individual accounts and participants may choose to allocate the respective funds among various mutual funds.

TOTAL RETURN AND ANNUALIZED RATES OF RETURN

The company has made the following contributions to the profit-sharing plan for Eddie and Tina for each of the related years:

	Eddie	Tina
2018	None yet	None yet
2017	$15,000	$3,600
2016	$0	$0
2015	$13,605	$3,265
2014	$10,366	$2,488
2013	$8,954	$2,369
2012	$25,000	$0

All contributions are made on December 31 of the indicated year.

Statement of Cash Flows

Eddie and Tina Topplemeir

For the Year Ending December 31, 2017

CASH INFLOWS

Salaries			
Eddie		$100,000	
Tina		24,000	
	Total salaries	$124,000	

Investment income

Brokerage account		$3,050	
Tina's investment portfolio		4,771	
Savings account		618	
Boys' education fund		1,062	
	Investment income	$9,501	
Total cash inflows			**$133,501**

CASH OUTFLOWS

Living expenses

Food		$4,300	
Clothing		4,000	
Entertainment		6,500	
Utilities, cable, and phone		5,000	
Auto maintenance		1,200	
Church		2,000	
Home mortgage		14,934	
Auto loan		18,818	
Credit card		4,300	
	Total living expenses	$61,052	

Insurance

Health premiums		$2,400	
Auto premiums		1,660	
Life premiums		520	
Homeowners premium including endorsement		950	
Disability		1,677	
	Total insurance	$7,207	

Taxes

Property (residence)		$5,550	
Federal income (withholding)		35,379	
State income (withholding)		4,122	
Payroll (FICA)		9,486	
	Total taxes	$54,537	
Total cash outflows			**$122,796**
Net cash flow			**$10,705**

Statement of Financial Position

Eddie and Tina Topplemeir

As of December 31, 2017

ASSETS[1]			LIABILITIES AND NET WORTH		
	Liquid assets			**Short-term liabilities**	
JT	Checking[2]	$2,500	S2	Credit cards	$4,300
JT	Savings[3]	15,450			
S1	Cash value life insurance	5,000			
	Total liquid assets	$22,950			
	Invested assets			**Long-term liabilities**	
S1	First Mutual Growth Fund[4]	$7,950	JT	Home mortgage	$144,981
S1	Brokerage account[5]	100,000	S1/S2	Auto loans	40,069
S2	Tina's investment portfolio	210,000	S1	Margin loan[6]	7,500
S2	Boys' education fund	22,747		Total long-term liabilities	$192,550
S1	Eddie's profit-sharing plan	80,000			
S2	Tina's profit-sharing plan	12,000		**Total liabilities**	$196,850
S1	Eddie's IRA[7]	9,000			
	Total invested assets	$441,697			
	Use assets				
JT	Home	$185,000		**Net worth**	$552,797
S1/S2	Automobiles	53,000			
S1	Boat	10,000			
S2	Furs and jewelry	7,000			
JT	Furniture and household	30,000			
	Total use assets	$285,000		**Total liabilities**	
	Total assets	**$749,647**		**and net worth**	**$749,647**

Notes to financial statements:

[1] All assets are stated at fair market value.

[2] The checking account is a non-interest-bearing account.

[3] The savings account earns 4% per year.

[4] See mutual fund detail.

[5] Brokerage account is stated at gross value, which does not include the margin loan of $7,500.

[6] The margin loan is for the brokerage account. The interest rate is currently 8%.

[7] Eddie's IRA is currently invested in CDs at a local bank.

S1 = Eddie's separate property

S2 = Tina's separate property

JT = joint tenancy with right of survivorship

INFORMATION REGARDING ASSETS AND LIABILITIES

Investment Income

Brokerage account

Money market	$300
Bonds	3,350
Margin interest	(600)
Total	$3,050

Tina's investment portfolio

Bonds	$1,300
Stocks	3,471
Total	$4,771

Savings account	$618
Boys' education fund	$1,062
TOTAL	$9,501

House

Principal residence	January 1, 2015 (purchase)
FMV (current)	$185,000
Original loan	$148,000
Term	30 years
Interest rate	9.5%
Payment	$1,244.46
Remaining mortgage	$144,981
Remaining term	27 years

Boat

The boat is a 90-horsepower fishing boat that was originally purchased for $10,000 and is owned outright.

Automobiles

	Eddie	Tina
Purchase price	$40,000	$35,000
Down payment	$0	$10,000
Term	48 months	48 months
Interest rate	7%	8%
Monthly payment	$957.85	$610.32
Payments remaining	33	20
Balance	$28,677.07	$11,392.23

Brokerage Account

Account Name: Eddie Topplemeir
Account Number: AB100402

	Balances			
Money market	Price/share	Shares	Current yield	FMV
Money market account	$1	6,667	4.5%	$6,667
Bonds	Maturity	Coupon	Cost basis	FMV
$10,000 US Treasury note	5	7.5%	$10,351.18	$10,000.00
$15,000 US Treasury bond	25	6%	$13,138.64	$10,579.83
$50,000 US Treasury bond	30	0%	$4,093.40	$3,982.02
$20,000 Davidson debenture	20	8.5%	$17,455.93	$16,288.44
			$45,039.15	$40,850.29
Stocks	Price/share	Shares	Cost basis	FMV
Stock 1*	$5.20	2,000	$10,000	$10,400
Stock 2*	$4.85	1,500	$6,750	$7,275
Stock 3*	$26	500	$11,250	$13,000
			$28,000	$30,675

* These stocks currently do not pay dividends.

Mutual funds	Price/share	Shares	Cost basis	FMV
Emerging Growth Fund	$21	500	$12,250	$10,500
Balanced Fund	$18	425	$8,925	$7,650
Municipal Bond Fund	$12	250	$3,500	$3,000
			$24,675	$21,150

Note: All distributions from these funds are automatically reinvested.

Options	Number of option contracts	Option premium paid	Exercise price	Expiration date	FMV
Stock 2 call options	5	$3	$5.50	July 2017	$486.37
Stock 3 put options	5	$5	$24	March 2017	$171.34
					$657.71

Total account value	**$100,000**
Margin loan balance	**$7,500**
Net account value	**$92,500**

First Mutual Growth Fund

Account Name: Eddie Topplemeir
Account Number: SN15135

Transaction	Date	Cost basis	Price/share	Shares	Total shares	Total value
Buy	04/01/16	$2,500	$25	100	100	$2,500
Buy	08/01/16	$4,000	$20	200	300	$6,000
Reinvest div	12/01/16	$500	$12.50	40	340	$4,250
Buy	02/01/17	$3,000	$15	200	540	$8,100
Buy	04/01/17	$2,000	$20	100	640	$12,800
Buy	06/01/17	$1,500	$25	60	700	$17,500
Sell	12/01/17	$11,880	$27	(440)	260	$7,020
Reinvest div	12/01/17	$1,080	$27	40	300	$8,100
Balance	12/31/17	—	$26.50	—	300	$7,950

Note: All distributions from this fund are automatically reinvested.

Tina's Investment Portfolio

Bonds

Bonds	Maturity	Duration	FMV
$10,000 US Treasury bonds	10	7.12 years	$10,000
$5,000 US Treasury bonds	20	9.95 years	$5,000
		Total value of bonds	$15,000

Stocks

Shares	Stock	$\bar{x}$	Beta	σ	R²	P/E ratio	Dividend yield	Basis	FMV
1,000	Stock A	6%	0.65	11%	75%	13.0	3.0%	$30,000	$38,000
575	Stock B	11%	0.75	9%	65%	14.0	3.7%	$45,000	$46,000
200	Stock C	7%	0.65	10%	30%	15.1	3.7%	$20,000	$17,000
500	Stock D	3%	0.70	8%	45%	25.2	0%	$11,000	$8,500
1,000	Stock E	25%	0.95	15%	70%	14.4	0%	$20,000	$18,000
1,250	Stock F	22%	1.10	18%	20%	11.1	0%	$23,000	$25,000
							Total value of stocks		$152,500

Mutual funds

Shares	Mutual fund	Style	$\bar{x}$	Alpha	Beta	σ	R²	Front-end load	Expense ratio	Basis	FMV
210	Fund A	MG	14%	3%	1.10	12%	57%	4.5%	0.71%	$2,500	$2,625
300	Fund B	LG	11.5%	0.5%	0.94	8%	81%	4.5%	1%	$5,000	$5,100
443	Fund C	MV	6%	(4%)	0.65	8%	42%	4.5%	1.5%	$10,000	$11,075
1,000	Fund D	MG	–6%	(10%)	0.70	20%	4%	4%	2%	$8,000	$7,500
320	Fund E	LG	4%	(3%)	1.10	5%	60%	5%	1.5%	$9,500	$8,000
410	Fund F	LG	7%	(2.5%)	0.90	3%	78%	3%	1.5%	$10,000	$8,200
								Total value of mutual funds			$42,500

Total portfolio value $210,000

Note: All distributions from the mutual funds are automatically reinvested.

$\bar{x}$	=	five-year average return	L =	large-cap
σ	=	standard deviation	M =	mid-cap
R²	=	coefficient of determination between the asset and the market	G =	growth
			V =	value

Questions

1. What is the character and amount of the taxable gain on the sale of the 440 shares of First Mutual Growth Fund (December 1, 2017), and how will it be classified for income tax purposes? Assume that the basis in the shares is determined using the FIFO method. (Round to the nearest dollar.)

   | | Capital Gain | |
	Short term	Long term
A.	$0	$3,380
B.	$1,780	$1,600
C.	$1,600	$1,780
D.	$1,200	$2,180

2. Which of the following methods are permitted for determining the basis of the 440 shares of First Mutual Growth Fund sold on December 1?

   1. FIFO method
   2. Specific identification method
   3. LIFO method
   4. Average cost method

   A. 1, 2, and 3
   B. 1, 2, and 4
   C. 1 and 4
   D. 1, 2, 3, and 4

3. Eddie and Tina are interested in maintaining an emergency fund to pay expenses in the event that Eddie loses his job. Which of the following would be the best option for their emergency fund?

   A. GNMA fund
   B. Money market fund
   C. Exchange-traded fund
   D. Hedge fund

4. Tina is considering the purchase of a van with 120,000 miles for $1,500 for her 16-year-old son, Brooks. Regarding collision coverage for this vehicle, what is the most appropriate risk management technique?

   A. Insure
   B. Subrogate
   C. Share
   D. Retain

5. The Topplemeirs should purchase separate insurance coverage in addition to their HO-2 policy for which of the following?

   1. Jewelry
   2. Boat
   3. Fur
   4. Fine art

   A. 1, 2, and 3
   B. 2 only
   C. 2, 3, and 4
   D. 1, 2, 3, and 4

6. Which of the following is the most appropriate strategy for the allocation of Tina's mutual funds?

   A. Because Tina has a relatively even balance between the growth and value styles, she should maintain this allocation.
   B. Although she has an even split between growth and value, she should sell an even amount of each of these groups to purchase an even amount of blend funds.
   C. She should sell some of the growth funds and buy more value and blend funds.
   D. She should sell all of her value funds and buy small company funds.

7. If one were to plot the current yields for Treasury securities given in the case, the derived yield curve is consistent with which of the following investment theories?

   1. Liquidity preference theory
   2. Market segmentation theory
   3. Expectations theory

   A. 1 and 2
   B. 2 only
   C. 2 and 3
   D. 1, 2, and 3

8. If interest rates for all maturities increase by 1%, what would be the approximate value of the bonds in Tina's investment portfolio?

   A. $13,759
   B. $13,887
   C. $14,324
   D. $15,000

9. What is the holding period return that Eddie would receive if the price of Stock 2 in the brokerage account increases to $7.50?

   A. 75%
   B. 67%
   C. 55%
   D. 44%

10. Tina has decided that the CDs and her investment account will be used to fund the cost of college for the boys. Tina wants to set aside enough of these assets to fund each boy's education and use the remainder to fund Emily's college education. Ignoring the transaction costs of selling the current assets, how much does she need to set aside for the boys' college education if she wants to invest in an even mix of 5-year and 10-year Treasury bonds? Assume all taxes will be paid out of current income.

    A. $223,711.15
    B. $219,568.33
    C. $211,463.02
    D. $194,714.06

11. How much of their current gross income are the Topplemeirs saving toward their retirement goal?

	Eddie	Tina
A.	$18,000	$3,840
B.	$6,000	$1,440
C.	$9,000	$2,160
D.	$0	$0

12. When Tina dies, which of the following assets will be considered income in respect of a decedent (IRD)?

    A. Life insurance Policy D owned by Tina
    B. Personal residence owned joint tenancy between Eddie and Tina
    C. Tina's investment portfolio
    D. Tina's profit-sharing plan

13. Which of the following correctly describe(s) the Topplemeirs' insurance situation?

    1. The Topplemeirs are underinsured for life insurance.
    2. The life insurance beneficiary designations need to be revised.
    3. None of the life insurance would be included in the probate estate because of the contractual nature of life insurance.

    A. 1 only
    B. 1 and 2
    C. 2 and 3
    D. 3 only

14. Which of the following is(are) the Topplemeirs' estate planning deficiency(ies)?

    1. Failure to plan for incapacity
    2. No provisions for the care of children
    3. Lack of wills

    A. 1 only
    B. 1 and 2
    C. 2 and 3
    D. 1, 2, and 3

15. After several meetings with Eddie and Tina, you are ready to communicate the recommendations. Which of the following is the first action Eddie and Tina should expect you to do right after you finish communicating your recommendations?

    A. Eddie and Tina should expect you to have checked with their accountant and taken their tax situation into consideration.
    B. Eddie and Tina should expect you to consider their possibilities of future pay increases.
    C. Eddie and Tina should expect you to listen attentively to their reaction to the planning recommendations.
    D. Eddie and Tina should expect you to have addressed their children's education funding.

16. Assuming that the Topplemeirs invest $10,000 in an S&P 500 Index fund, what is the probability that they will have a return greater than 3%?

    A. 16%
    B. 34%
    C. 84%
    D. 95%

17. What is the internal rate of return (rounded to the nearest 1/10 of a percent) that Eddie has earned on the assets held in the profit-sharing plan from December 31, 2012, to December 31, 2017?

    A. 2.3%
    B. 2.6%
    C. 2.9%
    D. 3.1%

18. Which of the following strategies would help the Topplemeirs reduce their current federal income tax liability?

    1. Have Eddie contribute to the Amadeus Section 401(k) plan
    2. Have Tina contribute to a Roth IRA
    3. Have both Eddie and Tina contribute to a single-premium deferred annuity
    4. Purchase a $1,000 computer for Eddie's business use and elect Section 179 expensing

    A. 1 only
    B. 1, 2, and 4
    C. 1 and 4
    D. 2 and 3

19. If Eddie died today, what amount of life insurance death benefits would be included in his probate estate?

    A. $0
    B. $75,000
    C. $100,000
    D. $275,000

20. Assuming Tina died today, which of the following statements is CORRECT?

    A. The death benefit of the whole life policy will be included in Tina's probate estate.
    B. The death benefit of the whole life policy will be considered a gift from Eddie to Brooks and Hunter.
    C. The group term policy will be included in Tina's probate estate.
    D. $22,000 of the group term policy death benefit will be subject to income tax to the beneficiaries.

ANSWER SUMMARY

1. B	6. C	11. D	16. C
2. B	7. D	12. D	17. D
3. B	8. B	13. B	18. A
4. D	9. B	14. D	19. B
5. B	10. A	15. C	20. B

SUMMARY OF TOPICS

1. Tax—Sale of Mutual Fund Shares
2. Tax—Sale of Mutual Fund Shares
3. Fundamentals—Emergency Fund
4. Insurance—Collision Coverage
5. Insurance—Personal Property/HO-2 Loss of Use Coverage
6. Investments—Allocation of Funds (Asset Allocation)
7. Investments—Yield Curve Theories
8. Investments—Bond Analysis
9. Investments—Calculation of Gains and Losses
10. Fundamentals—Education Funding
11. Retirement—Savings Rate
12. Estates—IRD
13. Insurance—Life Insurance Coverage
14. Estates—Planning Deficiencies
15. Fundamentals—Communicating the Recommendations
16. Investments—Probability of a Return
17. Investments—Internal Rate of Return
18. Tax—Reduction of Tax Liability
19. Estates—Probate Estate
20. Estates—Life Insurance Benefits

Solutions

Tax—Sale of Mutual Fund Shares

1. B

Purchase date	Sales date	Shares	Sales price	Purchase price	Short-term gain/loss	Long-term gain/loss
04/01/16	12/01/17	100	$2,700	$2,500		$200
08/01/16	12/01/17	200	5,400	4,000		1,400
12/01/16*	12/01/17	40	1,080	500	$580	
02/01/17*	12/01/17	100	2,700	1,500	1,200	
Total			$11,880	$8,500	$1,780	$1,600

*Long-term holding period rule: must be held for more than 12 months (sales price is $27 per share).

Tax—Sale of Mutual Fund Shares

2. B

The methods of determining basis include FIFO, specific identification, and the average cost method. Under the specific identification method, the taxpayer identifies specific shares to be sold and uses compounding basis for those shares. Generally, the shares with the highest basis would be selected. The average cost method calculates basis by determining the total basis for all shares owned and dividing the sum by the total number of shares.

Fundamentals—Emergency Fund

3. B

The money market fund would be the most appropriate investment for their emergency fund.

Insurance—Collision Coverage

4. D

Tina should not purchase collision coverage because of the low amount at risk and the high cost of the coverage.

Insurance—Personal Property/HO-2 Loss of Use Coverage

5. B

Boats are generally excluded from liability coverage under homeowners policies. A separate watercraft policy should be purchased. Their HO-2 policy includes an endorsement for furs and jewelry. The case does not specify that the couple owns fine art.

Investments—Allocation of Funds (Asset Allocation)

6. C

Allocation in dollars

	Value		Blend	Growth	
Large-cap				Fund	
				B	$5,100
				E	8,000
				F	8,200
				Total	$21,300
Mid-cap	Fund			Fund	
	C	$11,075		A	$2,625
				D	7,500
	Total	$11,075		Total	$10,125
Small-cap					

Allocation as a percentage

	Value	Blend	Growth
Large-cap			50.12%
Mid-cap	26.06%		23.82%
Small-cap			

Tina's portfolio is heavily concentrated in the growth style and is evenly split between large-cap and mid-cap companies. She should shift some of her investments to the value or blend style based on her risk tolerance.

Investments—Yield Curve Theories

7. **D**

The liquidity preference theory is based on the concept that longer-term bonds are more price sensitive to interest rate changes than shorter-term bonds. This theory also implies that investors pay a premium (i.e., lower yields) for shorter-maturity bonds to avoid the high interest rate risk associated with long-term bonds. Under this theory, long-term rates will generally be higher than short-term rates. Although the 30-year rate is slightly lower than the 25-year rate, the yield curve is still consistent with this theory. This theory argues that the yield curve should always slope upward and that any other shape is only a temporary aberration.

The market segmentation theory relies on the concepts of supply and demand for various maturities of borrowing and lending. Bonds with different maturities make up distinct markets. The markets for borrowing and lending can be broken into three categories.

Lenders in each market will match their assets, or lending, with their liabilities, or debts. Borrowers attempt to match the term of indebtedness with the period they need to borrow the funds.

Supply and demand in the various markets are believed to be independent, which allows for the shape of the yield curve to change over time. Based on this theory, the yield curve can take on almost any shape. The derived yield curve is consistent with this theory.

The expectations theory is based on the concept that long-term rates consist of a series of short-term rates. The long-term rates will be the average (or geometric mean) of the short-term rates.

Investments—Bond Analysis

8. **B**

Formula: $\dfrac{\Delta P}{P} = -D \left[\dfrac{\Delta y}{1 + y} \right]$

$-6.56\% = -7.12 \times \dfrac{0.01}{1.085}$ 10,000 T-bonds

$-9.13\% = -9.95 \times \dfrac{0.01}{1.09}$ 5,000 T-bonds

Note: The yield to maturity for each bond is determined by analyzing the current yield curve.

10,000 US Treasury Bonds		5,000 US Treasury Bonds	
Duration	7.12	Duration	9.95
YTM	8.5%	YTM	9%
Change in interest rates	1%	Change in interest rates	1%
Old price of bond	$10,000	Old price of bond	$5,000
Percentage change	−6.5622%	Percentage change	−9.1284%
New price of bond	$9,343.78	New price of bond	$4,543.58

Adjusted value of the bonds in Tina's investment portfolio: $9,343.78 + $4,543.58 = $13,887

Investments—Calculation of Gains and Losses

9. **B**

$$HPR = \frac{\$7.50 - \$4.50}{\$4.50} = \frac{\$3.00}{\$4.50} = 66.67\%$$

The holding period return is 67% (rounded).

The gain would be a capital gain (short-term or long-term depending on the holding period).

The beginning value of the stock is the cost basis of $6,750 divided by 1,500 shares, or $4.50.

Fundamentals—Education Funding

10. **A**

PMT	=	($25,000)
n	=	5
i	=	1.8868% {[(1.08 ÷ 1.06) – 1] × 100}
FV	=	$0
$PV_{AD@18}$	=	$120,455.30

Note: Ten-year bonds are yielding 8.5%. Therefore, 5-year bonds are yielding 7.5%, and the average yield is 8%.

		Brooks	**Hunter**
FV_{18}	=	$120,455.30	$120,455.30
n	=	2	6
i	=	1.8868	1.8868
PMT	=	$0	$0
PV	=	$116,035.28	$107,675.87

Therefore, Tina should set aside $223,711.15 to fund her boys' college education.

An alternate (and faster) method to calculate the answer is by using the uneven series of cash flows method. Using the HP 10BII/HP 10BII+:

0 CFj

0 CFj

25000 CFj

4 shift Nj

50000 CFj

25000 CFj

4 shift Nj

[(1.08 ÷ 1.06) – 1] × 100 = 1.8868 I/YR

shift NPV

Retirement—Savings Rate

11. **D**

Neither Eddie nor Tina participates in the Section 401(k) plan sponsored by their employer, and they do not make any other investments from current income designated for retirement.

Estates—IRD

12. D

Retirement plans are considered IRD assets.

Insurance—Life Insurance Coverage

13. B

Statement 3 is incorrect because the beneficiary designation on Policy B (Eddie's estate) subjects the proceeds to probate. Statement 2 is correct. None of the policies provide for Tina or Emily, and an estate is generally not a desirable beneficiary designation. Statement 1 is correct. If Eddie were to die, the only insurance proceeds available to his wife and dependents are $75,000. This amount is less than the Topplemeirs' current annual cash outlay requirement. The policy also names the estate as beneficiary, thereby subjecting the policy proceeds to possible creditor claims.

Estates—Planning Deficiencies

14. D

- There are no wills.
- There are no provisions for the care or guardianship of the children.
- There are no durable powers of attorney for health care.

Fundamentals—Communicating the Recommendations

15. C

At this stage in the financial planning process, you should be listening to Eddie and Tina's reaction to your recommendations. You should have already finished the other tasks before developing the recommendations.

Investments—Probability of a Return

16. C

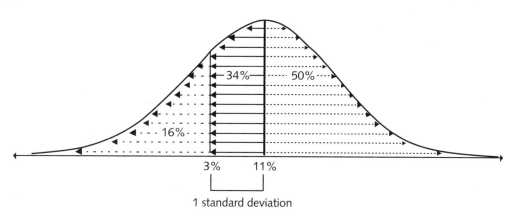

Because 3% is 1 standard deviation from the mean (11%), the probability of getting a return between 3% and 11% is 34% (½ of 68%). The probability of getting a return above 11% is 50%. Therefore, the probability of a return above 3% is 84% (50% + 34%).

Investments—Internal Rate of Return

17. D

Period	Cash flow	
0	($25,000)	
1	($8,954)	
2	($10,366)	
3	($13,605)	
4	$0	
5	$65,000	($80,000 – $15,000)
IRR	3.0745%	

Tax—Reduction of Tax Liability

18. A

Statement 1 is correct. Contributions to the Section 401(k) plan would be pretax, thereby reducing Eddie's compensation currently subject to state and federal income taxes.

Statement 2 is incorrect. Roth contributions are nondeductible.

Statement 3 is incorrect. Contributions to annuities are nondeductible.

Statement 4 is incorrect. Eddie is an employee of Amadeus. Therefore, his unreimbursed business expenses would be considered miscellaneous itemized deductions subject to the 2% of AGI floor.

Estates—Probate Estate

19. B

Eddie's probate estate will include the $75,000 death benefit from Policy B because Eddie's estate is the beneficiary.

Estates—Life Insurance Benefits

20. B

Because Eddie is the owner and the children are the beneficiaries, Eddie will have made a completed gift for federal gift tax purposes equal to the death benefit. However, the gift will be eligible for the gift tax annual exclusion.

The death benefit from the whole life policy will be excluded from Tina's probate estate because the proceeds are not payable to Tina's estate.

The death benefit from the group term policy will be excluded from Tina's probate estate because the death benefit will pass by contract to the beneficiaries.

The death benefit from the group term policy will be received by the beneficiaries income tax free.

Case Study 5: Robert and Robin Farrell

Case Study Facts

Robert and Robin Farrell have come to you, a CFP® professional, for help in developing a plan to accomplish their financial goals. From your initial meeting together, you have gathered the following information. Today is December 31, 2017.

PERSONAL INFORMATION

Robert Farrell (Age 65)

Robert owns Farrell's Animal Care Center, a local animal hospital with 25 employees. Robert has a salary of $250,000.

Robin Farrell (Age 50)

Robin is in excellent health. She works as a CPA for an international accounting firm, where she is currently a manager in the area of litigation support. She has a daughter, Payton, from a previous marriage, who is age 30 and living on her own. Robin has a salary of $50,000.

The Farrells

They have been married for 25 years.

Children

Robert and Robin have three children from their marriage.

Nicole—age 23

Ryan—age 21

Danielle—age 5

Marleen Burke

Robin's mother, Marleen, turned age 70 on December 1, 2017, and is a widow with substantial net worth. In addition to sizable holdings of real estate, stocks, and bonds, Marleen has $450,000 in her IRA rollover account as of December 31, 2017. (Her account grew by $25,000 during 2017.) Because she is in extremely poor health, she had an attorney draft a will leaving her entire estate to Robin. The will provides that in the event that Robin should predecease her, the entire estate will be left in trust for Robin's four children.

PERSONAL AND FINANCIAL OBJECTIVES

- Robert wants to sell his business during 2018 and retire. He expects to live 30 years.
- Robert wants to continue to transfer some of his wealth to his children. He will consider using the family limited partnership that is currently in place.

ECONOMIC INFORMATION

General

They expect inflation to average 4% annually both currently and for the long term.

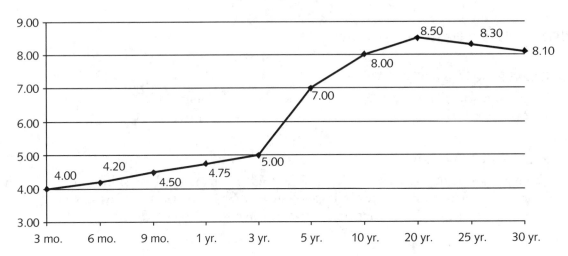

US Treasury

Current Yield Curve

Economic Outlook—Investments

	Expected returns (pretax)	Expected standard deviation
Aggressive stocks	18%	15%
Growth stocks	14%	10%
S&P 500	11%	8%
Bonds	8%	3%
Money markets	5%	1%
T-bills	4%	1%

Banking

The Farrells have favorable banking relationships and can borrow money at the following rates:

Type of loan	Rates
Installment loans—secured	6.5%
Personal signature bank loans	9%
Mortgage loan—30-year fixed	8.5%
Mortgage loan—15-year fixed	8%

INVESTMENT INFORMATION

They consider $100,000 adequate for an emergency fund. They indicate a moderate level of risk tolerance in investments.

INCOME TAX INFORMATION

The Farrells are in a marginal income tax bracket of 33% for federal and 6% for state. Capital gains are taxed at 15%/20% (depending on how much the capital gain would increase their AGI) at the federal level. (There is no special rate at the state level.)

In an effort to reduce their income tax liability, the Farrells would like to donate some cash and other assets to charity, but they are not certain as to which charity. They do not need cash flow from the donated assets and do not want to deal with administrative headaches. Although today is December 31, they would like to receive an income tax deduction for the current year if possible.

INSURANCE INFORMATION

Life Insurance	Policy 1	Policy 2
Insured	Robert Farrell	Robert Farrell
Face amount	$1.5 million	$250,000
Cash value	$25,000	$0
Type of policy	Whole life	Variable universal life
Annual premium	$4,500	$40,706 (single premium)
Beneficiary	Payton, Nicole, Ryan, Danielle	Robin Farrell
Contingent beneficiary	Robert's estate	Farrell Children's Insurance Trust
Policyowner	Farrell Children's Insurance Trust*	Robert
Settlement option	N/A	Single life annuity (guaranteed for 10 years)

* The original owner of the policy was Robert; however, he transferred the policy to the trust on June 30, 2017. William Bradley, who has been a friend of Robert since college, is the trustee of the Farrell Children's Insurance Trust. Interpolated terminal reserve at date of transfer was $25,000. The policy was purchased on January 1, 2006.

Robin has $100,000 of group term insurance provided through her employer. The primary beneficiary is Robert.

HEALTH INSURANCE

Robert

Currently he has a major medical health insurance plan through Farrell's Animal Care Center but will not be covered once the sale of the business has been finalized. Robert's health plan has the following features:

- $1,000 individual deductible
- $2,500 family deductible
- $3,500 stop-loss limit
- 80/20 coinsurance clause

Robin

Coverage is available through Robin's employer, but she is currently covered under Robert's policy.

Disability Insurance

Robert does not have disability insurance.

Robin has disability insurance provided by her employer. The policy provides for a benefit of 60% of gross pay with an own occupation definition and a 180-day elimination period. The policy covers both accidents and sickness. Benefits are payable to age 65.

Auto Insurance (Both Cars)

Type	PAP
Liability (bodily injury)	$100,000/$300,000
Property damage	$50,000
Medical payments	$1,000
Uninsured motorists	$100,000/$300,000
Collision deductible	$1,000
Comprehensive deductible	$500
Annual premium (2 cars)	$1,800

Homeowners Insurance

Type	HO-3
Dwelling	$700,000
Other structures	$70,000
Personal property	$350,000
Personal liability	$100,000
Medical payments	$1,000
Deductible	$1,000
Coinsurance requirement	80%
Annual premium	$2,200

Umbrella Insurance

The policy is for $3 million in coverage with a premium of $500 per year.

RETIREMENT INFORMATION

Robert

- Robert has a profit-sharing plan and a money purchase pension plan at Farrell's Animal Care Center, with a combined balance of $1.35 million. Contributions are made under the self-employed participant-owner rules.

- Robert also has an IRA with a balance of $30,000 (see details). This account was established in 1998.

- Robin is the beneficiary of all of Robert's retirement accounts.

Robin

- Robin has a Section 401(k) plan in which she is able to make elective deferrals of up to 20% of her salary. The accounting firm matches $.25 for each $1.00 she defers, up to 6% of her salary.

- Robert is the beneficiary of all of Robin's retirement accounts.

Robert and Robin

- They anticipate retiring today, and both expect to live until age 95.

- They have estimated that they need $250,000 per year, in today's dollars, for retirement. This amount would drop by 25% if only one were alive.

Asset Allocation

The Farrells plan to have a separate fund to provide for their retirement income. They expect to maintain a portfolio with the following asset allocation.

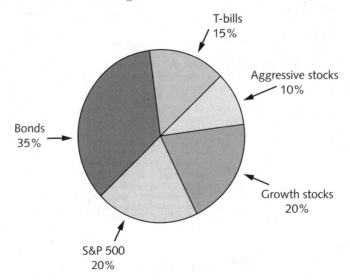

EDUCATION INFORMATION

Nicole and Ryan are both enrolled at a private college. The annual tuition is currently $30,000 per year for each child and is expected to increase by approximately 7% per year. This cost is being funded from current earnings and savings. They are concerned about funding Danielle's education because they are retiring and will not be working while Danielle is in school. They expect tuition to be $30,000 (today's cost) and to increase by 7% each year. They expect that Danielle, beginning at age 18, will attend four years of undergraduate and two years of graduate school. They would like to set aside money today, which would be invested in bonds, to fund the cost of Danielle's college education.

INFORMATION REGARDING WILLS, TRUSTS, AND ESTATES

Wills

Both Robert and Robin have wills. Each of the wills provides for all assets to be left in a QTIP trust with the surviving spouse as the income beneficiary and the children as the remaindermen. They think they need to have their wills updated.

The Farrell Family Trust

This trust was established in 2001 for the purpose of reducing the Farrells' estate tax. The primary beneficiaries of the trust are the four children, and the contingent beneficiary is the Heart Association. If a child were to die, his interest would pass to that child's heirs. If no heir exists, the interest would pass to the remaining children of the trust. If all children were to die without heirs, the Heart Association would receive the corpus of the trust. The trust is currently valued at $3 million.

The Farrell Children's Insurance Trust (All Four Children)

This trust was set up in early 2017 for the purpose of providing estate liquidity. On June 30, 2017, Robert Farrell transferred life insurance Policy 1 to the trust. There is a Crummey provision in the trust.

RARF Family Limited Partnership

P. K. Keller, one of the area's best estate planning attorneys, discussed the benefits of setting up a family limited partnership with the Farrells. With his help, the Farrells established RARF Family Limited Partnership (RARF FLP) in 2012. All of the assets transferred to the trust were Robert's separate property. Robert currently owns 100% of the RARF FLP but intends to begin transferring some ownership to his children and possibly to Robin.

Statement of Financial Position
Robert and Robin Farrell
As of December 31, 2017

	ASSETS[1]			LIABILITIES AND NET WORTH	
	Cash/cash equivalents			**Liabilities**	
Robert	Cash and checking[2]	$250,000	Robin	Credit card balances[7]	$15,000
Robert	Money market fund[3]	875,000	Robert	Short-term note	230,000
	Total cash/equivalents	**$1,125,000**		Total liabilities	**$245,000**
	Invested assets				
Robert	Profit-sharing plan	$1,350,000			
Robert	IRA—Robert	30,000			
Robin	Section 401(k) plan vested balance—Robin	150,000			
Robert	Growth mutual fund	53,100			
Robert	Due from RARF	70,500			
Robert	RARF Family Limited Partnership (see detail)	1,193,600			
Robert	Common stock portfolio[4]	100,000			
Robert	Farrell's Animal Care Center common stock[5]	2,250,000			
	Total invested assets	**$5,197,200**		Net worth	**$7,519,200**
	Use assets				
JT	Residence[6]	$1,000,000			
JT	Personal property	400,000			
JT	Autos	42,000			
	Total use assets	**$1,442,000**			
	Total assets	**$7,764,200**		**Total liabilities and net worth**	**$7,764,200**

Notes to financial statement:

[1] Presented at fair market value.

[2] Cash and checking earn 3% annually.

[3] Money market earns 5% annually.

[4] Publicly traded stock.

[5] The value is an approximation of the value of the business made by Dr. Farrell. The company is a C corporation with a basis of $25,000.

[6] Basis of home is $200,000 (Robert contributed 75% and Robin contributed 25% to the purchase of the house).

[7] Credit card interest rate is 18%.

Client name = separate property

JT = joint tenancy with right of survivorship

Statement of Cash Flows
Robert and Robin Farrell
January 1, 2017, to December 31, 2017

INFLOWS—ANNUAL		
Robert's salary	$250,000	
Robin's salary	50,000	
Dividend income	7,373	
Interest income	49,227	
Total inflows		$356,600
OUTFLOWS—ANNUAL		
Savings and investments	$56,600	$56,600
Fixed outflows		
Property taxes	20,000	
Homeowners insurance	2,200	
Utilities	7,800	
Telephone	600	
Auto insurance	1,800	
Gas/oil/maintenance	1,800	
Credit card payments	12,000	
Umbrella insurance	500	$46,700
Variable outflows		
Taxes	$119,691	
Food	7,800	
Medical/dental	2,000	
Clothing/personal care	6,000	
Child care	5,200	
Entertainment/vacation	10,000	
College	60,000	
Kindergarten	6,000	$216,691
Total outflows		$319,991
Net cash flow (surplus)		$36,609

INFORMATION REGARDING ASSETS AND LIABILITIES

Farrell's Animal Care Center

	Cash flows (NOI)
Year 1	$400,000
Year 2	$420,000
Year 3	$435,000
Year 4	$440,000
Terminal value at end of Year 4	$3 million*

* The terminal value was calculated by dividing the forecasted NOI for year 5 of $450,000 by an assumed discount rate of 15%.

Growth Mutual Fund

Account name: Robert Farrell

Date	Amount	Price/Share	Shares	Share Balance
2/1/16				0
3/1/16	$7,500	$15.00	500	500
4/1/16	7,500	18.75	400	900
5/1/16	1,000	20.00	50	950
6/1/16	1,000	20.00	50	1,000
7/1/16	1,000	25.00	40	1,040
8/1/16	1,000	25.00	40	1,080
9/1/16	1,000	25.00	40	1,120
10/1/16	1,000	20.00	50	1,170
11/1/16	1,000	25.00	40	1,210
12/1/16	1,000	25.00	40	1,250
3/1/17	2,300	23.00	100	1,350
6/1/17	4,800	24.00	200	1,550
9/1/17	3,000	30.00	100	1,650
12/1/17	4,200	28.00	150	1,800
12/15/17	2,700*	27.00	100	1,900

*Reinvest dividend

Account value as of 12/31/17: $53,100

Notes:

1. The NAV of the fund on December 31, 2016, was $26.

2. No dividends were paid in 2016.

3. A dividend of $1.50 per share was paid on December 15, 2017.

4. The NAV of the fund on December 31, 2017, was $27.9474.

Common Stock Portfolio

Account name: Robert Farrell

Stock	Expected return	Price/share	Total shares	Cost basis	FMV	Current dividend yield
A	25%	$25.55	1,250	$7,500	$31,937.50	3%
B	23%	$37.50	850	$10,000	$31,875.00	4%
C	15%	$87.00	175	$18,000	$15,225.00	0%
D	20%	$43.00	487.50	$16,000	$20,962.50	2.5%
	Total		2,762.50	$51,500	$100,000.00	

1. The standard deviation of the portfolio has been 10.9% in the past and is expected to be the same in the future.

2. Stocks were purchased as follows:

Stock A   3/5/00

Stock B   4/7/05

Stock C   6/30/17

Stock D   6/30/17

RARF Family Limited Partnership

Investment	FMV	Expected return	Standard deviation	Beta
Growth and Income Mutual Fund	$178,000	10.0%	9%	.92
Balanced Mutual Fund	246,500	8.5%	7%	.72
Foreign Mutual Fund	138,500	9.7%	15%	1.30
Brokerage Account A	216,000	11.2%	13%	1.22
Brokerage Account B	350,000	10.4%	10%	1.12
Total	$1,129,000			

Statement of Financial Position (RARF)
RARF Family Limited Partnership
As of December 31, 2017

ASSETS[1]

Cash/cash equivalent

Cash	$45,000	
Money market	55,000	
Total cash/cash equivalent		$100,000

Invested assets (see detail)

Growth and Income Mutual Fund	$178,000	
Balanced Mutual Fund	246,500	
Foreign Mutual Fund	138,500	
Brokerage Account A	216,000	
Brokerage Account B	350,000	
Total invested assets		$1,129,000

Use assets[2]

Computer equipment	$4,000	
Luxury auto	37,500	
Depreciation[3]	(6,400)	
Total use assets		$35,100
Total assets		$1,264,100

LIABILITIES

Due to Robert Farrell	$70,500	
Total liabilities		$70,500

Partner's capital		$1,193,600
Total liabilities and partner's capital		$1,264,100

Notes:

[1] All assets, other than use assets, are stated at fair market value.

[2] Use assets are listed at historical cost.

[3] Depreciation (computer = $4,000 and automobile = $2,400)

Questions

1. Farrell's Animal Care Center has been profitable for the past several years. Earnings in 2017 were $440,000. If a discount rate of 3% above the expected return for aggressive stocks is used, what would be the value of the business based on 2017 earnings under the capitalization of earnings approach?

    A. $1,904,762
    B. $2,095,238
    C. $2,444,444
    D. $2,933,333

2. Marleen Burke has engaged you to answer some questions about her IRA. Because of her financial stability and a sizable net worth, she intends to simply leave the funds in her IRA untouched. When she dies, she believes that this asset will get a step-up in basis for her heirs. Which of the following statements regarding her IRA is CORRECT?

    A. She must receive minimum distributions after attaining age 70½, but any amounts remaining in her IRA at her death will get a step-up in basis.
    B. She is correct in her belief, and this is a great strategy.
    C. She will be subject to minimum distribution penalties, but the IRA will receive a stepped-up basis at her death.
    D. The heirs will not receive a step-up in basis in the IRA, and she will be penalized if she does not take a minimum distribution when required by the Tax Code.

3. Which of the following statements regarding the RARF Family Limited Partnership is CORRECT?

    1. The Growth and Income Mutual Fund has a Treynor ratio of .06522.
    2. The Balanced Mutual Fund has a Treynor ratio of .06250.
    3. The Foreign Mutual Fund has a Treynor ratio of .04385.
    4. Among the three mutual funds in the portfolio, the Foreign Mutual Fund has the best risk-adjusted return based on the Treynor ratio.

    A. 1 only
    B. 2 and 4
    C. 2 and 3
    D. 1, 2, and 3

4. What is the dollar-weighted return from March 1, 2016, to December 31, 2016, for the Growth Mutual Fund (listed on the Statement of Financial Position)?

    A. 12.68%
    B. 21.82%
    C. 26.19%
    D. 53.55%

5. Which of the following statements explain the difference between time-weighted return and dollar-weighted return?

    1. Time-weighted return is primarily focused on how an investment has performed over a specific period without regard to the cash flows of specific investors.
    2. Time-weighted return is the same as dollar-weighted return.
    3. Dollar-weighted return is used primarily by mutual funds.
    4. Dollar-weighted return considers the return an investor receives from an investment based on the specific cash flows.

    A. 1, 2, and 4
    B. 1 and 3
    C. 1 and 4
    D. 2, 3, and 4

6. What was the gift tax valuation of the life insurance policy transferred to the Farrell Children's Trust?

    A. $11,000—because of the annual exclusion
    B. $25,000—interpolated terminal reserve
    C. $27,250—interpolated terminal reserve and ½ of the annual premium
    D. $29,500—interpolated terminal reserve plus the annual premium

7. What are the estate planning implications of having Robert's estate as the contingent beneficiary of life insurance Policy 1?

    A. There are no implications as long as the estate is simply the contingent beneficiary.
    B. It could cause inclusion of the proceeds in Robert's probate estate.
    C. There are no implications if Robert lives 3 years after transferring the policy to the trust.
    D. Because there are 4 beneficiaries, there is no problem.

8. Assume that you recommend Robert begin transferring ownership of the RARF Family Limited Partnership to Nicole and Ryan in 2018. You explain to Robert that if the transfer is implemented correctly, Robert can achieve certain gift and estate tax benefits. Assuming that Robert accepts your recommendation, which of the following steps would occur in the implementation of this strategy?

    1. Robert will begin gifting limited partnership interests to Nicole and Ryan.
    2. Nicole and Ryan will assume control over the partnership.
    3. Nicole and Ryan will give Robert collateral as security for the transfers.

    A. 1 only
    B. 1 and 2
    C. 2 and 3
    D. 3 only

9. The Farrells are currently designing an investment program to fund college for Danielle. Robert wants a portion of the investment portfolio to be invested in tax-exempt securities. Which of the following investments would produce interest or dividends that are free from federal income tax?

    A. Zero-coupon Treasury bonds

    B. State of Louisiana bonds with a 5% coupon rate

    C. Zero-coupon corporate bond with a duration of 7.3 years

    D. Series EE savings bonds

10. If Robert were to die today, which of the following assets would be included in his probate estate?

    A. Personal residence

    B. Profit-sharing plan

    C. RARF FLP

    D. Autos

11. Assume the Farrells decide to update their wills. Which of the following should be included in their new wills?

    1. Provision for guardians of minors

    2. Funeral instructions

    3. Transfer of IRA assets

    4. Attestation clause

    A. 1 and 2

    B. 1 and 4

    C. 2, 3, and 4

    D. 3 and 4

12. Assume that after evaluating the Farrells' objectives and financial status, you decide to recommend that Robert create a charitable remainder annuity trust (CRAT) and donate his ownership interest in Farrell's Animal Care Center to the CRAT instead of selling the business outright. Robert and Robin would be the income beneficiaries under the CRAT for their joint lifetimes, and the remainder interest will pass to Robert's favorite charity. You schedule a meeting with the Farrells to communicate your recommendation to them. You should do all of the following at this meeting EXCEPT

    A. verify that the Farrells accept the recommendation

    B. assure the Farrells that they will receive a fixed annual income from the CRAT for life

    C. make sure the Farrells understand that they cannot make additional contributions to the CRAT after it is established

    D. assure the Farrells that they can revise the CRAT in the future should their situation change

13. Assume that Marleen dies. Robin tells you that she does not want to receive Marleen's estate and prefers that it pass to her 4 children instead. You recommend that Robin file a qualified disclaimer. Assuming Robin accepts your recommendation, what steps are necessary in implementing the recommendation successfully?

    1. Robin must file the disclaimer with the executor.
    2. Robin must make the disclaimer in writing.
    3. Robin must make the disclaimer within 6 months of Marleen's death.
    4. Robin must avoid accepting any interest in or benefit from Marleen's estate before the disclaimer is made.

    A. 1, 2, and 4
    B. 2, 3, and 4
    C. 2 and 4
    D. 1, 2, 3, and 4

14. What is the expected weighted rate of return of the common stock portfolio?

    A. 20.69%
    B. 20.75%
    C. 21.78%
    D. 22.50%

15. What is the probability that Robert's common stock portfolio (listed on the Statement of Financial Position) will have a return above 10.88%?

    A. 34%
    B. 50%
    C. 68%
    D. 84%

16. Which of the following options are available to the Farrells to provide health insurance once Robert sells his business?

    1. Robert qualifies for Medicare Part A and Part B.
    2. Robin qualifies for Medicare as Robert's spouse.
    3. Danielle qualifies under COBRA to continue health insurance for 36 months.
    4. Robin qualifies under COBRA to continue health insurance for 36 months.

    A. 1 and 2
    B. 1, 2, and 3
    C. 1, 3, and 4
    D. 2 and 4

17. Using the Sharpe ratio, which of the RARF Family Limited Partnership accounts (mutual funds) has the highest risk-adjusted return?

    A.   Growth and Income Mutual Fund

    B.   Balanced Mutual Fund

    C.   Account A

    D.   Account B

18. Tom has always been Robert's favorite nephew. Robert has always thought of him as a son. Tom has worked closely with Robert at Farrell's Animal Care Center, and Robert considers him a top-notch veterinarian. Upon retirement, Robert is considering selling the business to Tom but is unsure how to structure the sale. Tom does not have sufficient cash to pay the purchase price in a lump sum. After discussing the sale further with Robert, you feel that a sale by installment note, self-canceling installment note (SCIN), or private annuity might possibly meet Robert's needs. Which of the following issues should you investigate before making a final recommendation to Robert?

    1.   Whether Robert wants the sale to be secured by collateral

    2.   Whether Robert wants Tom to continue making payments after Robert dies, if Robert dies before all payments have been made

    3.   Whether Robert foresees any health issues that might cause him to die prematurely

    4.   Whether Tom wants to deduct part of the payments under the sale as interest

    A.   1 and 3

    B.   2 and 4

    C.   1, 2, and 3

    D.   1, 2, 3, and 4

19. Assuming Robert's $250,000 variable universal life policy is classified as a modified endowment contract (MEC), all of the following statements regarding the policy are correct EXCEPT

    A.   the policy is classified as a MEC because too much premium has been paid into the policy

    B.   this policy has been funded with more premium than the sum of the net level premiums that are needed to result in a paid-up policy after 7 years

    C.   if Robert were to make a loan or withdrawal from the cash value of the policy, he would incur a 10% tax penalty in addition to any applicable income taxes

    D.   this policy is subject to LIFO income tax treatment for loans made from the policy

20. Based on the Farrells' charitable income tax planning goal, what would be the best strategy to implement today?

    A.   Charitable remainder annuity trust

    B.   Outright gift to charity

    C.   Private foundation

    D.   Donor-advised fund

21. Which of the following strategies will assist the Farrells in lowering their personal income tax liability for next year?

    A.   Donate their personal residence to charity, retaining a life estate

    B.   Contribute to a Section 529 plan to help fund Danielle's college education

    C.   Have the Animal Care Center purchase equipment and elect Section 179 expense

    D.   Have Robert purchase a Medigap insurance policy

ANSWER SUMMARY

1. B	6. C	11. B	16. C	21. A
2. D	7. B	12. D	17. A	
3. D	8. A	13. A	18. D	
4. D	9. B	14. C	19. C	
5. C	10. C	15. D	20. D	

SUMMARY OF TOPICS

1. Investments—Capitalized Earnings
2. Retirement—Traditional IRA
3. Investments—Treynor Ratio
4. Investments—Dollar-Weighted Return
5. Investments—Time-Weighted and Dollar-Weighted Returns
6. Estates—Gift Tax
7. Estates—Gifting Strategies
8. Estates—Family Limited Partnerships
9. Fundamentals—Education Funding Strategies
10. Estates—Probate Estate
11. Estates—Wills
12. Estates—CRAT
13. Estates—Qualified Disclaimers
14. Investments—Investment Returns
15. Investments—Normal Distribution
16. Insurance—Health Insurance
17. Investments—Sharpe Ratio
18. Estates— Intra-Family Transfers
19. Insurance—Modified Endowment Contracts
20. Tax—Charitable Contributions
21. Tax—Tax Planning

Solutions

Investments—Capitalized Earnings

1. **B**

Discount rate = 18% + 3% = 21%

$$\text{Value} = \frac{\text{earnings}}{\text{discount rate}} = \frac{\$440,000}{0.21} = \$2,095,238$$

Retirement—Traditional IRA

2. **D**

Marleen will be required to commence required minimum distributions from her IRA upon attainment of age 70½, and she will be subject to penalty if she does not take distribution of the required amount each year. Retirement accounts are considered income in respect of a decedent (IRD) assets and do not receive a step-up in basis at the owner's death.

Investments—Treynor Ratio

3. **D**

$$\text{Treynor Ratio} \quad \frac{\bar{r}_p - \bar{r}_f}{\beta_p}$$

Growth and Income Mutual Fund	$(.100 - .04) \div 0.92 = .06522$
Balanced Mutual Fund	$(.085 - .04) \div 0.72 = .06250$
Foreign Mutual Fund	$(.097 - .04) \div 1.30 = .04385$

Based on the Treynor ratio, the fund with the highest risk-adjusted performance is the Growth and Income Mutual Fund.

Investments—Dollar-Weighted Return

4. **D**

CF_0	($7,500)
CF_1	($7,500)
CF_2	($1,000)
CF_3	($1,000)
CF_4	($1,000)
CF_5	($1,000)
CF_6	($1,000)
CF_7	($1,000)
CF_8	($1,000)
CF_9	($1,000)
CF_{10}	$32,500 (1,250 shares @ $26)

IRR = 4.46% per month, which equates to 53.55% per year.

Investments—Time-Weighted and Dollar-Weighted Returns

5. **C**

The time-weighted return is primarily focused on how the investment has performed over a specific period without regard to cash flows of specific investors. The dollar-weighted return considers the return an investor receives from an investment based on his cash flows.

Estates—Gift Tax

6. **C**

The amount of the gift is the fair market value at the date of the gift. Because the policy has been in force for several years and further premiums are to be paid, the gift tax valuation may be approximated by adding to the interpolated terminal reserve the proportionate part of the gross premium last paid before the gift (unearned premium), which covers the period extending beyond the gift (i.e., $2,250— ½ of the yearly premium). The interpolated terminal reserve is equal to $25,000, and the valuation for gift taxation is $27,250.

Estates—Gifting Strategies

7. **B**

The contingent beneficiary status could cause the proceeds to be included in Robert's probate estate at his death, exposing the proceeds to claims of creditors.

Estates—Family Limited Partnerships

8. **A**

Statement 1 is correct. With an FLP, the senior family member gifts limited partnership interests to the younger family members over time and retains ownership of the general partnership interest.

Statement 2 is incorrect. With an FLP, the senior family retains control over the FLP by virtue of ownership of the general partnership interest.

Statement 3 is incorrect because the interests in an FLP are transferred to younger family members by gift, so there is no need for security for the transfers.

Fundamentals—Education Funding Strategies

9. **B**

Although the Treasury bonds are zero-coupon bonds, the taxpayer will still be responsible for paying federal income tax on the accrued interest each year.

Interest on municipal bonds is not taxed at the federal level.

Although the corporate bonds are zero-coupon bonds, the taxpayer will still be responsible for paying federal income tax on the accrued interest each year.

Series EE bonds are not taxed if the proceeds are used for education purposes. However, the tax benefit of Series EE bonds is phased out at certain AGI levels, and the Farrells are well above those levels.

Estates—Probate Estate

10. **C**

The FLP interest will be included in the probate estate. The personal residence and autos pass outside of probate because of the right of survivorship, and the profit-sharing plans bypass probate because of the beneficiary designation.

Estates—Wills

11. **B**

   Statements 1 and 4 are correct.

   Statement 2 is incorrect. The will is often read after the funeral.

   Statement 3 is incorrect. IRA assets will pass to the IRA beneficiaries automatically, regardless of the will.

Estates—CRAT

12. **D**

   A CRAT must be irrevocable, so the Farrells will not be able to revise the CRAT once it is established. All the other statements are correct.

Estates—Qualified Disclaimers

13. **A**

   Statements 1, 2, and 4 are correct. Statement 3 is incorrect because the disclaimer must be filed within 9 months of Marleen's death, not 6.

Investments—Investment Returns

14. **C**

	Fair market value	Percentage of portfolio	Expected return	Expected weighted return
Stock A	$31,937.50	31.94%	25%	7.98%
Stock B	31,875.00	31.88%	23%	7.33%
Stock C	15,225.00	15.22%	15%	2.28%
Stock D	20,962.50	20.96%	20%	4.19%
Total	$100,000.00	100.00%		21.78%

Investments—Normal Distribution

15. **D**

Sixty-eight percent of outcomes will fall within 1 standard deviation of the mean. Because 10.88% is 1 standard deviation from the mean of 21.78% (expected weighted average), the probability of having a return between 10.88% and 21.78% is 34% (½ of 68%), and the probability of a return above 10.88% is 84% [34% plus 50% (probability to the right of the mean)].

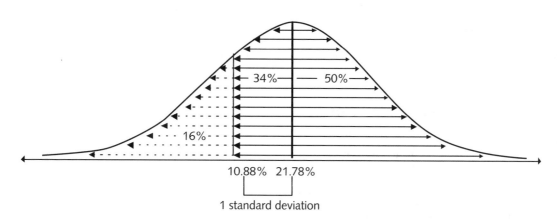

Insurance—Health Insurance

16. **C**

Robert is age 65 and qualifies for Medicare. Danielle, a dependent (under age 18) of someone qualifying for Medicare, and Robin, as the spouse, are both covered under COBRA for 36 months.

Investments—Sharpe Ratio

17. **A**

According to the Sharpe ratio, the Growth and Income Mutual Fund has the highest return.

Sharpe ratio $\dfrac{\overline{r}_p - \overline{r}_f}{\sigma_p}$

Growth and Income Mutual Fund $\dfrac{.10 - .04}{.09} = 0.67$

Balanced Mutual Fund $\dfrac{.085 - .04}{.07} = 0.64$

Account A $\dfrac{.112 - .04}{.13} = 0.55$

Account B $\dfrac{.104 - .04}{.10} = 0.64$

Estates—Intra-Family Transfers

18. **D**

All of these statements are correct. Statement 1 is correct because a private annuity is not suitable if Robert wants the sale to be secured by collateral.

Statement 2 is correct because a SCIN or a private annuity is not suitable if Robert wants Tom to continue making payments if Robert dies before all payments have been made.

Statement 3 is correct because the possibility that Robert might die prematurely will affect whether a SCIN or a private annuity is a suitable recommendation.

Statement 4 is correct because a private annuity is not suitable if Tom wants to deduct part of the purchase price as interest.

Insurance—Modified Endowment Contracts

19. **C**

Robert is over 59½ years old and would not be subject to the 10% penalty for loans or withdrawals from the MEC.

Tax—Charitable Contributions

20. **D**

A donor-advised fund is easy to set up and administer and would allow an immediate income tax deduction (subject to the charitable deduction rules for income tax), even though they are not certain of the charity at this time.

A CRAT would provide them with an annuity payment, which is not needed. In addition, it would be difficult to establish a CRAT today, which is the goal.

They do not know to which specific charity they would like to donate.

Private foundations are expensive and have restrictions and regulatory requirements.

Tax—Tax Planning

21. **A**

If they donated their personal residence to charity, retaining a life estate, they would receive an immediate income tax deduction equal to the present value of the remainder interest in the residence (subject to the charitable deduction rules for income tax).

Contributions to a Section 529 plan are nondeductible.

Farrell's Animal Care Center is a C corporation, so the Farrells will not receive a personal income tax benefit from deductions received by the corporation.

Premiums for the Medigap insurance must be combined with other medical expenses and are subject to the 10% of AGI floor. The Farrells projected retirement income of $250,000 makes a medical expense deduction unavailable until those expenses exceed $25,000. Generally speaking, this would not be a definite expense that would reduce their income tax liability next year.

Case Study 6:
Paul and Kristi Roth

Case Study Facts

Today is December 31, 2017. Paul and Kristi Roth have come to you, a CFP® professional, for help in developing a plan to accomplish their financial goals. From your initial meeting together, you have gathered the following information.

PERSONAL BACKGROUND AND INFORMATION

Paul Roth (Age 45)

Paul owns an 80% interest in a closely held company, Roth Printing. He has recently been diagnosed with diabetes and is considering selling or transferring some or all of the business to his son, Anthony, and retiring earlier than age 65.

Kristi Roth (Age 34)

Kristi is the office manager of Blue Moon, a paper supply store with 45 employees.

The Roths

Paul and Kristi met at Blue Moon when Paul purchased paper for Roth Printing. They have been married for two years. They live in a community property state but have a prenuptial agreement declaring that all property is separate.

The Children

Paul and Kristi have no children of their own, but Paul has two children from a prior marriage. His ex-wife is deceased. Paul's children are Julia, an 18-year-old full-time college student, and Anthony, age 25, who works in the printing business with Paul.

PERSONAL AND FINANCIAL OBJECTIVES

- Retire before age 65
- Provide adequate retirement income
- Avoid or minimize any death taxes at the death of the first spouse
- Minimize any death taxes at the death of the second spouse
- Provide adequate estate liquidity

ECONOMIC INFORMATION

- They expect inflation to average 4% annually, both currently and long term.
- They each expect salaries and net income to increase at 4% annually, both currently and long term.
- They believe the S&P 500 index is a good measure of the market's overall performance. The index's historical rate of return of 12% is expected to continue into the future.

ASSUMED TREASURY YIELD CURVE

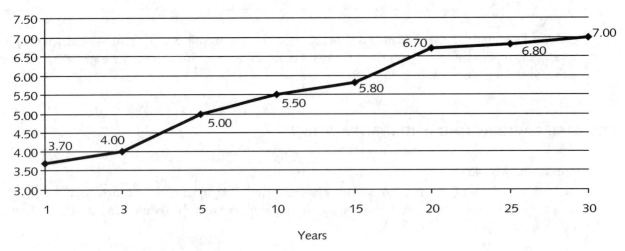

Years

Economic Outlook—Investments

	Expected Return	Expected standard deviation
Small company stocks	13.0%	15%
Large company stocks	11.0%	12%
S&P 500	12.0%	12%
Corporate bonds	8.5%	6%
30-year Treasury bonds	7.0%	5%
T-bills	3.7%	2%

INSURANCE INFORMATION

Life Insurance

	Policy 1	Policy 2	Policy 3[1]
Insured	Paul	Paul	Kristi
Face amount	$500,000	$150,000	$28,000
Policy type	Whole life	Term	Group term
Cash value	$15,000	$0	$0
Annual premium	$5,000	$150	$28
Beneficiary	Kristi	Kristi	Paul
Owner	Paul	Paul	Kristi
Contingent beneficiary	Estate of Paul Roth[2]	Estate of Paul Roth[2]	Anthony and Julia

[1] Kristi's group term policy is employer provided. No premiums have been paid for 2018.

[2] Paul listed his estate as the contingent beneficiary because he was concerned about his wife's ability to pay off their debts if he died.

Health Insurance

Kristi has a major medical health insurance plan provided by her employer, Blue Moon. Kristi and Paul are both covered by her plan. The plan has the following provisions:

- $1,500 individual deductible/$3,000 family deductible
- Maximum out-of-pocket limit—individual: $4,000, family: $6,000
- 80/20 coinsurance provision

NOTE: Julia is also covered under this plan and is eligible to continue coverage until age 26. Roth Printing does not have a health insurance plan. Anthony is currently covered under his wife's group health insurance policy.

Disability Insurance

Kristi has disability income coverage provided by her employer (60% of gross pay monthly benefit, own occupation definition of disability, 90-day elimination period, and benefits are paid until age 65). Roth Printing does not provide disability insurance to its employees. Paul has purchased an individual disability income policy. This policy includes an *own occupation* definition of disability, 65% of gross pay monthly benefit, and 180-day elimination period. The premium for this policy is $2,500 per year, and the policy provides benefits to age 65.

Auto Insurance

	Paul and Kristi's autos	Julia's auto
Policy type	PAP	PAP
Liability (bodily injury)	$100,000/$300,000	$50,000/$100,000
Property damage	$50,000	$25,000
Medical payments	$1,000	$1,000
Physical damage, own car	Actual cash value	Actual cash value
Uninsured motorists	$100,000/$300,000	N/A
Collision deductible	$1,000	$1,000
Comprehensive deductible	$500	$500
Annual premium	$1,800 (2 autos)	$1,350

Homeowners Insurance

	Personal residence	Beach condo
Policy type	HO-3	HO-6
Dwelling	$150,000	N/A
Other structures	$15,000	$1,000
Personal property	$75,000	$75,000
Personal liability	$100,000	$100,000
Medical payments	$1,000	$1,000
Deductible	$250	$500
Coinsurance requirement	80%	80%
Annual premium	$1,500	$1,100

Umbrella Liability Insurance

The policy provides coverage up to $2 million, and the premium is $300 per year.

INVESTMENT INFORMATION

The Roths have a required and expected rate of return of 9%. They consider themselves to be moderate to moderate-aggressive investors, and they consider $50,000 adequate for an emergency fund.

INCOME TAX INFORMATION

The Roths are in the 25% marginal income tax bracket for federal income tax purposes. Long-term capital gains will generally be taxed at 15%/20% depending on the Roth's AGI in the year of the transaction. They live in a state without a state income tax.

RETIREMENT INFORMATION

Kristi is eligible to participate in her employer's Section 401(k) plan but has chosen not to participate. Her employer provides a dollar-for-dollar match up to 3% of a participant's gross salary.

Paul does not have a retirement plan at Roth Printing but usually makes IRA contributions for Kristi and himself. Each IRA has the other spouse designated as beneficiary.

Paul has several retirement accounts from previous employers, all of which consist of qualified plan assets.

Paul and Kristi would both like to retire before Paul reaches age 65. They believe that together they would need about $75,000 (in today's dollars) pretax income during their retirement. This amount would decrease by 1/3 at the death of the first spouse.

Although Paul is battling diabetes, they believe his condition is manageable and expect him to live to age 95. Kristi also expects to live to age 95.

GIFTS, ESTATES, TRUSTS, AND WILLS INFORMATION

Gifts

Neither Paul nor Kristi has made a previous taxable gift.

Estates

Paul and Kristi estimate that funeral expenses will be $25,000 each and administrative expenses will be $40,000 each.

Wills

Paul and Kristi both have wills that leave $100,000 outright to each child, with the remainder of the estate going to the surviving spouse.

Statement of Cash Flows
Paul and Kristi Roth
For the Year Ending December 31, 2017

CASH INFLOWS

Salary—Paul	$60,000	
Salary—Kristi	32,800	
Investment income[1]	10,362	
Rental income	2,100	
Total cash inflows		$105,262

CASH OUTFLOWS

Savings

Savings—IRA contributions	$6,000
Money market account reinvestment	104
Bond mutual fund	750

Ordinary living expenses

Food	$4,800
Clothing	2,500
Travel	3,500
Home entertainment	1,500
Utilities	3,000
Telephone	3,600
Auto maintenance	400
Pool service	700
Lawn service	840
Church	2,500
Total ordinary living expenses and savings	$30,194

Other payments

Automobile payment	$7,200
Mortgage payment (principal residence)	11,747
Mortgage payment (beach condo)	12,943
Total other payments	$31,890

Insurance premiums

Automobile	$3,150
Disability	1,200
Homeowners	2,600
Life	5,150
Umbrella	300
Total insurance premiums	$12,400

Taxes

Federal income tax	$21,633
FICA—Kristi ($32,800 @ 7.65%)	2,509
FICA—Paul ($60,000 @ 7.65%)	4,590
Property tax (principal residence)	500
Property tax (beach condo)	300
Total taxes	$29,532

Total outflows	$104,016
Net cash flow (surplus)	$1,246

(Continued on next page)

Notes:

	¹Investment income:	Checking	$0
		Savings	764
		Roth Printing stock	0
		Equity brokerage account	1,594
		Bond mutual fund*	750
		Bond brokerage account	6,354
		High Tech stock	800
		Fox stock	100
		Total	$10,362

*All distributions are automatically reinvested in the fund.

Statement of Financial Position
Paul and Kristi Roth
As of December 31, 2017

	ASSETS[1]			LIABILITIES[10] AND NET WORTH		
	Cash and cash equivalents					
JT	Checking[2]	$5,000		**Current liabilities**		
JT	Checking[3]	8,000	Paul	Automobile		$19,000
JT	Savings[4, 5]	25,475	Kristi	Credit cards		3,500
	Total cash and equivalents	$38,475		Current liabilities		$22,500
	Invested assets					
Paul	Stock in Roth Printing[6]	$160,000		**Long-term liabilities**		
Paul	Equity brokerage account	58,121	JT	Mortgage on residence		$139,150
Paul	Bond mutual fund	136,000	Paul	Mortgage on beach condo		107,627
Paul	Brokerage account	100,000		Long-term liabilities		$246,777
Paul	High Tech stock[7]	20,000				
Kristi	Fox stock[8]	5,000		**Total liabilities**		$269,277
Paul	Pension plan #1[9]	34,594				
Paul	Pension plan #2[9]	98,676				
Paul	IRA rollover[9]	65,078				
Paul	IRA	14,650				
Kristi	IRA	17,350				
Paul	Cash value life insurance	15,000				
	Total invested assets	$724,469		**Net worth**		$980,667
	Use assets					
JT	Personal residence[3]	$180,000				
Paul	Beach condo	120,000				
JT	Personal property[3]	100,000				
Paul	Automobiles	87,000				
	Total use assets	$487,000				
	Total assets	$1,249,944		**Total liabilities and net worth**		$1,249,944

Notes to financial statements:

[1] Assets are stated at fair market value with the exception of Roth Printing stock.

[2] Joint tenancy with right of survivorship with spouse. Checking account does not earn interest.

[3] Joint tenancy with right of survivorship with son, Anthony. Checking account does not earn interest. Paul contributed 100%.

[4] Joint tenancy with right of survivorship with spouse.

[5] The current rate for savings account is 3%.

[6] This is Paul's estimate at what Roth Printing is worth. His basis is $25,000.

[7] 2,000 shares at $10 per share. The current dividend is $.40 per share and is expected to grow at 3% per year.

[8] 100 shares.

[9] All pension plans have the spouse of participant as named beneficiary.

[10] All liabilities go with the associated asset for title purposes.

Title designations:

Client name = separate property

JT = joint tenancy with right of survivorship

INFORMATION REGARDING ASSETS AND LIABILITIES

High Tech Stock

This stock was given to Paul as a Christmas present several years ago by Paul's brother, David. David's basis in the stock was $13,500, and the value at the date of the gift was $25,000. See the footnote on the Statement of Financial Position.

Bond Mutual Fund

The bond fund was inherited from Paul's Uncle Fred, who died on December 10, 2017, at which time the fund was valued at $148,000. Uncle Fred had just invested $145,000 in the fund on November 1, 2017. All distributions are automatically reinvested in the fund. Since Paul inherited the fund there have been no cash distributions. The fund earned $6,000 in 2017, of which $750 was earned after Fred's death, but unfortunately, the fund is valued at only $136,000 today because of fluctuations in interest rates.

Bond Brokerage Account

Description	Maturity	Coupon[1]	Cost basis	FMV
10,000 US T-bills	1	N/A	$9,640	$9,643.20
20,000 US T-bonds	30	8%	20,000	22,494.47
10,000 US T-bonds	20	0%	1,313	2,625.30
20,000 Small Co. bonds[2]	20	9%	20,000	24,271.01
15,000 Weak Co. junk bonds[3]	25	9%	15,000	3,000.47
25,000 Texas municipal bonds	15	6%	25,000	27,616.29
			$90,953	$89,650.74
Money market account[4]				10,349.26
Account value as of 12/31/17				$100,000.00

Notes:

[1] Assume all coupon payments are made semiannually.

[2] Bonds are investment quality.

[3] Bonds are noninvestment quality.

[4] Money market account yield is 1% and is automatically reinvested.

Equity Brokerage Account[1]

Stock	Shares	Beta	Standard deviation	Dividend yield	Average return	Cost Basis	FMV
Big Co.	1,000	0.88	12.5%	4%[2]	12.5%	$8,046.47	$14,500
Small Co.	1,000	1.24	18%	0%	15%	10,724.35	12,333
Oil Co.	1,000	1.00	10%	3.5%[3]	8%	11,135.70	15,150
Auto Co.	1,000	1.12	10%	3%[2]	10%	12,124.72	16,138
					Total	$42,031.24	$58,121

Notes:

[1] The stock portfolio has a correlation coefficient with the market of 0.80.

[2] The expected dividend growth rate is zero.

[3] The dividend growth rate is expected to remain at 3%.

Fox Stock

Kristi inherited the stock in 2014 from her great aunt, Joyce, who bought the stock when the price was $42 per share. When Joyce died, she left Kristi 50 shares of Fox stock. Kristi knows that when Joyce died, Fox stock closed at $35 per share, with a high price of $38 and low price of $34. The stock has since split 2 for 1 and has a current dividend yield of 2%.

Personal Residence

The Roths purchased their personal residence for $175,000 nine months ago. They made a down payment of 20%. They were able to obtain a mortgage loan rate of 7.5% financed over 30 years. The monthly payment is $978.90, with a remaining balance of $139,150.39.

Beach Condo

Paul purchased the beach condo three years ago for $150,000 with a 20% down payment. The balance was financed over 15 years at 7%. The monthly payment is $1,078.59, and they have made 30 payments. The balance on the loan is $107,627.07. Since the purchase, Paul has paid $9,200 in restoration costs. The Roths personally use the condo often in both the winter and summer. Paul and Kristi also let some of their friends rent the condo during the year. This year, they rented the condo to Paul's best friend for one week and to Kristi's sister for a long weekend (five days).

Questions

1. Paul consults you, a CFP® professional, for help in reviewing his current estate planning. After receiving and analyzing the documents from Paul, you have come to some conclusions. Which of the following statements accurately describes Paul's current estate plan?

   1. The estate as contingent beneficiary on life insurance does not address Paul's concerns of debt payment at his death.
   2. The will arrangement adequately protects both children regarding inheritance.
   3. A QTIP trust would be useful in this case.
   4. The plan has inadequate provisions for addressing Paul's potential incapacity.

   A. 1, 3, and 4
   B. 2 and 4
   C. 3 and 4
   D. 1, 2, 3, and 4

2. Which of the following assets would be included in Kristi's probate estate if she died today?

   A. Savings
   B. Life insurance policy
   C. Fox stock
   D. Personal residence

3. Paul is considering selling the bond fund because it is not performing well and expects to receive net proceeds of $136,000 from the sale. He is concerned, however, about the tax consequences of the sale. What would be the tax consequences of this sale, assuming that it takes place on April 15, 2018?

   A. No gain or loss
   B. $12,000 long-term capital loss
   C. $12,750 long-term capital loss
   D. $15,000 long-term capital loss

4. Assume that Paul needs retirement income from Roth Printing. In addition, he wants to make certain he will not be subject to gift tax on the transfer, and he wants the transaction to be secured by collateral. Which of the following devices or methods can be used to accomplish his goals?

   1. Self-canceling installment note (SCIN)
   2. Private annuity
   3. Charitable remainder annuity trust (CRAT)
   4. Grantor retained annuity trust (GRAT)

   A. 1 only
   B. 1, 2, and 3
   C. 1 and 4
   D. 2, 3, and 4

5. Assuming they can earn their required rate of return, how much capital do they need when Paul is age 65 to provide for both of them in retirement? (Round to the nearest thousand and assume they are both living and expected to live to age 95.)

    A. $1,343,000
    B. $2,707,000
    C. $7,526,000
    D. $2,942,000

6. Concerning investment risk within the bond portfolio, which of the following statements are CORRECT?

    1. All of the bonds except the T-bills are subject to reinvestment rate risk.
    2. None of the bonds are subject to foreign currency risk.
    3. All of the bonds are subject to interest rate risk.
    4. Only Small Co. bonds and Weak Co. bonds are subject to default risk.
    5. All of the bonds except the T-bills are subject to liquidity risk.

    A. 1, 2, 3, and 5
    B. 1, 3, and 4
    C. 2, 3, and 4
    D. 2, 3, and 5

7. How could Paul protect his gain in Big Co. stock without actually selling his stock?

    1. Sell Big Co. short
    2. Sell a put option on Big Co.
    3. Purchase a put option on Big Co.
    4. Purchase a call option on Big Co.
    5. Sell a call option on Big Co.

    A. 1 and 3
    B. 2 and 4
    C. 3 only
    D. 3 and 5

8. Based on the value of the bonds in the bond portfolio, what have interest rates been doing during the holding period?

    A. Interest rates have been increasing.
    B. Interest rates have been stable.
    C. Interest rates have been decreasing.
    D. The answer cannot be determined based on the information provided.

9. Based on the information contained in the case facts, rank the order of the risk-adjusted performance of the stocks in the brokerage account, highest to lowest, using the Sharpe ratio. (Use the T-bill rate as the risk-free rate of return.)

   A.   Big Co., Auto Co., Small Co., Oil Co.
   B.   Oil Co., Auto Co., Big Co., Small Co.
   C.   Oil Co., Auto Co., Small Co., Big Co.
   D.   Big Co., Oil Co., Auto Co., Small Co.

10. Concerning the Roths' brokerage account, which of the following statements is(are) CORRECT?

   1.   Sixty-four percent of the change in the account can be explained by the market.
   2.   The entire account movement can be explained by the market.
   3.   The portfolio is sufficiently diversified such that there is almost no unsystematic risk exposure within the portfolio.
   4.   Unsystematic risk accounts for more than 1/3 of total risk.

   A.   1 and 3
   B.   1 and 4
   C.   2 only
   D.   2 and 3

11. Roth Printing used a cross-purchase life insurance program to provide protection in the event of death of a principal shareholder. Paul owns 80%; two other individuals (X and Y) own 10% each. How many policies do they have and for what amounts? Assume that Roth Printing is valued at $350,000.

   1.   Six policies were purchased.
   2.   Paul must own 2 policies of $140,000 each.
   3.   X must own a policy on Paul for $280,000.
   4.   Y must own a policy on Paul for $140,000 and on X for $17,500.
   5.   Each must own a policy with a face amount of $350,000.

   A.   1 and 4
   B.   2 and 3
   C.   3 and 4
   D.   5 only

12. If Kristi were to sell the Fox stock today for the value on the Statement of Financial Position, what would be the income tax consequence?

   A. $800 short-term capital gain
   B. $1,500 short-term capital gain
   C. $2,900 long-term capital gain
   D. $3,200 long-term capital gain

13. Paul has been increasingly concerned about his finances. Because he has been overwhelmed with personal issues, he wants to wait to make an IRA contribution to his traditional IRA for this year. Can Paul make a contribution for this year in the next year?

    A.   Yes. He can make a deductible contribution on or before April 15 next year.

    B.   Yes. He can make a contribution anytime in the next year for the current year.

    C.   Yes. He can make a contribution if he has not already filed his income tax return for this year, but it is not deductible because the Roth's earnings exceed the applicable phaseout threshold.

    D.   Yes. He can make a contribution if he has not already filed his income tax return for this year, but it is not deductible because his wife is covered by an employer-sponsored plan.

14. Paul and Kristi have the following income and expenses from the rental of the condo during the year:

Rental income	$2,100.00
Interest expense	$7,733.41
Property tax	$300.00
Depreciation	$4,800.00
Utilities expense	$1,000.00

    What is the income tax treatment of the above items on their federal income tax return?

    A.   Schedule E loss of $11,733

    B.   Schedule E loss of $11,733 suspended under the passive activity rules

    C.   No taxable income; claim the interest and tax on Schedule A of Form 1040

    D. $2,100 income (claimed as other income on Form 1040)

15. Paul had surgery as an outpatient in January of this year to remove a small tumor from his arm. He incurred $5,200 in expenses. How much of this total will not be paid by Paul's health insurance policy? (Assume this is his first claim of the year.)

    A. $1,040

    B. $1,440

    C. $1,840

    D. $2,240

16. How many option contracts should Paul buy or sell to fully hedge his position in Big Co. stock?

    A.   He should buy 10 put option contracts to protect his long position.

    B.   He should buy 1,000 put option contracts to protect his long position.

    C.   He should sell 10 call option contracts to protect his position.

    D.   He should sell 1,000 call option contracts to protect his position.

17. Blue Moon is considering establishing a health savings account (HSA) for its employees. Which of the following statements regarding an HSA is(are) CORRECT?

    1. Blue Moon does not qualify for an HSA because there are too many employees.

    2. Blue Moon qualifies for an HSA because its plan has high deductibles that meet the requirements of the Internal Revenue Code.

    3. Contributions by Kristi to an HSA would be deductible from her taxable income, and distributions used to pay qualified medical expenses are excludable from income.

    4. If Blue Moon elects to fund the HSA, contributions are deductible to the corporation and excludable from Kristi's income.

    A. 1 and 2

    B. 2 and 3

    C. 2, 3, and 4

    D. 1, 2, 3, and 4

18. Which of the following statements regarding the High Tech stock is(are) CORRECT?

    1. The stock is overvalued in the secondary market by approximately 46% using the constant growth dividend discount model.

    2. Because David and Paul are related parties and the FMV of the stock exceeded the donor's basis on the date of the gift, Paul will have a basis of $13,500 for losses and $25,000 for gains.

    3. This investment is inappropriate given their conservative risk tolerance.

    A. 1 only

    B. 1 and 3

    C. 2 only

    D. 1, 2, and 3

19. Before beginning a new venture for Roth Printing, Paul consults you, a CFP® professional, about the net present value (NPV) and the internal rate of return (IRR) of the new project. Paul tells you that he has a 10% required rate of return for the new project and provides expected inflows and outflows of the investment. After performing an NPV analysis on the new project, you tell Paul the NPV is positive. What will the IRR be for this project?

    A. Less than 0%

    B. Between 0% and 10%

    C. Equal to 10%

    D. Greater than 10%

20. Paul is considering the purchase of a business overhead expense (BOE) insurance policy for the printing business. The business will purchase the policy and pay the premiums. Which of the following statements regarding this arrangement is CORRECT?

    A. Benefits will be paid during the disability period to replace Paul's salary.

    B. Premiums are not deductible as a business expense.

    C. Benefits are often paid until age 65, unless a lifetime option is selected.

    D. Benefits received from the policy are taxable.

21. When Paul and Kristi engaged your services as a CFP® professional for comprehensive financial planning, the couple had some strong concerns about the confidentiality of their financial records. Paul has a friend who had been subject to identity theft and Paul was understandably concerned about his own information. You tell the couple that all of their information is treated as confidential and only some information may be disclosed to others. For which of the following is it permissible for you to disclose information about Paul and Kristi to others?

    1. The Roths' personal attorney who reviews their wills after you and notes some deficiencies in their current will provisions.

    2. A staff member in your office who prepares some of the documents for the Roth's financial plan recommendations.

    3. You consult with your supervisor on the plan recommendations for the Roths.

    A. 1 only
    B. 1 and 3
    C. 2 and 3
    D. 1, 2, and 3

ANSWER SUMMARY

1. A	6. D	11. A	16. A	21. D
2. C	7. A	12. D	17. C	
3. C	8. C	13. A	18. A	
4. A	9. A	14. C	19. D	
5. D	10. B	15. D	20. D	

SUMMARY OF TOPICS

1. Estates—Estate Planning
2. Estates—Probate Estate
3. Tax—Basis of Inherited Property
4. Estates—Estate Planning
5. Retirement—Needs Analysis
6. Investments—Types of Investment Risk
7. Investments—Option Strategies
8. Investments—Bond Valuation Concepts
9. Investments—Sharpe Ratio
10. Investments—Coefficient of Determination
11. Insurance—Business Uses of Insurance
12. Tax—Basis of Inherited Property
13. Retirement—Traditional IRA
14. Tax—Itemized Deductions
15. Insurance—Health Insurance
16. Investments—Hedging Strategies
17. Insurance—Health Savings Accounts
18. Investments—Constant Growth Dividend Discount Model and Risk Tolerance
19. Fundamentals—Time Value of Money
20. Insurance—Disability Insurance
21. Fundamentals—Rules of Conduct

Solutions

Estates—Estate Planning

1. A

   ■ Because Kristi is the primary beneficiary of Paul's life insurance policies, Paul's reason to make the estate the contingent beneficiary does not address his concern about Kristi's ability to pay their debts after his death. As it stands, Kristi would have to predecease Paul for the life insurance proceeds to go to the estate. The estate should rarely be the beneficiary of life insurance policies because this arrangement subjects the proceeds to potential claims of estate creditors. An irrevocable life insurance trust (ILIT) would be better suited to own the insurance policies. If Paul died today, the estate would have barely enough liquid assets (excluding pension and IRA funds) to pay bequests and debts, without considering final expenses and funeral costs. A loan from an ILIT to provide liquidity would solve estate liquidity issues.

   ■ The will arrangement does not fully protect the children from a prior marriage. A QTIP trust would provide more protection for the children. Because of Kristi's age, however, the children may not receive funds for many years.

   ■ There are no durable powers for health care.

   ■ There are no advance medical directives.

Estates—Probate Estate

2. C

   The Fox stock is included in the probate estate. The other assets will pass by contract or right of survivorship.

Tax—Basis of Inherited Property

3. C

   Paul's adjusted tax basis is $148,750, which is the fair market value on Uncle Fred's date of death ($148,000) plus the reinvested income of $750 from 2017 received by Paul after Fred's death but reinvested into the fund. If Paul sells the bond fund for $136,000, he will produce a long-term capital loss of $12,750 for 2018. All inherited property is considered long term.

Estates—Estate Planning

4. A

   The SCIN solves the gift tax problem and allows the seller (Paul) to take collateral as security.

   The CRAT should be used only if Paul needs retirement income and has charitable intentions. The GRAT, private annuity, and installment sale (SCIN) all allow Paul to transfer the stock to his son Anthony. Paul will have made a taxable gift at the time of the GRAT's creation. The private annuity is best suited for a person who is not in good health and does not allow the extra security of collateral that can be used in a SCIN.

Retirement—Needs Analysis

5. **D**

The total amount needed at age 65 is $2,942,000 (rounded).

This calculation is best solved for using the uneven series of cash flows method. Keystrokes for the HP 10BII/HP 10BII+ are shown below.

Step 1:

75000 CFj

75000 CFj

29 shift Nj

50000 CFj

11 shift Nj

$[(1.09 \div 1.04) - 1] \times 100 = 4.8077$ I/YR

shift NPV

result: 1,342,803.0818

Step 2:

1,342,803.0818 +/– PV

0 PMT

20 N

4 I/YR

FV

result: 2,942,246.9090

rounded to the nearest thousand: $2,942,000

Investments—Types of Investment Risk

6. **D**

Only statements 2, 3, and 5 are correct.

- Small Co., Weak Co., and the Texas municipal bonds are considered to have default risk.
- All of the bonds, except the T-bills and zero-coupon bonds, are subject to reinvestment rate risk.
- None of the bonds is subject to foreign currency risk.
- All of the bonds are subject to interest rate risk.
- All of the bonds, except the T-bills, are subject to liquidity risk.

Investments—Option Strategies

7. **A**

Paul has two choices. He can either sell the stock short, called *shorting against the box*, or purchase a put option. Selling a call will not protect his gain but only limit a loss in the case that the stock price declines. The constructive sale rules have greatly limited the usefulness of the shorting-against-the-box technique for tax purposes.

Investments—Bond Valuation Concepts

8. **C**

The increase in the fair market value (FMV) of the bonds is a clear indication that interest rates have been declining. The most likely reason the Weak Co. bonds have such a high YTM and low fair market value is that the company must be in poor financial condition.

Investments—Sharpe Ratio

9. **A**

$$\frac{\bar{r}_p - \bar{r}_f}{\sigma}$$

Using a risk-free rate of return of 3.7% (52-week T-bill rate)

Big Co. = (.125 − .037) ÷ .125 = .7040

Auto Co. = (.10 − .037) ÷ .10 = .6300

Small Co. = (.15 − .037) ÷ .18 = .6278

Oil Co. = (.08 − .037) ÷ .10 = .4300

Investments—Coefficient of Determination

10. **B**

Coefficient of determination is calculated by squaring the correlation coefficient

Systematic risk:

$0.8^2 = 0.64$

Therefore, 64% of the change in the Roths' brokerage account can be explained by the market.

Unsystematic risk:

100% − 64% (systematic risk) = 36%

Insurance—Business Uses of Insurance

11. **A**

Paul's ownership interest is 80% ($280,000) or $140,000 for each policy owned by X and Y. X would also own a policy on Y for $17,500, and Y would own a policy on X for $17,500. Paul would own a policy on X of $17,500 and on Y of $17,500. Total number of policies equals 6.

	X	Y	Paul
Ownership interest	$35,000	$35,000	$280,000
X's policies	$0	$17,500	$140,000
Y's policies	$17,500	$0	$140,000
Paul's policies	$17,500	$17,500	$0

Tax—Basis of Inherited Property

12. **D**

First, determine the adjusted tax basis. The adjusted tax basis is the fair market value at the date of death, determined as the average of the high and low of the day [($38 + $34) ÷ 2] = $36.

The stock has split (2 for 1); therefore, the adjusted tax basis is $18 per share.

All capital gains or losses from inherited stock are deemed to be long term.

Sales price	=	$5,000
Adjusted tax basis (100 × $18)	=	(1,800)
Long-term capital gain	=	$3,200

Retirement—Traditional IRA

13. **A**

Paul can make a contribution until April 15 of the next year and it is deductible for the current year. A contribution made by April 15 will be deemed to be made in the previous year. Because Kristi is not participating in her Section 401(k) plan, she is not considered covered by a qualified plan. Therefore, if Paul makes the IRA contribution by April 15 of next year, it will qualify as a current year deductible contribution regardless of their income.

Tax—Itemized Deductions

14. **C**

- Because the property is rented less than 15 days, it is considered a personal use asset, not a mixed-use vacation home.
- The income does not have to be included in taxable income because the property was rented for fewer than 15 days.
- The interest and property taxes are deductible on Schedule A. None of the other expenses are deductible.

Insurance—Health Insurance

15. **D**

Expense	$5,200
Deductible	(1,500)
Net expense	$3,700
Coinsurance (20%)	× 20%
Coinsurance amount	$740

The total amount payable by Paul is $2,240 ($1,500 deductible + $740 coinsurance).

Investments—Hedging Strategies

16. **A**

Generally, an option contract gives the owner the right to put (sell) or call (buy) 100 shares of an underlying stock. Paul will need to buy 10 put option contracts (1,000 divided by 100) to protect his long position in Big Co. stock.

Insurance—Health Savings Accounts

17. C

Statement 1 is incorrect. An employer can establish an HSA regardless of the number of employees. Statement 2 is correct. The limits for family coverage for 2017 are at least a $2,600 annual family deductible and maximum out-of-pocket expenses of $13,100. Statements 3 and 4 are correct.

Investments—Constant Growth Dividend Discount Model and Risk Tolerance

18. A

The intrinsic value of the stock using the constant growth dividend discount model is as follows:

$$\frac{\$.40 \times (1 + .03)}{.09 - .03} = \$6.87$$

The amount the stock is overvalued is as follows:

$$\frac{\$10.00 - \$6.87}{\$6.87} = 45.56\%$$

Statement 2 is incorrect. Paul's basis is $13,500 for gains and losses. The basis would be higher, however, if David had paid gift tax on the gift. Statement 3 is incorrect. This investment is appropriate given their moderate to moderate-aggressive risk tolerance.

Fundamentals—Time Value of Money

19. D

An NPV greater than zero implies that the IRR of the cash flows is greater than the discount rate used to discount the future cash flows. An NPV of zero implies that the discount rate used is equal to the IRR for the cash flows. A negative NPV implies that the discount rate used is greater than the true IRR of the cash flows.

Insurance—Disability Insurance

20. D

The company will receive an income tax deduction when paying premiums on a BOE policy. Therefore, the benefits will be taxable when received.

Business overhead expense insurance will not provide a benefit for the replacement of the owner's salary.

Benefits are typically paid for 1 to 2 years.

Fundamentals—Rules of Conduct

21. D

All of these situations are appropriate instances where some disclosure of a client's confidential information may be needed in order to adequately perform services. Rule 3.1 states "A certificant shall treat information as confidential except as required in response to proper legal process; as necessitated by obligations to a certificant's employer or partners; to defend against charges of wrongdoing; in connection with a civil dispute; or as needed to perform the services."

Case Study 7: Tom and Erin Ackerman

Case Study Facts

Tom and Erin Ackerman have come to you, a CFP® professional, for help in developing a plan to accomplish their financial goals. Assume today is December 31, 2017, and you have gathered the following information.

PERSONAL BACKGROUND AND INFORMATION

Tom Ackerman (Age 56)

Tom owns his own business, a coat store, with Schedule C net income of $50,000 in the current year. Tom has no employees other than his son, Justin, who works with him full time.

Erin Ackerman (Age 51)

Erin is a professor of psychology at State University, where she has been employed full time for 17 years. Her W-2 income of $65,000 for nine months of teaching is paid ratably over 12 months at $5,416.67 per month.

The Ackermans

Tom and Erin have been married for five years. Both are in excellent health. They provide some support for Erin's father, Stanley, who is in a nursing home, but they do not claim him as a dependent for tax purposes.

The Children

Tom and Erin have twin children, Tom Jr. and Mary (age 4).

Tom has two children, Justin (age 23) and Riley (age 12) from a previous marriage.

Justin works full time in the coat store.

PERSONAL AND FINANCIAL OBJECTIVES

- To retire when Tom is age 62 and Erin is age 57
- To increase their tax-advantaged savings
- To be free of all mortgage debt at retirement
- To implement suitable estate planning techniques and integrate charitable intentions into the plan
- To transfer the coat business to Justin at death or retirement

ECONOMIC INFORMATION

- They expect inflation to average 4% over the long term.
- Historical and projected return on the market is 12%.
- Historical and projected standard deviation of the market is 14%
- 90-day T-bills are yielding 3%, 30-year T-bonds are yielding 5%.

INSURANCE INFORMATION

Life Insurance

	Policy #1	Policy #2
Insured	Tom	Erin
Face amount	$200,000	$200,000
Cash value	$0	$0
Policy type	Term	Group term
Annual premium	$1,600	Partially employer paid; Erin pays $20/month
Beneficiary	Erin	Debra (Erin's mother)
Contingent beneficiary	None	None
Policyowner	Tom	Erin
Settlement option chosen	Life annuity	None

Health Insurance

Persons covered	Family
Policy type	Comprehensive major medical/State University plan
Coverage	80/20 coinsurance, $2,500 stop-loss limit
Deductible	$500 family deductible
Annual premium	100% employer paid

Automobile Insurance

Policy type	Personal auto policy
Liability limits	$100,000/$300,000/$50,000
Medical payments	$3,000/person/accident
Uninsured motorists	$50,000/accident
Physical damage, own car	Actual cash value
Collision deductible	$250
Comprehensive deductible	$250
Annual premium for two cars	$1,000

Homeowners Insurance

Personal Residence	
Policy type	HO-3 Special Form
Dwelling coverage limit	$196,000
Personal property	$98,000
Personal liability	$100,000/occurrence
Medical payments	$5,000/person/occurrence
Deductible	$250
Premium (annual)	$1,000
Other	80% coinsurance requirement

Residential Rental Property	
Policy type	HO-3
Personal liability	$300,000/occurrence
Medical payments	$2,000/person/occurrence
Deductible	$500
Premium (annual)	$850
Other	$15,000 covers renters with an endorsement

Disability Income Policy (Long Term)

Insured	Erin
Definition of disability	Own occupation
Premium	Employer pays 60%; Erin pays 40%; total $600/year
Elimination period	90 days
Monthly benefit	60% of gross pay (currently $3,250 per month)

Section 79 Costs for Group Term Insurance
(Costs per $1,000 of protection for one month)

Age	Cost
45 through 49	$.15
50 through 54	$.23
55 through 59	$.43

INCOME TAX INFORMATION

The Ackermans file married filing jointly. They are in the 25% federal marginal income tax bracket. They live in a state with no state income tax. Justin and Riley are claimed as dependents by Tom's former wife, Dorinda.

RETIREMENT INFORMATION

Savings

The Ackermans are saving $15,700 annually, consisting of $10,000 of IRA contributions, $3,750 ($4,750 – $1,000 received in cash) in reinvested dividends, and $1,950 annually into Erin's Section 403(b) retirement plan.

Titling of retirement accounts	Beneficiary designation
Tom's IRA	Erin
Erin's IRA	Tom
Erin's Section 403(b) plan	Tom

Social Security Benefits

Tom's Social Security benefits at full retirement age are estimated to be $18,500 per year (in today's dollars). Erin's Social Security benefit at full retirement age is estimated to be $23,000 per year.

Retirement Plan

State University provides a Section 403(b) plan and contributes 7% of Erin's salary to the plan. Erin has elected to contribute an additional 3% after tax to the plan.

GIFTS, ESTATES, TRUSTS, AND WILL INFORMATION

Tom's Will

Tom's will leaves his automobile and the coat business to Justin and everything else to Erin. Erin is the executrix for the estate. The residuary legatee is to pay all administrative expenses, costs, and taxes. Indebtedness goes with the respective assets.

Erin's Will

Erin's will leaves everything to Tom.

Statement of Cash Flows
Tom and Erin Ackerman
January 1, 2017–December 31, 2017

INFLOWS

Tom's Schedule C net income	$50,000	
Erin's salary	65,000	
Dividend income from equity portfolio	4,750	
Rental property income (net of management fees)	12,000	
Interest income from bonds	5,000	
Total inflows		**$136,750**

OUTFLOWS

Savings and investments	$15,700	
Fixed outflows		
Payments to Dorinda	$6,000	
Mortgage—principal residence (P&I)	19,498	
Taxes—principal residence	1,800	
Insurance—principal residence	1,000	
Mortgage—rental (P&I)	14,591	
Rental property operating costs	1,200	
Taxes—rental property	2,800	
Rental property association dues	1,600	
Rental property insurance premium	850	
Auto note payment	5,928	
Auto insurance premium	1,000	
Life insurance premium (Policies 1 and 2)	1,840	
Disability insurance premium	240	
Total fixed outflows	$58,347	
Variable outflows		
Taxes	$25,038	
Food (including dining out)	4,800	
Transportation	2,600	
Clothing/personal care	2,800	
Entertainment/vacations	4,000	
Medical/dental	2,000	
Utilities and household expenses	2,000	
Church donations	520	
Miscellaneous	68	
Total variable outflows	$43,826	
Total outflows		**$117,873**
Net cash flow (surplus)		**$18,877**

Tax detail:	Total self-employment tax Tom	$7,065	($50,000 x .9235 x .153)
	FICA Erin	$4,973	
	Fed W/H	$13,000	
		$25,038	

Statement of Financial Position
Tom and Erin Ackerman
As of December 31, 2017

ASSETS[1]			LIABILITIES AND NET WORTH	
Cash and cash equivalents			**Liabilities[4]**	
JT	Cash and checking	$15,000	JT Automobile	$14,750
JT	Money market	20,000	Mortgage rental property[2]	99,330
	Total cash and equivalents	$35,000	Mortgage personal residence[3]	153,115
			Total liabilities	$267,195
Invested assets				
Tom	Proprietorship	$400,000		
Tom	IRA	40,000		
Erin	IRA	50,000		
Tom	Equity stock portfolio	135,000		
Erin	Bond portfolio	40,000		
JT	Rental real estate[2]	160,000		
Erin	Retirement plan	80,000		
	Total invested assets	$905,000	**Net worth**	**$1,057,805**
Personal use assets				
JT	Residence[3]—dwelling	$260,000		
JT	Residence[3]—land	20,000		
Erin	Coin collection	25,000		
JT	Automobiles	20,000		
JT	Personal property	60,000		
	Total personal use assets	$385,000		
Total assets		**$1,325,000**	**Total liabilities and net worth**	**$1,325,000**

Notes to financial statements:

[1] Assets are stated at fair market value.

[2] Rental property refinanced in 2014 at 10.5% for 15 years. The first payment was due January 15, 2015.

[3] Personal residence financed December 1, 2015, for $165,000 at 8.5% fixed for 15 years. Replacement value for insurance purposes has been determined to be $260,000.

[4] Liabilities are stated at principal only.

Client name = separate property
JT = joint tenancy with right of survivorship

INFORMATION REGARDING ASSETS AND LIABILITIES

Proprietorship

This business was purchased by Tom 10 years ago for $100,000. No additional capital contributions have been made.

Equity Portfolio

Mutual fund	Shares	FMV	Basis	Beta	Standard deviation
A	1,000	$25,000	$10,000	1.3	25%
B	2,000	$40,000	$40,000	1.0	15%
C	6,000	$60,000	$45,000	0.9	20%
D	200	$10,000	$15,000	1.2	18%

Notes:

The portfolio has a correlation of 0.50 with the market.

The portfolio has had a historical return of 14% with a volatility of approximately 18% as measured by standard deviation.

Bond Portfolio

The bond portfolio was a gift to Erin from her Uncle Stirling five years ago. The value of the portfolio at the time of the gift was $28,000. Stirling paid gift tax of $10,000 on the gift. The bonds currently yield 7.5% annually. Stirling had originally paid $33,000 for the bonds.

Rental Property

The rental property was purchased in January 1986 for $110,000. The current tax basis of the rental property is $0 plus land cost of $10,000. The property is used exclusively as a rental.

Coin Collection

The coin collection was acquired from Erin's mother as a gift. At the time of the gift, her mother's tax basis was $5,000 and the fair market value of the collection was $30,000. At the time of the gift, Erin's mother had already used her annual exclusion for gifts to Erin in a previous gift. Erin's mother paid gift tax of $5,000 on this gift.

Divorce Decree

Tom was divorced from Dorinda five years ago and remarried the same year. His divorce decree required payments to Dorinda of $500 per month for support until Riley is age 18. The payments will then be reduced to $300 per month for five more years. In the event of Dorinda's early death, payments are to be made to her estate for the remainder of the 15-year period.

Questions

1. What is the amount of the payments to Dorinda that Tom and Erin can deduct as alimony on their current federal income tax return?

   A. $0
   B. $2,400
   C. $3,600
   D. $6,000

2. What amount will be included in Erin's W-2 as a result of her group term insurance?

   A. $174
   B. $240
   C. $270
   D. $414

3. You have completed an analysis of the Ackermans' insurance documentation. In which of the following areas have you noted risk exposure that you recommend be corrected?

   1. Homeowners policy
   2. Health policy
   3. Disability income insurance for Tom
   4. Personal liability umbrella coverage

   A. 1, 3, and 4
   B. 2, 3, and 4
   C. 3 only
   D. 3 and 4

4. If Erin were to become disabled on March 31 of next year and remain disabled for the remainder of the year, how much would she collect in disability benefits?

   A. $0
   B. $19,500
   C. $22,750
   D. $26,000

5. How much of Erin's disability benefits would be taxable if she were to become disabled on March 31 of next year and remained disabled for the balance of the year?

   A. $0
   B. $4,000
   C. $7,800
   D. $11,700

6. If the Ackermans were to have a fire in their personal residence that resulted in a loss of $20,000, how much of the loss would be reimbursed by the insurance company?

   A. $14,827
   B. $18,596
   C. $18,611
   D. $20,000

7. Erin and Tom have consulted you for advice on the taxation of her investments. If Erin were to sell the bond portfolio today for the value on the statement of financial position, what should you tell them about the tax consequences of the sale?

   A. No gain or loss
   B. $3,000 short-term capital gain
   C. $2,000 long-term capital gain
   D. $7,000 long-term capital gain

8. What is Erin's adjusted tax basis in the coin collection?

   A. $5,000
   B. $9,167
   C. $10,000
   D. $30,000

9. Which of the following describing the investment characteristics of the coin collection is CORRECT?

   A. Illiquid
   B. Lack of marketability
   C. Diverse investment
   D. Appropriate hedge for stocks and bonds

10. Assume the Ackermans make a $10,000 contribution ($5,000 each) to traditional IRA accounts for this year. What amount of their IRA contributions is deductible?

    A. $0
    B. $2,500
    C. $5,000
    D. $10,000

11. Assume Erin is hurt in an auto accident, but she has sufficient disability coverage to cover her recovery period. Under which principle can she still collect from the negligent party?

    A. Negligence per se
    B. Collateral source rule
    C. Vicarious liability
    D. Constructive receipt

12. If Tom were to die today, which of the following assets would be excluded from Tom's probate estate?

    A. Proprietorship
    B. Stock portfolio
    C. Rental property
    D. All are included in the probate estate

13. In 2018, Tom decides to take early retirement and sell the coat business to Justin. Tom tells you that Justin does not have enough cash to pay the purchase price in full and will need to purchase the business in installments. He also says that he wants Justin to provide collateral as security and that he wants to ensure that Justin pays the entire purchase price even if Tom dies before all payments have been made. However, he does not want Justin to have to pay more than FMV for the business regardless of how long Tom lives after the sale. Tom says that Justin is agreeable to all of these requirements. Which of the following recommendations is most suitable to meet Tom's objectives?

    A. Private annuity
    B. Installment note
    C. Self-canceling installment note (SCIN)
    D. Bargain sale

14. Assume you are analyzing the Ackermans' current estate planning arrangements to help you develop recommendations for improvement. Which of the following would you identify as planning deficiencies in Tom's current estate plan?

    1. Absence of guardianship and support provisions for children
    2. Absence of marital deduction planning
    3. Absence of charitable planning
    4. Absence of incapacity planning

    A. 1, 2, and 4
    B. 1 and 3
    C. 1, 3, and 4
    D. 2 and 3

15. Assume Tom wins the lottery next year and receives a lump-sum distribution of $20 million. Which of the following devices could be used to improve his estate plan?

    1. Create an irrevocable life insurance trust (ILIT)
    2. Create a charitable remainder trust for selected charities
    3. Start an annual gifting program
    4. Create a standby trust to manage assets on incapacity

    A. 1 and 2
    B. 1, 3, and 4
    C. 2, 3, and 4
    D. 1, 2, 3, and 4

16. What is the implied capitalization rate for the rental property? Assume depreciation is $2,000 per year.

    A. 7.5%
    B. 4.3%
    C. 3.5%
    D. 2.2%

17. What is the Treynor ratio for the equity portfolio?

    A. 0.0818
    B. 0.0877
    C. 0.0100
    D. 0.1072

18. The Ackermans would like to evaluate how well their portfolio has performed on a risk-adjusted basis. Based on a previous analysis, they know that their portfolio has an alpha of +2%. Based on this information, which of the following statements is CORRECT?

    A. The equity portfolio has clearly outperformed the market because it has a positive alpha of 2%.
    B. Although alpha is positive and is an absolute measure of performance, the equity portfolio did not outperform the market when total return and total risk are considered as in the Sharpe ratio.
    C. Because both alpha and Treynor of the equity portfolio are higher than those for the market, the equity portfolio is superior on a risk-adjusted basis.
    D. Because alpha for the market is 3% and alpha for the equity fund is 2%, the market portfolio has superior performance.

19. Which of the following statements regarding the Ackermans' rental real estate property is CORRECT?

    A. The loss from the rental property can be deducted this year only to the extent of the Ackermans' investment income.
    B. There will be no alternative minimum tax consequences resulting from the Ackermans' ownership of the rental property.
    C. If the Ackermans sold the rental property for its current fair market value, any gain on the sale would be taxed at a favorable 15% capital gain rate.
    D. There is a loss from the rental property, which may be deductible this year against the Ackermans' ordinary income.

20. You have finished an analysis of the Ackermans' wills and have asked the couple to come into your office to review the findings. You point out that Tom has effectively disinherited all of the children except Justin. Erin states that she is capable of taking care of the children, including providing for Riley if something happens to Tom. You also tell Erin she has done the same thing for her own children by leaving everything to Tom and making no provisions for her minor children. When you ask the couple what would happen to the children, including Justin who is still a minor, if they both died at the same time, the couple realized there was more estate planning to be done. Which of the following recommendations would help the Ackermans?

    1. Add a simultaneous death clause to both wills.

    2. Provide for guardianship for any children who are still minors at the date of death.

    3. Establish an ILIT to purchase life insurance on both parents to provide support and education funds for the children.

    4. Provide for springing durable powers of attorney for both property and health care in case of incapacity.

    A. 1 only

    B. 1 and 4

    C. 2 and 3

    D. 1, 2, 3, and 4

ANSWER SUMMARY

1. A	6. B	11. B	16. C
2. A	7. D	12. C	17. D
3. A	8. B	13. B	18. B
4. B	9. A	14. C	19. D
5. D	10. C	15. D	20. D

SUMMARY OF TOPICS

1. Tax—Adjustments
2. Insurance—Group Term Life Insurance
3. Insurance—Analysis of Risk Exposures
4. Insurance—Disability Income Insurance
5. Tax—Disability Income Benefits
6. Insurance—Homeowners
7. Tax—Basis of Gift Property
8. Tax—Basis of Gift Property
9. Investments—Collectibles
10. Retirement—Traditional IRA
11. Insurance—Liability
12. Estates—Probate Estate
13. Estates—Intra-Family Transfers
14. Estates—Estate Planning
15. Estates—Estate Planning
16. Investments—Capitalized Earnings
17. Investments—Treynor Ratio, Weighted Beta
18. Investments—Performance Measures
19. Tax—Rental Real Estate
20. Estates—Wills

Solutions

Tax—Adjustments

1. **A**

Payments to an ex-spouse are deductible as alimony only if there is no requirement for payments to be paid after the death of the recipient spouse. Payments to a spouse that are required to be made to the estate of that spouse after death are disqualified as alimony.

Insurance—Group Term Life Insurance

2. **A**

Erin's W-2 will include the excess of $200,000 over $50,000, multiplied by the rate found in the schedule in Section 79 of the Internal Revenue Code, less payments she makes toward the policy premium.

Section 79: $.23 per $1,000 per month ($150 \times \$.23 \times 12 = \$414$).

$414 – $240 = $174

The $240 equals a payment of $20 per month by Erin × 12 months.

Insurance—Analysis of Risk Exposures

3. **A**

The Ackermans are deficient in disability income insurance for Tom.

Health insurance appears to be adequate. Additional information is needed regarding health insurance after retirement.

The Ackermans need a personal liability umbrella policy of $1–2 million.

The homeowners policy is deficient because the dwelling has a replacement value of $260,000 and they only carry $196,000 of coverage. They need a minimum coverage of $208,000 (80% of replacement value) to avoid a coinsurance penalty. The value of the land is $20,000. Additionally, they would need an endorsement for the coin collection.

Insurance—Disability Income Insurance

4. **B**

The elimination period is 90 days. She would begin collecting 60% of $5,416.67 per month beginning in July and collect for a total of 6 months.

$3,250 × 6 months = $19,500

Tax—Disability Income Benefits

5. **D**

Erin pays 40% of the premiums; therefore, that portion of the benefits received would be nontaxable to Erin because she did not receive a tax deduction for the premiums she paid for the coverage. The remainder (60%) would be taxable because the premiums were paid and deducted by her employer.

$3,250 × 40% = $1,300 × 6 = $7,800 nontaxable

$3,250 × 60% = $1,950 × 6 = $11,700 taxable

Comment: Because a portion of the benefit is taxable, the benefit of 60% of gross pay may be inadequate.

Insurance—Homeowners

6. **B**

$18,596 of the loss would be reimbursed by the insurance company.

The loss amount is $20,000.

$260,000 × .80 = $208,000 required coverage under the coinsurance requirement

[($196,000 ÷ $208,000) × $20,000] – $250 deductible = $18,596

Tax—Basis of Gift Property

7. **D**

Erin's adjusted tax basis must be determined.

Sale price	$40,000		
Basis for gains	(33,000)	Basis for losses	$28,000
Long-term capital gain	$7,000		

The donee's basis in a gift is the donor's basis, except when the fair market value at the date of the gift is less than the donor's basis, in which case the donee has a double basis (the fair market value for losses and the donor's basis for gains). Gift tax paid on *appreciation* of the asset in the hands of the donor may be added pro rata to the basis of the donee. In this situation, there was no appreciation as of the date of the gift and, therefore, the pro rata share of the gift tax cannot be added to basis. Stirling's original basis was $33,000.

Tax—Basis of Gift Property

8. **B**

The donee's basis in a gift is generally the donor's basis ($5,000). In addition, the donee can add the pro rata share of gift tax paid by the donor on the portion of the fair market value that represents appreciation [(appreciation ÷ FMV) × gift tax paid = basis adjustment]. The annual exclusion was not available for this gift.

$5,000 + [($25,000 ÷ $30,000) × $5,000] = $9,167

Investments—Collectibles

9. **A**

A coin collection is illiquid.

Retirement—Traditional IRA

10. **C**

Tom can make a deductible contribution of up to $6,500 for 2017 ($5,500 maximum deductible contribution plus $1,000 catch-up because he is 50+). A couple with one spouse who is an *active participant* in a qualified plan will not have to consider adjusting the deduction for the other spouse until their combined MAGI exceeds $186,000. No deduction is allowed for the spouse of an active participant if their combined MAGI exceeds $196,000. Erin's contribution is not deductible because she is an *active participant* in a qualified plan and their joint MAGI exceeds $119,000 (the 2017 phaseout for taxpayers married filing jointly).

Insurance—Liability

11. **B**

The collateral source rule provides that damages assessed against an individual should not be reduced by the existence of other sources of recovery available to the injured party, such as insurance.

Estates—Probate Estate

12. **C**

The rental property would be excluded from the probate estate.

	Total	Probate assets	Liabilities	Comment
Cash and cash equivalents	$35,000	$0	$0	JTWROS
Proprietorship	400,000	400,000	0	
Tom's IRA	40,000	0	0	Beneficiary
Stock portfolio	135,000	135,000	0	
Rental property	160,000	0	49,665	JTWROS
Personal residence	280,000	0	76,558	JTWROS
Autos	20,000	0	0	JTWROS
Personal property	60,000	0	0	JTWROS
Life insurance	200,000	0	0	Beneficiary
		$535,000	$126,223	

Estates—Intra-Family Transfers

13. **B**

An installment note is the most suitable recommendation because it provides for payments to be made over time, allows collateral as security, and does not cancel at the seller's death. A private annuity is not suitable because it does not allow collateral, payments cease at the seller's death, and the buyer may end up paying more than FMV if the seller lives longer than expected. A SCIN is not suitable because payments cease at the seller's death and the buyer may end up paying more than FMV if the seller lives longer than expected. A bargain sale is not suitable because a bargain sale is a sale for less than FMV.

Estates—Estate Planning

14. **C**

Statement 1 is correct because Tom's existing will does not contain guardianship and support provisions for his minor children.

Statement 2 is incorrect; Tom's assets currently fall far below the current federal estate tax exemption amount, so there is no reason to incorporate marital deduction planning in his estate plan.

Statement 3 is correct; although one of the Ackermans' goals is to integrate charitable intentions into their estate plan, there are no arrangements currently in place to do so.

Statement 4 is correct because Tom's current plan contains no arrangements, such as a power of attorney for health care, to provide for his potential incapacity.

Estates—Estate Planning

15. D

1. Having an ILIT as the owner of each insurance policy will protect the insurance proceeds from possible claims by creditors of the estate and keep the proceeds out of Tom's gross estate. The life income beneficiary would be the spouse who could disclaim. The principal beneficiaries could be the children.

2. Place sufficient assets in a charitable remainder trust to satisfy the Ackermans' charitable giving plans.

3. Annual gifting can be completed without incurring gift tax.

4. A standby trust that springs upon incapacity will ensure that the assets are managed properly during incapacity.

Investments—Capitalized Earnings

16. C

Rental income (net)		$12,000
Operation costs	$1,200	
Taxes	2,800	
Association dues	1,600	
Insurance premiums	850	
Total expenses		(6,450)
Net operating income		$5,550

FMV = $160,000 (from balance sheet)

$$\text{Implied capitalization rate} = \frac{\$5,550}{\$160,000} = 3.469\%$$

Note: Neither depreciation nor mortgage interest is used in determining the value of the real estate.

Investments—Treynor Ratio, Weighted Beta

17. D

$$\text{Treynor ratio} = \frac{\overline{r_p} - \overline{r_f}}{\beta_p} = \frac{.14 - .03}{1.0259} = .1072$$

Weighted portfolio beta:

Fund	FMV	Beta	Product
A	$25,000	1.3	$32,500
B	40,000	1.0	40,000
C	60,000	.9	54,000
D	10,000	1.2	12,000
Total	$135,000		$138,500

Weighted beta = $138,500 ÷ $135,000 = 1.0259

Note: The 90-day T-bill rate of 3% is used as the risk-free rate.

Investments—Performance Measures

18. **B**

R^2 (coefficient of determination) is an indication of the percentage of returns, which is attributable to the market as well as the percentage of systematic risk within the portfolio. Because R^2 equals 25% (0.5^2), systematic risk represents only 1/4 of the total risk within the portfolio. Because R^2 is so low and beta measures only systematic risk, beta will not be a reliable measure of risk. Similarly, because Treynor and alpha both rely on beta as the risk measure, neither performance measure should be used. The Sharpe ratio uses standard deviation as the measure of risk. Because standard deviation measures total risk, the Sharpe ratio is the preferred measure.

$$\text{Sharpe ratio for the portfolio} = \frac{\overline{r_p} - \overline{r_f}}{\overline{\sigma_p}} = \frac{.14 - .03}{.18} = 0.6111$$

$$\text{Sharpe ratio for the market} = \frac{\overline{r_m} - \overline{r_f}}{\sigma_m} = \frac{.12 - .03}{.14} = 0.6429$$

Because the Sharpe ratio for the market is higher than that of the portfolio, the market has a higher risk-adjusted rate of return.

Tax—Rental Real Estate

19. **D**

Up to $25,000 of rental real estate losses are deductible against ordinary income. The $25,000 loss allowance is phased out $1 for every $2 by which AGI (excluding the rental property) exceeds $100,000. Depending on the Ackermans' AGI (excluding the rental property), the loss on the rental property may be fully deductible.

Losses up to $25,000 from rental properties can be deducted directly against ordinary income, subject to AGI limits.

Residential real estate placed in service before 1998 must be depreciated over 40 years to avoid AMT. Because the Ackermans are currently assigning a book value of zero to the rental property building, they have fully depreciated that portion of the property that is the building on an accelerated basis. There will be an AMT adjustment for the depreciation.

Because the rental property is depreciable real property, the portion of any gain on the sale of the rental property that represents depreciation recapture will be taxed at a 25% rate.

Estates—Wills

20. **D**

All of these are ways to better prepare for the death of one or both of the parents. When a planner communicates the recommendations, educating the client on the findings and the available alternatives will help the client understand why the planner is making the recommendations. The Ackermans did not understand the effects of their current wills until their CFP® professional explained them.

Case Study 8: Barry and Kay Blocker

Case Study Facts

Today is December 31, 2017. Barry and Kay Blocker have come to you, a CFP® professional, for help in developing a plan to accomplish their financial goals. From your initial meeting together, you have gathered the following information.

PERSONAL BACKGROUND AND INFORMATION

Barry Blocker (Age 67)

Barry Blocker's date of birth is May 11, 1950. He has been employed for 20 years as a partner at Blocker Securities (Blocker). He participates in a profit-sharing plan at Blocker under the self-employed participant rules. He was previously employed for 20 years as a broker with Semper Investors, Inc., where he participated in the Section 401(k) plan.

Kay Blocker (Age 67)

Kay Blocker's date of birth is January 10, 1950. She has volunteered at the Boys and Girls Clubs of America and the Associated Charities for the past 15 years.

The Blockers

The Blockers have been married 42 years. Both Barry and Kay are currently in good health, although Barry had knee replacement surgery eight years ago. Barry's life expectancy is 17 years. Kay's life expectancy is 20 years. Their joint life expectancy is 26 years.

Children

Katie	Age 39	2 children
Denise	Age 36	5 children
Lauren	Age 30	4 children
Jessica	Age 29	3 children
Barry, Jr.	Age 18	No children

All of the girls are healthy, employed, married, and not living with Barry and Kay. Barry Jr. is an unemployed, single, high school graduate, living with his parents.

PERSONAL AND FINANCIAL OBJECTIVES

- Barry plans to sell his share of the business.
    - He will sell half of his share of the business to his key employee, Andrew Byland.
    - He will sell the other half to his daughter Katie, who is the senior broker in the firm.
- Barry plans to retire immediately and travel around the world with his wife.
- After traveling around the world, Barry plans to return to the business as a self-employed consultant on a fee basis beginning January 1, 2019. He expects to earn $250,000 per year in consulting fees.
- Barry's grandchild, Beau (Katie's younger child), was born with a serious physical disability; Barry plans to give Beau $2 million in trust.

ECONOMIC INFORMATION

- The couple expects inflation (CPI) to average 4% annually.

- Expected stock market returns are 10% annually, as measured by the S&P 500 Index, with a standard deviation of 10%.

- The 90-day T-bill is yielding 3.5%.

- The 30-year Treasury bond is yielding 7.5%.

- Current mortgage rates are 7.5% for 15 years and 8% for 30 years. If the Blockers refinance their mortgage, closing costs (3% of the mortgage) will be paid from separate funds at closing.

INSURANCE INFORMATION

Life Insurance

Neither spouse has life insurance.

Health Insurance

Barry's business provides major medical health insurance coverage for both Kay and himself during employment and subsequent retirement.

- 80/20 coinsurance

- $250 deductible per person

- $2,000 family stop-loss limit

Disability Insurance

Neither spouse has disability insurance.

Homeowners Insurance

They have an HO-3 policy on the primary residence and vacation homes.

	Residence	Vacation Home 1	Vacation Home 2
Dwelling Coverage	$750,000	$700,000	$600,000
Coinsurance requirement	80%	80%	80%
Deductible	$250	$250	$250

Personal Liability Umbrella Policy

$3 million coverage limit

Automobile Insurance

$250,000/$500,000/$100,000; no comprehensive or collision coverage

Insurance Premiums

- Car insurance: $6,000 per year for all three automobiles
- Homeowners insurance: $7,500 per year (includes all three homes)
- Boat insurance: $1,200 per year (also covered under the umbrella liability policy)
- Umbrella liability policy: $1,000 per year

INVESTMENT INFORMATION

- The Blockers have a required rate of return of 8%.
- The Blockers have a medium to high risk tolerance but see little need to take excessive risks because of their net worth.
- Barry plans to sell 4,468 shares of Q-Mart stock to his daughter Jessica, who is an employee of Q-Mart. Barry anticipates that the stock will appreciate greatly in the upcoming years. The stock was purchased four years ago for $26.66 per share and is currently trading at $11.25 per share.

INCOME TAX INFORMATION

- Barry and Kay are currently in the highest federal income tax bracket.
- They also pay state income taxes of 9.5%.
- For personal income tax reporting, Barry has a $700,000 salary.
- They do not reside in a community property state.

RETIREMENT INFORMATION

- The Section 401(k) plan has a balance of $600,000, consisting of a portfolio of small-cap funds. This portfolio is projected to average a return of 16% over the next 20 years, with a standard deviation of 8%.
- His scheduled Social Security retirement benefit is $27,600 next year and will increase at the expected CPI of 4%.
- Barry's company has a profit-sharing plan that makes contributions for Barry as a self-employed plan participant. His company contributes $12,000 per year into the plan. The contributions to this plan have been made out of the company's profits. The balance is a result of an annual contribution of $12,000, with a 7% average return since July 1, 1998.
- Barry and Kay will continue to collect $200,000 per year in rental proceeds from Commercial Property A.
- Barry will receive $50,000 per year from the charitable remainder annuity trust that owns Commercial Property B.

GIFTS, ESTATES, TRUSTS, AND WILL INFORMATION

Gifts

The following are Barry Blocker's lifetime gifts.

- Barry established a 5% charitable remainder annuity trust (CRAT) this year and funded it with an apartment building (Commercial Property B) he inherited from his grandfather. The initial valuation of the trust was $1 million, and the initial income in the first year is projected to be $50,000 beginning next year. The charitable remainder beneficiary is the Chicago Art Institute.

■ Although the trust document has not been finalized, Barry is working with an attorney to draft an irrevocable trust for the benefit of his grandchild, Beau, who is the younger child of Katie. Barry will contribute $2 million to the trust. Under the provisions of the trust, Katie will receive income from the trust for the rest of her life, and the remainder of the trust will pass to Beau at Katie's death. The trustee will have the authority to make distributions of trust principal during Katie's lifetime to Beau as deemed fit.

■ Kay has not made any taxable gifts during her lifetime and has not split any gifts with Barry.

Estates

For the purpose of estimating estate liquidity needs of both spouses:

■ last illness and funeral expenses are expected to be $250,000 each (terminal illnesses anticipated); and

■ estate administration expenses are estimated at $200,000 each.

Wills

Mr. and Mrs. Blocker have simple wills. They have left all probate assets to each other. Each will also includes a six-month survivorship clause. Debts and taxes are to be paid from the residue of the estate. If Kay predeceases Barry or fails to survive him for more than six months, his entire estate goes to his five children in equal and undivided 1/5 shares. If any of his children predecease him or fail to survive him for more than six months, or disclaim or fail to accept any property bequeathed to him or her, his or her share of the property will pass to the grandchildren. If the heirs have no children, then the property passes to the surviving heirs. Kay is named as Barry's executrix.

Statement of Cash Flows

Barry and Kay Blocker

January 1, 2017–December 31, 2017

CASH INFLOWS

Salary	Barry's salary		$700,000
Rental income			200,000
Dividend income	Barry	$5,000	
	Kay	1,500	
	Total dividend income		6,500
Interest income[1]			1,000
Total inflows			**$907,500**

CASH OUTFLOWS

Mortgage payments	Primary residence	$37,030	
	Vacation home 1	45,181	
	Vacation home 2	79,308	
	Total mortgage payments		$161,519
Insurance premiums	Homeowners	$7,500	
	Auto	6,000	
	Boat	1,200	
	Umbrella	1,000	
	Total insurance premiums		$15,700
Miscellaneous expenses	Credit card payments	$2,400	
	Entertainment	50,000	
	Food	14,400	
	Clothes	30,000	
	Utilities	24,000	
	Charity	90,000	
	Total miscellaneous expenses		$210,800
Taxes	Property taxes	$84,000	
	Payroll taxes[2]	408,375	
	Total taxes		$492,375
Total outflows			**$880,394**
Net cash flow (surplus)			**$27,106**

Notes to financial statements:

[1] Next year's projected income of $50,000 from the CRAT is not included in the statement of cash flows but should be included in any projections for 2018.

[2] Payroll taxes includes FICA and state and federal withholding.

Statement of Financial Position

Barry and Kay Blocker

As of December 31, 2017

ASSETS[1]			LIABILITIES AND NET WORTH		
			Liabilities[2]		
Cash/cash equivalents			**Current liabilities**		
JT	Cash	$100,000	Kay	Credit card 1	$1,000
			Kay	Credit card 2	15,000
Total cash/cash equivalent		$100,000	**Total current liabilities**		$16,000
Invested assets			**Long-term liabilities**		
Barry	Blocker Securities	$5,000,000	JT	Mortgage—primary	$258,630
Kay	Investment portfolio	500,000	JT	Mortgage—vacation 1	369,428
Barry	Deferred annuity	233,047	JT	Mortgage—vacation 2	687,444
Barry	Section 401(k) plan	600,000		**Total long-term liabilities**	$1,315,502
Barry	Self-employed profit-sharing plan	526,382		**Total liabilities**	$1,331,502
Barry	Investment portfolio	4,000,000			
JT	Commercial Property A	1,500,000			
Total investments		$12,359,429			
Personal-use assets			**Net worth**		$15,087,927
JT	Primary residence[3]	$1,300,000			
JT	Vacation home 1[4]	800,000			
JT	Vacation home 2[5]	700,000			
JT	Personal property/furniture	875,000			
Barry	Auto 1	80,000			
Barry	Auto 2	55,000			
Kay	Auto 3	40,000			
Kay	Yacht	110,000			
Total personal use		**$3,960,000**			
Total assets		**$16,419,429**	**Total liabilities and net worth**		**$16,419,429**

Notes to financial statements:

[1] Assets are stated at fair market value.

[2] Liabilities are stated at principal only.

[3] Replacement value of the dwelling: $1 million

[4] Replacement value of the dwelling: $700,000

[5] Replacement value of the dwelling: $575,000

Property ownership:

JT   = Joint tenancy with right of survivorship
Client name = Separate property

INFORMATION REGARDING ASSETS AND LIABILITIES

Blocker Security Investments

Barry is a 50% partner.

- Market value of Barry's interest: $5 million
- Adjusted tax basis: $1 million
- Transfer of business (sale)
  - 50%: 10-year installment sale to Andrew Byland for a down payment of 20% on January 1, 2018, and monthly payments beginning February 1, 2018, at 10% interest
  - 50%: self-canceling installment note (SCIN) to Katie

Primary Residence

- Jointly owned—purchased 15 years ago
- Market value: $1.3 million
- Original purchase price: $300,000
- Current 30-year mortgage at 12% interest; payment: $3,085.84 per month

Vacation Home 1

- Jointly owned—purchased in December in the year before last
- Market value: $800,000
- Original purchase price: $400,000
- Current 15-year mortgage at 7.75% interest; payment: $3,765.10 per month

Vacation Home 2

- Jointly owned—purchased this year
- Market value: $700,000
- Original purchase price: $700,000
- Current 15-year mortgage at 7.8% interest; payment: $6,608.99 per month

Commercial Property A

- Original site of business
- Fair market value: $1.5 million
- Adjusted basis: $200,000

Single Premium Deferred Annuity

- Barry purchased this annuity on July 1, 1983, for $60,000. The current fair market value is $233,047.
- Earnings rate of 6% compounded annually is expected in the near term.
- Annuity start date is January 1, 2019, at which time the fair market value is projected to be $247,030 and will consist of monthly payments made over 15 years.

- If Barry dies before the annuity start date, Kay is named beneficiary.
- If he dies after the annuity start date, Kay will receive a 100% survivor payout.

Summary of Indebtedness

Asset	Date of first payment	Mortgage amount	Term/ years	Interest rate	Monthly payments	Remaining payments	Remaining balance
Primary residence	4/1/03	$300,000	30	12%	($3,085.84)	183	$258,629.77
Vacation home 1	1/1/16	$400,000	15	7.75%	($3,765.10)	156	$369,427.87
Vacation home 2	7/1/17	$700,000	15	7.8%	($6,608.99)	174	$687,443.57
Total							$1,315,501.21

Detailed Investment Portfolios

Barry's Portfolio					
Description	Acquired	Shares	Adjusted basis	Beta	Current FMV
Seers	8/10	16,325	$201,633	0.9	$830,214
Q-Mart	1/13	4,468	$119,117	1.2	$50,265
Cannon, Inc.	2/15	22,249	$400,188	1.4	$2,230,462
*RC, Inc.	9/15	3,742	$67,181	1.5	$222,600
WW Grain	10/17	4,257	$221,435	1.2	$311,293
Circuitville Stores	9/17	10,561	$304,062	1.2	$355,166
Total			$1,313,616		$4,000,000

* The RC, Inc. stock is Section 1244 Small Business Stock.

Kay's Portfolio					
Description	Acquired	Shares	Adjusted basis	Beta	Current FMV
Tanet Health Care	1/11	2,542	$30,504	0.6	$50,209
Bay Bank, Inc.	2/15	1,500	$120,000	0.5	$167,250
Macrosoft	9/15	589	$53,010	0.7	$66,189
Zeenith	10/16	22,190	$177,520	0.8	$216,352
Total			$381,034		$500,000

Questions

1. Assume today Barry sells the Q-Mart stock to Jessica for the current fair market value. What is Barry's tax consequence from this transaction?

    A. STCG of $50,265
    B. STCL of $68,852
    C. LTCL of $68,852
    D. No gain or loss

2. Assume that Barry sells the Q-Mart stock to Jessica for the current fair market value as of December 31, 2017, and Jessica resells the Q-Mart stock at $16.50 per share in November of the following year through her broker. What is the tax consequence to Jessica?

    A. No gain or loss
    B. STCG of $23,457
    C. LTCG of $23,457
    D. STCL of $45,395

3. If Barry sells all of his RC, Inc. stock this year at the current fair market value, what will be the tax treatment?

    A. LTCG of $155,419
    B. Ordinary income of $100,000 and LTCG of $55,419
    C. Ordinary income of $100,000 and STCG of $55,419
    D. Ordinary income of $100,000 and carryover of $55,419 ordinary income

4. If Barry sells all of his RC, Inc. stock this year at the current fair market value, what would the tax treatment be if the stock was Section 1202 stock purchased 9/15/15 instead of Section 1244 stock?

    A. No gain or loss
    B. LTCG of $105,419
    C. LTCG of $116,564
    D. LTCG of $155,419

5. Which of the following techniques could be used to limit which assets are included in Barry's probate estate?

   1. Totten trust
   2. Revocable living trust
   3. Pay-on-death arrangements (POD)

   A. 1 and 3
   B. 2 only
   C. 2 and 3
   D. 1, 2, and 3

6. In your early meetings with Barry and Kay, the couple asked you to evaluate their current insurance situation. You have completed your analysis and have come to several conclusions. Which of the following statements regarding your analysis of the Blockers' insurance situation is(are) CORRECT?

   1. They have a serious disability insurance deficiency.
   2. The homeowners policy is appropriate and adequate.
   3. The umbrella liability policy is inadequate.
   4. They are underinsured for life insurance.

   A. 1, 2, and 4
   B. 2, 3, and 4
   C. 3 only
   D. 1, 2, 3, and 4

7. Assume that Barry begins a consulting career in 2018 instead of waiting until the following year and expects to have taxable earned income of $250,000 per year. Which of the following statements regarding the results of his consulting activities is CORRECT? (Assume the Social Security earnings limits do not change for 2018.)

   A. He will lose Social Security benefits of $1 for every $3 earned over $44,880.
   B. He will lose Social Security benefits of $1 for every $2 earned over $16,920.
   C. He will lose all of his Social Security benefits.
   D. None of these are correct.

8. Kay and Barry are meeting with you today. You have completed a thorough analysis of the Blockers' investments and have developed some recommendations for the couple's investment planning. Which of the following investment planning recommendations would you communicate to Kay and Barry?

    1. You recommend that they should diversify their portfolio because a significant amount of their wealth is invested in only a few stocks.

    2. Because the Blockers can tolerate a high level of risk, their current portfolio is allocated properly and you have no recommendations for reallocation of investments in their portfolio.

    3. Because of their high tax bracket, you recommend the Blockers consider investing in tax-free securities, such as municipal bonds.

    4. For several stocks, you recommend they not sell those securities because their cost basis in those stocks is low.

    A. 1 and 3
    B. 2 and 4
    C. 2, 3, and 4
    D. 1, 2, and 3

9. If Barry were to refinance his primary residence on January 2, 2018, at current mortgage rates for 15 years, how much would his monthly payment decline?

    A. $614.16
    B. $616.38
    C. $688.31
    D. $2,397.53

10. Assume Barry begins his consulting business in 2019. Which of the following statements regarding his ability to defer taxes using a qualified retirement plan (assume plan limits will be the same as the current year) is(are) CORRECT?

    I.   He can contribute the maximum amount to a profit-sharing plan for a self-employed plan participant-owner.

    II. A Section 401(k) plan will allow him to shelter more than a profit-sharing plan.

    A. I only
    B. II only
    C. Both I and II
    D. Neither I nor II

11. Which of the following transfers will NOT result in Barry making a taxable gift? For purposes of the annual exclusion and lifetime applicable credit amount, assume they take place in 2017.

    1. Barry pays each grandchild's private school tuition directly to the school ($6,000 each).
    2. Barry pays City Hospital for the hospital bill of a friend ($15,000).
    3. Barry gives a distant cousin money for law school tuition ($25,000).
    4. Barry pays Barry Jr.'s tuition directly to Horizon College ($30,000).

    A. 1, 2, and 4
    B. 1 and 3
    C. 1, 3, and 4
    D. 1, 2, 3, and 4

12. With regard to the installment sale portion of Barry's interest in Blocker Securities to Andrew Byland, how much, if any, of the down payment is taxable to Barry in 2018, and what is the character of the down payment?

    A. No taxable income; a return of basis
    B. Capital gain of $400,000
    C. Ordinary income of $250,000 and capital gain of $150,000
    D. Ordinary income of $500,000 and capital gain of $300,000

13. Calculate the total monthly installment payments that Andrew Byland will make to Barry during 2018. (Round to the nearest dollar.)

    A. $288,329
    B. $290,732
    C. $314,541
    D. $317,162

14. If Barry dies on January 1 of next year and Kay survives him by 6 months, which of the following statements regarding the installment sale to Andrew Byland is CORRECT?

    A. Nothing will be included in Barry's gross estate.
    B. The present value of the remaining notes payable will be included in Barry's gross estate.
    C. Only the remaining unrecognized gain will be included in Barry's gross estate.
    D. The unpaid principal balance of the notes and any unpaid accrued interest as of Barry's date-of-death will be included in Barry's gross estate.

15. What is the likelihood that the return on the investments in Barry's Section 401(k) plan will be below the Blockers' required rate of return?

    A. 0%
    B. 8%
    C. 16%
    D. 24%

16. Barry and Kay are considering the purchase of a joint and survivor (second-to-die) life insurance policy for the purpose of wealth replacement, for the assets that were transferred to the CRAT, and to help to create estate liquidity. Which of the following is(are) the most appropriate owner(s) for the policy?

    A. The children should own the policy to have cash to pay estate taxes or make loans to the estate.
    B. Kay should own the policy because Barry's estate is overqualified.
    C. An irrevocable life insurance trust should be created to purchase and own the policy to exclude the proceeds from Kay's and Barry's gross estates.
    D. Barry and Kay should own the policy jointly to keep control over the cash value accumulation.

17. If Barry dies on December 31, 2018, how much of an annual Social Security benefit will Kay expect to receive for 2019?

    A. $13,300
    B. $20,700
    C. $27,600
    D. $28,704

18. Which of the following statements is CORRECT?

    A. As a result of setting up the CRAT, Barry is eligible for a charitable income tax deduction (subject to AGI limitations) this year equal to the PV of the remainder interest in the trust.
    B. If Barry dies in March of next year (after the sale of his business), the value of the installment note and the SCIN will be included in his estate.
    C. Commercial Property B will be included in Barry's probate estate if he dies next year.
    D. Payments received from the CRAT will be income tax free to Barry.

19. Barry recently attended an investment seminar about the concepts of business risk and concentrated portfolios. He has already addressed the issue of Blocker Securities by entering into 2 transactions. However, he would like to consider minimizing the risk attributable to owning $2.2 million of Cannon, Inc. Which of the following would be a good method for dealing with his concentrated portfolio?

    1. Transfer the stock to an exchange-traded fund
    2. Establish an employee stock ownership plan
    3. Establish a zero-cost collar

    A. 1 only
    B. 1 and 2
    C. 1 and 3
    D. 3 only

20. Assume that the Blockers ask you for advice on arranging their estates to minimize the effect of transfer taxes when they die. Based on your knowledge of the estate tax, you understand that the estate tax laws, including the estate tax rates and exemptions, can vary from year to year. Your assumption is that the tax laws will continue to fluctuate in the future. Which of the following statements regarding your obligations in making estate planning recommendations for the Blockers is(are) CORRECT?

1. You can make reasonable assumptions concerning future tax rates in formulating your recommendations.

2. Your recommendations must be consistent with any assumptions you have made concerning future tax rates.

3. In presenting your recommendations to the Blockers, you should indicate that future legislative changes could affect the intended outcome of the recommendations.

4. In presenting your recommendations to the Blockers, you should communicate any assumptions that are critical to their understanding of the recommendations.

A. 1 and 4

B. 3 only

C. 1, 2, 3, and 4

D. 1 and 2

ANSWER SUMMARY

1. D	6. C	11. A	16. C
2. A	7. D	12. B	17. D
3. A	8. A	13. B	18. A
4. D	9. C	14. D	19. D
5. D	10. C	15. C	20. C

SUMMARY OF TOPICS

1. Tax—Related-Party Transaction
2. Tax—Related-Party Transaction
3. Tax—Section 1244 Stock
4. Tax—Section 1202 Stock
5. Estates—Minimization of the Estate
6. Insurance—Analysis of Risk Exposures
7. Retirement—Social Security Benefits
8. Investments—Portfolio Diversifications
9. Fundamentals—Mortgage Refinancing
10. Retirement—Qualified Retirement Plans
11. Estates—Gift Tax Compliance
12. Tax—Installment Sale
13. Fundamentals—Time Value of Money
14. Estates—Gross Estate
15. Investments—Normal Distribution
16. Estates—Use of Life Insurance in Estate Planning
17. Retirement—Social Security Benefits
18. Estates—Inclusion in the Estate
19. Investments—Strategies for Dealing with Concentrated Portfolios
20. Fundamentals—Planner Assumptions

Solutions

Tax—Related-Party Transaction

1. **D**

   Barry has an economic loss of $68,852 that would be realized but not recognized because this is a related-party transaction. Thus, there would be no gain or loss associated with this transaction.

Tax—Related-Party Transaction

2. **A**

   Because Jessica sold the stock at $16.50 per share, she has a realized gain of $5.25 per share. None of this gain is recognized by Jessica because she can offset her realized gain with an equivalent amount of Barry's previously disallowed loss of $15.41 per share ($26.66 – $11.25). Barry's remaining disallowed loss of $10.16 per share cannot be used by either Barry or Jessica.

Tax—Section 1244 Stock

3. **A**

   Barry would have a long-term capital gain of $155,419. Although this is Section 1244 stock (small business stock), the Section 1244 rules apply only to losses, not gains. The treatment of Section 1244 stock for gains is the same as any ordinary stock transaction.

Sale price	$222,600
Adjusted tax basis	(67,181)
Long-term capital gain	$155,419

Tax—Section 1202 Stock

4. **D**

   Although there is a 100% gain exclusion for Section 1202 stock purchased after 9/27/10, Barry has not met the 5-year holding period. Therefore, the stock is taxed as a normal LTCG.

Estates—Minimization of the Estate

5. **D**

   All of these techniques could be used to limit which assets are included in Barry's probate estate.

Insurance—Analysis of Risk Exposures

6. **C**

   The amount of coverage under their homeowners policy is inadequate because it does not satisfy the 80% coinsurance requirement. They do not need life insurance because of their high net worth and liquidity. They are retired, so they have no need for disability income insurance. Given that their net worth exceeds $15 million, their umbrella liability coverage of $3 million is inadequate. Only statement 3 is correct.

Retirement—Social Security Benefits

7. **D**

The earnings test does not apply to individuals who have attained full retirement age. Barry has reached full retirement age so he will not lose his Social Security benefits even if he has earned income.

Investments—Portfolio Diversifications

8. **A**

Only Statements 1 and 3 are correct. Diversification of their portfolio and investment in tax-free securities are highly recommended.

Fundamentals—Mortgage Refinancing

9. **C**

$3,085.84 (current payment) – $2,397.53 (new payment) = $688.31 savings per month.

PV	=	–$258,630	Current mortgage balance
n	=	180 (15 × 12)	Term
i	=	0.625 (7.5 ÷ 12)	Interest rate
PMT_{OA}	=	$2,397.53	New payment

Retirement—Qualified Retirement Plans

10. **C**

Both statements are correct. Barry can defer approximately 20% [because he is self-employed (.25 ÷ 1.25 = 20%)]. This deferral will allow him to reach the maximum annual additions limit.

Because salary deferrals do not count against the 25% plan limit, lower income earners generally can increase their overall contribution to a retirement plan by also contributing to a Section 401(k) plan. Salary deferrals do count against the annual additions limit. Barry is over age 65, and catch-up contributions are not included in the annual additions limit. He can defer more with a Section 401(k) plan.

Estates—Gift Tax Compliance

11. **A**

Statement 3 is not a qualified transfer and is subject to gift tax because the tuition was not paid directly to the law school. Statements 1, 2, and 4 are qualified transfers; therefore, they are not taxable gifts.

Tax—Installment Sale

12. B

Of the $500,000 down payment, $400,000 is taxable as a capital gain.

Sale price	$2,500,000	Gross profit percentage	$\dfrac{\$2,000,000}{\$2,500,000} = 0.8$
Adjusted basis	($500,000)		
Gain	$2,000,000		

Down payment	$2,500,000
	× 0.2
	$500,000
Gross profit percentage	× 0.8
Recognized gain	$400,000

Fundamentals—Time Value of Money

13. B

n	=	120 (10 × 12)
i	=	0.8333 (10 ÷ 12)
PV	=	–$2,000,000 (80% × $2,500,000)
PMT_{OA}	=	$26,430.15
		× 11 payments in 2018
Total payments	=	$290,731.62 (rounded to $290,732)

Estates—Gross Estate

14. D

The unpaid principal balance of the notes and any unpaid accrued interest as of Barry's date of death will be included in Barry's gross estate.

Investments—Normal Distribution

15. C

- 68% of outcomes fall within 1 standard deviation.

- Because 8% is 1 standard deviation to the left of the mean, the probability of having a return below 8% will be 16% (50% – 34%).

- 50% represents ½ of the area under the curve.

- 34% represents ½ of the area within 1 standard deviation.

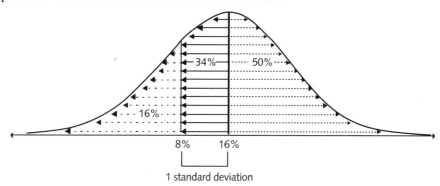

Estates—Use of Life Insurance in Estate Planning

16. C

Although the children's ownership of the policy would keep the proceeds outside of Kay or Barry's gross estate, the best answer is the irrevocable life insurance trust. If a child were to die owning the policy, a portion of the policy's cash value would be includable in the child's estate.

Retirement—Social Security Benefits

17. D

Kay will step into Barry's place and receive $28,704 ($27,600 × 1.04). Kay is a nonworking, age-appropriate spouse and will therefore receive 100% of Barry's primary insurance amount. The 1.04 adjustment is made to increase the amount for inflation at the rate stated in the scenario.

Estates—Inclusion in the Estate

18. A

The grantor is eligible for an immediate income tax deduction (subject to AGI limitations) when the CRAT is established.

The SCIN will cancel upon Barry's death and therefore will not be included in his estate.

The property Barry transferred to the CRAT will be excluded from Barry's probate estate.

The CRAT payments will be taxable to Barry.

Investments—Strategies for Dealing with Concentrated Portfolios

19. **D**

Exchange-traded funds are like open-ended mutual funds that trade like closed-end funds. The Cannon stock cannot be transferred to an exchange-traded fund.

There is no indication that Barry has control of Cannon to make a decision to establish an ESOP. There is also no indication that he owns a large portion of the stock.

A zero-cost collar is an effective method for limiting downside risk with minimal cost. A zero-cost collar is a strategy that is used to protect a gain in a long position of a stock. The collar consists of a long position in stock, a long put option, and a short call option. The investor purchases a put option to protect against downside risk and sells a call option to generate premium income to cover the cost of the put option's premium.

Fundamentals—Planner Assumptions

20. **C**

All of these statements are correct.

Statement 1 is correct under Practice Standard 300-1, which provides that a practitioner should utilize reasonable economic assumptions, such as inflation rates and tax rates, in analyzing a client's financial status.

Statement 2 is correct under Practice Standard 400-2, which states that recommendations must be consistent with any personal and economic assumptions.

Statements 3 and 4 are both correct under Practice Standard 400-3, which governs the presentation of financial planning recommendations to clients.

Case Study 9:
Ida Klar

Case Study Facts

Today is December 31, 2017. Ida Klar has come to you, a CFP® professional, for help in developing a plan to accomplish her financial goals. From your initial meeting together, you have gathered the following information.

PERSONAL BACKGROUND AND INFORMATION

Ida Klar (Age 69)

Ida is a retired homemaker. She is a recent widow. Ida's 70th birthday will be March 1, 2018. Ida is in fair health.

Gerard Klar (Deceased)

Ida was married to Gerard Klar, who died on November 1 of this year at age 69 after a brief battle with cancer. His date of birth was June 1, 1948.

Gerard was employed 45 years as a supervisor at ABC Co., Inc. (ABC) before retiring at age 65. The Klars were married for 50 years.

Children

Ida has two children from her marriage to Gerard: Robert (age 50) and Bryan (age 49). Robert and Bryan are each married, healthy, employed, and self-sufficient.

Grandchildren

Robert and his wife, Gloria, have one daughter, Sharon (age 18). Sharon is currently a senior in high school and will be a freshman at Private University in the fall. The cost of tuition for Private University is currently $25,000 annually. Ida would like to pay Sharon's tuition for this year. As a high school graduation present, Ida is paying for Sharon's trip to Europe this summer. The total cost of this trip is $3,000.

Bryan and his wife, Tara, have one son, Owen (age 17). Owen is a junior in high school. Owen needs orthodontic work that will cost $6,000. Ida would like to pay for Owen's orthodontic work. Ida is also considering gifting stock worth $9,000 to Owen.

PERSONAL AND FINANCIAL OBJECTIVES

- Generate sufficient income ($30,000 per year in today's dollars, including Social Security benefits)
- Consider acquiring a smaller residence
- Explore long-term nursing care alternatives (annual cost in today's dollars: $40,000)
- Donate to the American Cancer Society
- Provide for her children and grandchildren

- Pay Sharon's tuition ($25,000)
- Gift stock to Owen ($9,000)
- Pay for Owen's orthodontic work ($6,000)
- Send Sharon to Europe ($3,000)

ECONOMIC INFORMATION

- Inflation is expected to be 4% annually.
- She is not subject to state income tax.
- The economy is growing slowly; however, stocks are expected to grow at 9.5%.
- Bank lending rates are as follows:

  —15-year mortgages: 7.5%

  —30-year mortgages: 8%

  —Secured personal loan: 10%

Minimum Distribution Divisors (Uniform Distribution Table)

Age	Distribution period
70	27.4
71	26.5

INSURANCE INFORMATION

Life Insurance

Irrevocable Life Insurance Trust (ILIT)

Gerard created an ILIT 10 years ago. The only asset in the trust is a permanent life policy with a face value of $200,000. The income beneficiary of the ILIT is Ida. She is also the trustee and has a general power of appointment over the trust assets. The remainder beneficiaries are the grandchildren.

Health Insurance

Gerard and Ida were both covered under Medicare Part A and Medicare Part B.

INVESTMENT INFORMATION

Ida's investment risk tolerance is low.

INCOME TAX INFORMATION

The Klars filed federal income taxes as married filing jointly last year. Ida and Gerard have always lived in a community property state.

RETIREMENT INFORMATION

Gerard had a profit-sharing plan with ABC with Ida designated as the beneficiary. The plan will permit a beneficiary to take a lump-sum distribution as one of its options. Gerard's account is currently valued at $150,000. As the beneficiary, Ida can choose to receive a life annuity or a lump-sum payment from the plan.

Ida currently has an IRA with Gerard as her named beneficiary.

Ida is the named beneficiary on Gerard's IRA.

Both Gerard and Ida began receiving Social Security benefits on their respective 65th birthdays. Gerard's benefit for this year was $1,200 per month until his death in November, and Ida's benefit for this year is $600 per month.

GIFTS, ESTATES, TRUSTS, AND WILL INFORMATION

Gerard's will left all of his probate assets to Ida. His estate is currently in probate. The grandchildren are named as equal contingent beneficiaries.

Ida does not have a will.

Statement of Financial Position

Gerard (Deceased) and Ida Klar

As of December 31, 2017

	Assets[1]			Liabilities and Net Worth		
	Cash and equivalents			**Liabilities[2]**		
CP	Cash	$25,000	Ida	Credit cards[3]		$20,000
CP	Savings account	20,000				
	Total cash and equivalents	$45,000		Total liabilities		$20,000
	Invested assets					
Gerard	Stocks	$20,000				
Ida	IRA	40,000				
Gerard	IRA	50,000				
CP	Profit-sharing plan	150,000		**Net worth**		$1,180,000
	Total invested assets	$260,000				
	Personal use assets					
CP	Primary residence[4]	$600,000				
Ida	Vacation home[5]	200,000				
CP	Auto	18,000				
CP	Furniture and personal property	77,000				
	Total use assets	$895,000				
	Total assets	**$1,200,000**		**Total liabilities and net worth**		**$1,200,000**

Notes to financial statements:

[1] Assets are stated at fair market value.

[2] Liabilities are stated at principal only. All liabilities are community property.

[3] Interest rate is 18.3%.

[4] The primary residence was originally purchased for $110,000. There have been no additions or upgrades.

[5] The vacation home was inherited by Ida from her mother. Adjusted tax basis is $125,000.

Other notes to financial statements:

The income beneficiary of the ILIT is Ida. Remainder beneficiaries are the grandchildren. Ida has a general power of appointment over the trust assets. The trustee has the power to invade corpus for health, education, maintenance, and support (HEMS) for the grandchildren. The ILIT is not listed on the statement of financial position.

Property ownership:

Client name = Separate property

CP   = Community property

INFORMATION REGARDING REAL ESTATE ASSETS

Primary Residence

- Purchased on April 1, 1978
- Original purchase price: $110,000

Vacation Home

- Owned by Ida (fee simple)
- Inherited by Ida from her mother 17 years ago with a fair market value of $125,000 at the time of the mother's death
- Current fair market value: $200,000
- Located in a noncommunity property state; all payments for repairs and maintenance have been made using community property assets

Questions

1. Which of the following statements regarding Ida's options for Gerard's IRA are CORRECT?

    1. Ida can leave Gerard's IRA intact and receive distributions over her remaining single life expectancy, beginning in 2018.
    2. Ida can roll Gerard's IRA over to her own IRA and name the grandchildren as beneficiaries.
    3. Ida can take a complete distribution from Gerard's IRA with a step-up in basis to the fair market value at the date of Gerard's death.
    4. Ida must withdraw the entire balance of Gerard's IRA over a period not to exceed 5 years.

    A. 1 and 2
    B. 2 and 3
    C. 2, 3, and 4
    D. 2 and 4

2. When must Ida receive her first distribution from her IRA?

    A. April 1, 2018
    B. December 31, 2018
    C. April 1, 2019
    D. December 31, 2019

3. Calculate Ida's probate estate as of today, assuming Ida elected the life annuity option from Gerard's profit-sharing plan.

    A. $980,000
    B. $1,050,000
    C. $1.2 million
    D. $1.4 million

4. Gerard's death has made Ida aware of her own inadequate planning for incapacity and death. Which of the following planning devices should Ida consider immediately for her own estate planning?

    1. Effective disclaimer for assets in Gerard's estate
    2. Springing durable power of attorney for property
    3. Create a will
    4. Qualified terminable interest property (QTIP) election by executor of Gerard's estate

    A. 1 and 2
    B. 1, 2, and 3
    C. 3 and 4
    D. 1, 2, 3, and 4

5. Ida is considering selling her personal residence. What is Ida's adjusted tax basis for the personal residence?

   A. $355,000
   B. $490,000
   C. $500,000
   D. $600,000

6. Ida would like to set up qualified tuition plans (QTPs) for college tuition expenses for both Sharon and Owen today. If Ida did not want to use any of her applicable credit amount in making the transfer, what is the total amount she could contribute to the plan this year and still avoid making a taxable gift?

   A. $14,000
   B. $28,000
   C. $56,000
   D. $140,000

7. Ida is considering making a charitable contribution for the benefit of the American Cancer Society and wants her grandchildren to receive income from the property for an extended period. Which of the following charitable devices may be appropriate to meet Ida's objective?

   1.   Charitable remainder annuity trust
   2.   Charitable remainder unitrust
   3.   Pooled income fund
   4.   Charitable lead trust

   A.   1 or 2
   B.   1, 2, and 3
   C.   2, 3, and 4
   D.   1, 2, 3, and 4

8. If Ida exercised her right to take a lump-sum cash distribution from Gerard's profit-sharing plan on January 1, 2018, what would be the net proceeds from the plan distribution?

   A. $60,000
   B. $75,000
   C. $120,000
   D. $150,000

9. For which of the following Social Security benefits does Ida currently qualify?

    1. $255 death benefit
    2. Widow's share of retirement benefit
    3. Caretaker's benefit
    4. Medicare

    A. 1, 2, and 4
    B. 1 and 4
    C. 2 and 3
    D. 1, 2, 3, and 4

10. What happens to Ida's IRA upon her death, assuming she makes no changes to the account?

    1. The heirs will receive a step-up in basis.
    2. The IRA is in her probate estate.
    3. The IRA is subject to income tax upon distribution.

    A. 1 only
    B. 2 only
    C. 2 and 3
    D. 1, 2, and 3

11. Assuming that Ida has taken a lump-sum distribution from Gerard's profit-sharing plan, which combination of the following investments is appropriate for Ida?

    1. Long-term bonds (average maturity 23 years)
    2. Short-term bonds (average maturity 3 years)
    3. Money markets
    4. T-bills
    5. Growth stocks
    6. Treasury notes
    7. Intermediate bonds (average maturity 10 years)

    A. A combination of 1, 2, 6, and 7
    B. A combination of 2, 3, 6, and 7
    C. A combination of 2, 4, 5, and 6
    D. A combination of 2, 5, 6, and 7

12. How could Ida benefit each grandchild without incurring transfer taxes or using any of her applicable credit amount?

    1. Pay Sharon's tuition directly to the school
    2. Transfer $15,000 to Owen and use a gift-splitting election
    3. Give Sharon the money for her trip to Europe
    4. Pay the dentist directly for Owen's orthodontic work

    A. 1, 2, and 3
    B. 1, 3, and 4
    C. 1 and 4
    D. 2, 3, and 4

13. What is Ida's federal income tax filing status for 2017, 2018, 2019, and 2020, assuming she does not remarry?

	2017	2018	2019	2020
A.	MFJ	S	S	S
B.	MFJ	QW	QW	S
C.	MFJ	QW	QW	HH
D.	QW	QW	HH	HH

    MFJ = married filing jointly
    QW = qualifying widow
    HH = head of household
    S   = single

14. How much will Ida's monthly Social Security benefit be next year?

    A. $600
    B. $900
    C. $990
    D. $1,200

15. On November 1, 2018, Ida decides to sell the personal residence for the fair market value as of December 31, 2017. What will be her tax consequences?

    A. No gain or loss
    B. $240,000 long-term capital gain
    C. $345,000 realized gain, but exempt from tax
    D. $490,000 long-term capital gain

16. Ida is very concerned about her long-term health and is enrolled in Medicare Part B. Which of the following benefits is(are) covered under Medicare Part B?

    1. Hospice care
    2. Medical supplies
    3. Outpatient hospital services for diagnosis
    4. Physicians' fees

    A. 1 and 2
    B. 1, 2, and 3
    C. 2, 3, and 4
    D. 4 only

17. Ida is worried that she will need long-term custodial care because although her mother lived at home until age 95, she needed assistance with bathing, dressing, and toileting once she became 75 years old. Ida is worried that there will be no family member around to care for her. Which of the following would provide Ida with such continued assistance in her home?

    1. Medigap
    2. Medicare Part A and Part B
    3. Medicare HMO
    4. Long-term care insurance

    A. 1 and 2
    B. 1, 3, and 4
    C. 3 and 4
    D. 4 only

18. At her death, Ida wants to maximize her benefit to the American Cancer Society and at the same time maximize benefits to her children and grandchildren. Which of the following assets would be best left to the American Cancer Society?

    A. The IRAs
    B. The vacation home
    C. The stocks
    D. The primary residence

19. Ten years ago, Gerard and Ida gave their grandchildren stock in a US domestic corporation that is publicly traded. The earnings have been steady but unremarkable over the years, returning dividends of about $1,200 for each grandchild last year. Because of an important advance in technology in the last year, the company is growing rapidly, and in 2017 paid $2,300 in dividends to each child. What are the income tax implications of the dividends in 2017?

    A. The grandchildren will be taxed at Ida's marginal tax rate for the dividends.
    B. The grandchildren will owe no tax, but the parents will owe tax on a portion of the dividends.
    C. The grandchildren will owe tax at their rate on a portion of the dividends and will owe tax at their parent's marginal tax rate on a portion of the dividends.
    D. The grandchildren will owe tax at their own marginal tax rate on the entire amount of the dividends.

20. Ida has decided that after Gerard passed away, she needs to get some help with her finances, particularly with her investments. Which of the following would be the most important document(s) you would want to receive before making any recommendations?

    A.   Ida's credit card statements

    B.   Gerard's profit-sharing plan statement with ABC, of which Ida is the beneficiary

    C.   Ida's Social Security statement

    D.   Ida's investment policy statement

ANSWER SUMMARY

1. A	6. D	11. B	16. C
2. C	7. B	12. B	17. D
3. B	8. C	13. A	18. A
4. B	9. A	14. D	19. C
5. D	10. C	15. A	20. D

SUMMARY OF TOPICS

1. Retirement—IRA
2. Retirement—Minimum Distributions
3. Estates—Probate Estate
4. Estates—Estate Planning
5. Tax—Personal Residence
6. Estates—Gifting and Educational Funding
7. Estates—Charitable Trust
8. Retirement—Pension Distribution
9. Retirement—Social Security Benefits
10. Retirement—IRA Beneficiary
11. Investments—Selection
12. Estates—Gifting
13. Tax—Filing Status
14. Retirement—Social Security Benefits
15. Tax—Sale of Personal Residence
16. Insurance—Medicare
17. Insurance—Long-Term Care
18. Estates—Charitable Giving
19. Tax—Kiddie Tax
20. Fundamentals—Financial Planning Process

Solutions

Retirement—IRA

1. **A**

Statements 1 and 2 are correct. Because Gerard died before his required beginning date, Ida (spousal beneficiary) has the following choices with respect to Gerard's IRA.

- Ida can receive distributions over her remaining life expectancy, using her single life expectancy. Distributions must begin in the year in which Gerard would have reached age 70½.

- Ida can roll the IRA balance over and wait until she attains age 70½ to begin taking minimum distributions.

- Ida can *elect* to distribute the entire account balance within 5 years after Gerard's death (5-year rule). This election can be made only if the plan provisions allow the 5-year rule.

Statement 3 is incorrect. There is no step-up in basis to fair market value at death for IRAs because assets held in an IRA at death are considered to be income in respect of a decedent (IRD) assets. Statement 4 is incorrect because Ida is not required to withdraw the entire account balance over 5 years or less.

Retirement—Minimum Distributions

2. **C**

Because her 70th birthday is March 1, 2018, she will be age 70½ on September 1, 2018. Therefore, her first distribution must be made by April 1, 2019.

Estates—Probate Estate

3. **B**

Assets	Probate estate	
Cash	$25,000	
Savings	20,000	
Stocks	20,000	
IRA (Gerard)	50,000	No subsequent or contingent beneficiary
IRA (Ida)	40,000	No subsequent or contingent beneficiary
Profit-sharing plan	0	Ida had a life annuity only
Personal residence	600,000	
Vacation home	200,000	
Auto	18,000	
Furniture	77,000	
ILIT	0	Grandchildren are the remainder beneficiaries
Total	**$1,050,000**	

Estates—Estate Planning

4. **B**

Ida could disclaim any portion of the probate assets she received from Gerard's estate for which the grandchildren are contingent beneficiaries, in effect gifting to the grandchildren now.

A springing durable power of attorney for property would be wise at her age. Ida should create a will to properly dispose of her assets and insure her charitable and personal intentions are carried out in the event of her death. Without a will, she would die intestate and property will pass according to state law. She should also execute a springing durable power of attorney for health care and a living will as part of her overall estate planning.

The QTIP election is unnecessary in Gerard's estate because there are no children from a previous marriage or a need to control the assets from the grave. There is no real benefit here, and it would limit Ida's control over the assets.

Tax—Personal Residence

5. **D**

$600,000. Ida receives a step-up in basis on both halves of community property at Gerard's death.

Estates—Gifting and Educational Funding

6. **D**

For gift tax purposes, contributions to a QTP can be treated as though they were made ratably over a 5-year period, allowing an individual to use 5 years' worth of annual exclusions on an initial contribution. Because the annual exclusion for 2017 is $14,000, Ida can contribute up to $140,000 [($14,000 × 5) × 2].

Estates—Charitable Trust

7. **B**

Statements 1, 2, and 3 are correct. CRATs and CRUTs both provide for income to be paid to the beneficiaries and the remainder interest to charity. A pooled income fund works similarly to CRATs and CRUTs but is managed by the charity. A CLT is designed to pay income to the charity and transfer the remainder interest to a family member or the grantor. The pooled income fund can provide only a life interest, not for a term certain.

Retirement—Pension Distribution

8. **C**

$120,000. There is a mandatory 20% withholding of federal income taxes on distributions from qualified plans.

$150,000 × .80 = $120,000

Retirement—Social Security Benefits

9. **A**

Statement 3 is incorrect. Ida is not a caretaker of a dependent child under age 16. The remaining statements 1, 2, and 4 are correct.

Retirement—IRA Beneficiary

10. **C**

Statements 2 and 3 are correct. The IRA is her own property and will be included in her probate estate because she has no living named beneficiary. IRAs are subject to federal income tax upon distribution and do not receive a step-up to FMV at death because IRAs are considered to be income in respect of a decedent (IRD).

Investments—Selection

11. **B**

The process of elimination should be used to answer this question. Long-term bonds (Statement 1) are inappropriate for her age. Growth stocks (Statement 5) are inappropriate for her low risk tolerance. Therefore, the best combination of investments is short-term bonds, money markets, Treasury notes, and intermediate bonds. T-bills (Statement 4) may have been an appropriate investment selection; however, T-bills are included in combination with other inappropriate investments (5 growth stocks).

Estates—Gifting

12. **B**

Statements 1, 3, and 4 are correct.

Statement 2 is incorrect. Because Gerard has died, the gift-splitting election is not available. The amount transferred to Owen exceeds the annual exclusion and is, therefore, a taxable gift, requiring Ida to use some of her applicable exclusion amount.

Statement 3 is correct because the cost of the trip to Europe is less than the annual exclusion and, therefore, is not a taxable gift.

Tax—Filing Status

13. **A**

Ida's filing status is married filing jointly for the 2017 tax year (the year of the death of the spouse). This MFJ election should always be coordinated with the executor of the deceased spouse's estate. After 2017, she will be required to file as single because she has no qualifying dependent child.

Retirement—Social Security Benefits

14. **D**

Ida will receive 100% of Gerard's primary insurance amount (PIA) as a result of his death. Essentially, she steps into his place. If he had begun benefits before full retirement age, she would have been subject to a reduced benefit amount.

Tax—Sale of Personal Residence

15. **A**

There will be no gain or loss. The basis of the community property assets is the fair market value at Gerard's death ($600,000).

Insurance—Medicare

16. **C**

Hospice care is covered under Medicare Part A, not Part B.

Insurance—Long-Term Care

17. **D**

Only long-term care insurance will provide the kind of coverage that Ida seeks.

Estates—Charitable Giving

18. **A**

The IRAs would not be taxable to the charity but would be income taxable to other beneficiaries. The other assets could receive a stepped-up basis to fair market value at Ida's death and, therefore, would be better left to the children or grandchildren. Because of the stepped-up basis, these assets would probably generate little gain if the children or grandchildren sold them shortly after Ida's death.

Tax—Kiddie Tax

19. **C**

In 2017, Sharon is a student under age 24 and Owen is a dependent under age 19, so both are subject to the kiddie tax rules. They will both pay tax on a portion of the dividends at their own tax rate and pay tax on a portion of the dividends based on their parents' marginal tax rate. The calculation is:

$2,300	unearned income
− 1,050	standard deduction
− 1,050	taxed at the child's marginal tax rate
$ 200	taxed at the parents' rate

Neither the parents of the grandchildren nor Ida incur any tax liability for the dividend income.

Fundamentals—Financial Planning Process

20. **D**

The most important document to evaluate before making any investment planning recommendations is Ida's investment policy statement. The other statements may be used to help evaluate and analyze Ida's current financial strategy.

Case Study 10: Billy Joe and Danielle Hobart

Case Study Facts

Billy Joe and Danielle Hobart have come to you, a CFP® professional, for help in developing a plan to accomplish their financial goals. From your initial meeting, you have gathered the following information. Assume today is December 31, 2017.

PERSONAL BACKGROUND AND INFORMATION

Billy Joe Hobart (Age 60)

Billy Joe is employed as vice president of a large spice manufacturer and has been with the company 25 years. He participates in the company's defined benefit pension plan. Billy Joe's first wife died several years ago.

Danielle Hobart (Age 29)

Danielle owns two businesses: Shape Spa and Enchanted Flower Garden.

Billy Joe and Danielle Hobart

Billy Joe and Danielle married on July 4, 2015 and have no children together.

Billy Joe's Children

Taylor—age 34

Kennedy—age 33

McKenzie—age 32

Samantha—age 31

All are healthy, employed, married, and not living with Billy Joe and Danielle. Taylor has two children, Tom and Melissa.

PERSONAL AND FINANCIAL GOALS

- Danielle plans to sell her businesses.
- Billy Joe plans to retire on January 1 of next year (his life expectancy is 25.75 years).
- They plan to sell their primary residence.
- They plan to refinance the mortgage on their vacation home.
- They plan to travel extensively before deciding where to permanently relocate.

ECONOMIC INFORMATION

- They expect inflation to average 3% (CPI) annually over both the short term and the long term.
- Expected return on the S&P 500 Index is 11%.
- T-bills are currently yielding 5%.

- Current mortgage rates are as follows:
    - —15-year fixed: 6.75%
    - —30-year fixed: 7.25%
- Closing costs are expected to be 3% of any mortgage amount.
- They will pay any closing costs separately.

INSURANCE INFORMATION

Life Insurance

	Policy 1	Policy 2
Insured	Billy Joe	Danielle
Owner	Billy Joe	Danielle
Beneficiary	In equal shares to the surviving children of the insured and to the surviving children of deceased children of the insured, per stirpes	Billy Joe Hobart, husband of the insured
Face amount	$150,000	$150,000
Cash value	$0	$0
Type of policy	Term	Term
Settlement option	Lump sum	Lump sum
Premium (annual)	$450	$150

Health Insurance

Billy Joe's employer currently provides group health insurance for both Billy Joe and Danielle. The employer will continue to provide health insurance during retirement.

Disability Insurance

Neither Billy Joe nor Danielle has disability insurance.

Homeowners Insurance

They have an HO-3 policy on both their primary residence and vacation home.

	Residence	Vacation home
Dwelling coverage limit	$175,000	$150,000
Coinsurance requirement	80%	80%
Deductible	$250	$250

Personal Liability Umbrella Policy

$3 million coverage limit

Automobile Insurance

$250,000/$500,000/$100,000 liability coverage; comprehensive and collision coverage, each with a $500 deductible

INVESTMENT DATA

- Their emergency fund is adequate at $40,000.

- They have a moderate risk tolerance.

- Billy Joe's IRA investment portfolio is currently valued at $200,000, with $100,000 invested in low- to medium-risk equity mutual funds. Danielle is the beneficiary.

- The remaining $100,000 is invested in staggered maturity short-term Treasury notes.

- Billy Joe expects to use the income and some of the principal from the $100,000 to make up any shortfall between his retirement needs and his defined benefit plan annuity for the period until Social Security benefits are received (two years at age 62).

- Billy Joe is currently earning 6.5% on the $100,000 invested in Treasury notes and expects this earnings rate to continue until the notes mature.

INCOME TAX INFORMATION

Billy Joe and Danielle file a joint federal income tax return and are marginal 28% federal income taxpayers but pay no state income tax.

RETIREMENT INFORMATION

Billy Joe

- Has an employer-provided defined benefit pension plan that will pay him a joint and survivor annuity equal to 80% of a single life annuity at retirement age 60 or older. There is no reduction for retirement at age 60 or older.

- The defined benefit formula is 1.25% times the number of years of service multiplied by the last salary with no offset for Social Security (Billy Joe's final salary for this year was $100,000).

- The present value of his projected annual Social Security benefits at full retirement age is $26,000 per year. Social Security benefits are expected to increase directly with the inflation rate.

- Billy Joe is expected to retire on January 1 of next year. He has three options from which to select regarding the form of benefits from his defined benefit pension plan:

    —Lump sum payout of $400,000

    —Single life annuity of $2,865 per month beginning on January 1 of next year

    —Joint and survivor annuity of $2,292 per month beginning on January 1 of next year

GIFTS, ESTATES, TRUSTS, AND WILL INFORMATION

Gifts

Lifetime taxable gifts made are as follows:

- Ten years ago, Billy Joe gifted $200,000 to each of his four children. The $800,000 was put in an irrevocable trust. During the same year, he gave $10,000 to each child (a total of $40,000). He paid gift taxes of $75,000 at the time. He inherited the $915,000 ($800,000 + $40,000 + $75,000) as the primary legatee after his mother's death 10 years ago. The successor legatees were his mother's four grandchildren, the children of Billy Joe.

- Danielle has made no taxable gifts during her lifetime.

Estates

For purposes of estimating estate settlement costs (of either spouse):

- Last illness and funeral are estimated at $20,000
- Estate administration expense is estimated at $30,000

Wills

Billy Joe and Danielle have simple wills leaving all probate assets to each other. Debts and taxes are to be paid from the inheritance of the surviving spouse.

Statement of Financial Position
Billy Joe and Danielle Hobart
As of December 31, 2017

ASSETS[1]			LIABILITIES & NET WORTH[2]		
Cash/cash equivalents			**Liabilities**		
JT	Cash (money market)	$40,000	Current:		
			Billy Joe Bank credit card 1		$5,000
	Total cash/cash equivalents	$40,000	Danielle Bank credit card 2		7,000
			Danielle Bank credit card 3		8,000
			Billy Joe Auto note 1		10,000
Invested assets			Danielle Auto note 2		10,000
Danielle Shape Spa		$300,000	Current liabilities		$40,000
Danielle Enchanted Flower Garden		100,000			
Danielle Danielle's Investment Portfolio		90,000	Long term:		
Billy Joe SPDA		110,801	Mortgage—primary residence		$150,000
Billy Joe IRA		200,000	Mortgage—vacation home		120,000
Billy Joe Defined benefit plan (vested benefits)		400,000	Long-term liabilities		$270,000
	Total investments	$1,200,801			
Personal use assets			**Total liabilities**		$310,000
JT	Primary residence[3]	$300,000			
JT	Vacation home[3]	180,000			
JT	Personal property and furniture	100,000	**Net worth**		$1,552,801
Billy Joe Auto 1		20,000			
Danielle Auto 2		22,000			
	Total personal use	$622,000			
Total assets		$1,862,801	**Total liabilities and net worth**		$1,862,801

Notes to financial statements:

[1] All assets are stated at fair market value.

[2] Liabilities are stated at principal only.

[3] For the purposes of homeowners insurance, the replacement value is $250,000 for the primary residence and $160,000 for the vacation home.

Titles and ownership information:

Client name = Separate property

JT = Joint tenancy with right of survivorship

INFORMATION REGARDING ASSETS AND LIABILITIES

Assets

1. *Shape Spa* (Danielle 100% shareholder of the C corporation)

- Fair market value $300,000
- Original and current tax basis $75,000 (acquired by purchase seven years ago)
- Danielle has agreed to sell the company for $300,000 on April 1, 2018. Terms are 20% down on April 1 and the balance paid in equal monthly installments over 10 years at 11% interest beginning May 1, 2018.

2. *Enchanted Flower Garden* (Danielle 100% shareholder of C corporation—Section 1244 stock)

- She started the business 10 years ago, and her tax basis is $250,000.

3. *Single premium deferred annuity* (SPDA) (Billy Joe's)

- Acquired January 1, 1982, for $25,000; current fair market value is $110,801.
- Contract had a contingent deferred sales charge of 5% for first seven years.
- Fixed earnings rate of 6% is compounded quarterly.
- Annuity start date is October 1, 2018, and will consist of quarterly payments over Billy Joe's life (Billy Joe's life expectancy is 25 years as of October 1, 2018).
- Danielle is the named beneficiary if Billy Joe dies before the annuity start date.

4. *Defined benefit plan*

- Vested benefits are valued at $400,000.
- In the event of Billy Joe's death before retirement benefits begin, the entire balance is paid directly to Danielle as his named beneficiary.

5. *Primary residence*

- Originally owned by Billy Joe, but one-half was given to Danielle when they were married.
- Fair market value is $300,000 with a cost basis of $140,000.
- The couple expects to pay 6% real estate commission on a sale.

6. *Vacation home*

- Fair market value is $180,000.
- Original mortgage was for 15 years at a 9% interest rate.
- Current payment is $1,522 per month (principal and interest).
- Current mortgage balance is $120,000, with a remaining term of 120 months.

7. *IRA Investments* (Billy Joe)

- Beneficiary is Danielle.

DANIELLE'S DETAILED INVESTMENT PORTFOLIO

Description	Quantity	FMV	Beta	Maturity (duration)	Coupon Payment	Yearly returns				
						'17	'16	'15	'14	'13
ABC Fund	200	$6,000.00	1.15			10%	15%	12%	6%	(5%)
Tex Oil	500	$10,000.00	.90			5%	6%	3%	7%	(6%)
Werner Brothers	1,250	$10,000.00	.85			5%	9%	8%	8%	(1%)
Silicon Graphics	400	$20,000.00	1.20			11%	15%	12%	10%	3%
Growth Fund	1,400	$21,000.00	1.15			5%	11%	14%	9%	2%
Treasury A	1	$929.64		2 (1.95)	$25.00					
Treasury B	2	$2,050.62		3 (2.74)	$50.00					
Treasury C	2	$2,272.28		5 (4.07)	$62.50					
Cash		$17,747.46								
Total		**$90,000.00**								

Note: The correlation coefficient between Danielle's portfolio and the market is 0.9. All bonds have a par value of $1,000. The coupon payment is expressed as a semiannual amount per bond.

Questions

1. Billy Joe and Danielle have decided to refinance the balance of their vacation home mortgage over the remaining life of the existing current mortgage. Closing costs will not be financed. If the interest rate is equal to the 15-year mortgage rate, what will be the monthly principal and interest payment if they refinance?

    A. $1,093.75
    B. $1,370.18
    C. $1,377.89
    D. $1,419.23

2. Assume Billy Joe and Danielle have sold their personal residence with a realized gain. They want to invest $100,000 of the gain, with the intent of using the investment toward the purchase of their next principal residence within a couple of years. Given their moderate risk tolerance, which of the following asset allocations would be the most appropriate for this investment?

    A. $50,000 Growth Fund, $25,000 Balanced Fund, $25,000 International Fund
    B. $50,000 Money Market, $25,000 Balanced Fund, $25,000 Bond Fund
    C. $50,000 Balanced Fund, $25,000 Growth Fund, $25,000 Bond Fund
    D. $75,000 Money Market, $25,000 Bond Fund

3. In the event of a $25,000 loss resulting from fire on the personal residence, how much will the homeowners insurance company pay?

    A. $20,000
    B. $21,625
    C. $21,875
    D. $25,000

4. Considering Danielle's current bond portfolio, which of the following risks is she NOT subject to if she holds the bonds to maturity?

    1. Purchasing power risk
    2. Reinvestment rate risk
    3. Exchange rate risk
    4. Default risk
    5. Financial risk

    A. 1 and 2
    B. 1, 3, 4, and 5
    C. 3, 4, and 5
    D. 1, 2, 3, 4, and 5

5. Is Danielle's portfolio of common stocks (including the mutual fund) subject to unsystematic risk?

    A. Yes, because unsystematic risk includes business risk, and common stocks naturally contain this risk.

    B. Yes, because the coefficient of determination of the portfolio is not at its maximum level.

    C. Yes, because unsystematic risk includes market risk, and all common stock and common stock portfolios are subject to market risk.

    D. No, because the portfolio contains enough stocks to be completely diversified.

6. Which of the following statements regarding the forthcoming sale of Shape Spa are CORRECT?

    1. The installment payments received by Danielle could cause a portion of Billy Joe's Social Security benefits to be taxable.

    2. If Danielle sells the spa to a related party, Danielle must recognize any remaining gain on the sale if the related party sells the spa within 2 years of purchase.

    3. If Billy Joe dies during the note term, the remaining unpaid principal balance plus any interest accrued and unpaid will be included in his estate.

    4. The down payment on the note will be taxed as part capital gain and part return of basis.

    A. 1, 2, and 4

    B. 1 and 3

    C. 2 and 4

    D. 1, 2, 3, and 4

7. Assume Billy Joe decides to withdraw $15,000 from his SPDA on January 1 of next year. What is the income tax effect of Billy Joe's proposed withdrawal?

    A. $15,000 is ordinary income.

    B. $3,384 is ordinary income.

    C. $11,615.55 is ordinary income, and there is a 10% early withdrawal penalty.

    D. $15,000 is return of basis and not taxable.

8. Assume Billy Joe decides to work as a consultant during 2019. Which of the following statements are CORRECT?

    1. Billy Joe will qualify for retirement benefits from Social Security during the year.

    2. Consulting income above a certain level will reduce his Social Security benefits by $1 for every $3 of earnings above a specified threshold.

    3. Consulting income will allow him to create a self-employed qualified plan.

    4. Regardless of his consulting income, up to 85% of his Social Security benefits may be included in taxable income.

    A. 1 and 2

    B. 1, 2, and 4

    C. 1, 3, and 4

    D. 2, 3, and 4

9. Billy Joe has asked you for more information regarding the single life annuity option in his defined benefit plan. Under what conditions can Billy Joe select a single life annuity from his defined benefit plan?

    A. He can select one only if he has adequate life insurance.
    B. He can select one only if Danielle waives her rights to a survivorship retirement benefit.
    C. He cannot select a single life annuity.
    D. He must be a US citizen.

10. Excluding the down payment, what is the total of the expected installment payments to be received by Danielle next year from the sale of Shape Spa? (Round to the nearest dollar.)

    A. $26,208
    B. $26,448
    C. $29,484
    D. $29,754

11. Which of the following statements regarding the SPDA is CORRECT if Billy Joe dies before the annuity starting date?

    A. The annuity will receive a step-up in basis to the FMV at Billy Joe's death.
    B. The annuity will not be included in his probate estate.
    C. The entire annuity amount will be taxable to the beneficiary as a capital gain.
    D. If Billy Joe dies next year and Danielle receives the full value of the annuity as a lump-sum payment, she is subject to regular income and a 10% penalty because she has not attained age 59 1/2.

12. Assume Billy Joe elects to take the lump-sum benefit from his defined benefit plan on January 1 and deposits the money into a non-interest bearing checking account until he decides what to do with the proceeds. He believes his after-tax earnings rate on an investment portfolio would be 10% and that inflation would be equal to the projected CPI. What inflation-adjusted single life monthly annuity could he create, assuming the payments were made at the beginning of each month and began on October 1 of next year?

    A. $2,083.33
    B. $2,207.74
    C. $2,759.68
    D. $2,775.31

13. If Billy Joe died today, what would be the value of his probate estate?

    A. $0
    B. $20,000
    C. $190,000
    D. $440,000

14. What is the modified duration of Danielle's bond portfolio? (Round each bond's YTM to the nearest whole percentage.)

    A. 2.8580
    B. 3.0389
    C. 3.1755
    D. 3.3333

15. Assuming Billy Joe and Danielle sell their primary residence for the fair market value today, what are the recognized tax consequences, assuming they have no plans to reinvest in a new residence and they take advantage of available elections?

    A. $35,000 LTCG
    B. $142,000 LTCG
    C. $142,000 gain excluded
    D. $160,000 LTCG

16. Billy Joe is contemplating gifting his life insurance policy to his children who are the current beneficiaries. Which valuation for gift tax purposes of such a gift is CORRECT?

    A. The interpolated terminal reserve
    B. The replacement cost
    C. The interpolated terminal reserve plus unearned premiums
    D. The unearned premiums at the date of the gift

17. You have reviewed the Hobarts' insurance coverage for catastrophic coverage and estate planning. Which of the following represent deficiencies in their insurance arrangements that you should communicate to the couple?

    1. Lack of disability insurance for Danielle
    2. Insufficient auto insurance
    3. Insufficient umbrella liability coverage
    4. Insufficient life insurance for estate liquidity at Billy Joe's death

    A. 1, 2, and 3
    B. 1, 2, and 4
    C. 4 only
    D. 1, 2, 3, and 4

18. Which of the following risks should Danielle be concerned about with regard to her investment portfolio?

    1. Systematic risk
    2. Unsystematic risk
    3. Market risk
    4. Reinvestment rate risk
    5. Interest rate risk
    6. Default risk

    A. 1, 2, 3, 4, and 5
    B. 1, 2, and 6
    C. 3, 4, 5, and 6
    D. 1, 2, 3, 4, 5, and 6

19. Which of the following bonds could Danielle purchase if she wants to increase the duration of her bond portfolio?

    1. Bond 1: 3-year, zero-coupon bond selling for $772.18 (duration = 3 years)
    2. Bond 2: 3-year bond selling for $923.32 with an annual coupon of $75 (duration = 2.385 years)
    3. Bond 3: 4-year bond selling for $983.80 with an annual coupon of $85 (duration = 3.55 years)

    Note: All bonds have a maturity value of $1,000.

    A. 1 only
    B. 2 only
    C. 3 only
    D. 1, 2, or 3

20. Billy Joe is interested in purchasing Treasury securities. Which of the following statements regarding the original issue of Treasury securities is CORRECT?

    A. T-bills are sold in denominations of $100, and T-notes are sold in denominations of $10,000.
    B. T-notes may be issued at a discount.
    C. T-notes have semiannual coupon payments.
    D. Both T-bills and T-notes have semiannual coupon payments.

21. What is the tax treatment next year of the down payment made on April 1 of that year when Danielle sells Shape Spa, assuming that she treats the sale as an installment sale?

    A. Long-term capital gain of $225,000
    B. Return of capital of $60,000
    C. Long-term capital gain of $45,000
    D. Ordinary income of $6,600

22. Assume that Danielle sells Enchanted Flower Garden for its fair market value on December 31 of this year. What is the effect of this transaction on the Hobarts' joint tax return for this year?

    A. $50,000 ordinary loss
    B. $100,000 ordinary loss
    C. $150,000 long-term capital loss
    D. $100,000 ordinary loss and a $50,000 long-term capital loss

23. Assume that Danielle sells Shape Spa on an installment sales basis. What are the investment risks associated with the installment notes?

    1. Default risk
    2. Reinvestment rate risk
    3. Interest rate risk
    4. Purchasing power risk

    A. 1 and 2
    B. 1, 2, and 3
    C. 2, 3, and 4
    D. 1, 2, 3, and 4

24. You have been asked by Billy Joe and Danielle for recommendations on funding the education of their grandchildren. Billy Joe's oldest child, Taylor, has 2 children. Billy Joe and Danielle want to contribute a lump sum of $20,000 toward the children's higher education expenses. Which of the following recommendations accomplishes the Hobarts' goal?

    1. The lump sum can be deposited in a Coverdell Education Savings Account, which provides tax-deferred growth
    2. The contribution is considered a completed gift, and with Billy Joe and Danielle using the split gift annual exclusion, no gift tax is owed
    3. A QTP would be appropriate and allows the contributor to select among different investment strategies when the initial contribution is made

    A. 1 and 2
    B. 1 and 3
    C. 2 and 3
    D. 1, 2, and 3

25. Danielle is considering adding XYZ Company stock to her investment portfolio. She just read the annual report for the XYZ Company. What form of the efficient market hypothesis best supports this action?

    A. Weak form
    B. Semistrong form
    C. Strong form
    D. Super strong form

26. What could Billy Joe have done 10 years ago to avoid his current estate situation and still have achieved the same result as his initial gifting?

    A. He could have orally disclaimed the inheritance from his mother.

    B. He could have given a written disclaimer to the executor directing that the monies should be paid to the successor legatees in trust.

    C. He could have given a written disclaimer, which would have been due 6 months after death.

    D. None of these.

27. If Taylor predeceased Billy Joe, which of the following situations representing the life insurance payout from Billy Joe's term policy upon Billy Joe's subsequent death is CORRECT?

    A. Taylor—$37,500; Kennedy—$37,500; McKenzie—$37,500; Samantha—$37,500

    B. Kennedy—$37,500; McKenzie—$37,500; Samantha—$37,500; Tom—$18,750; Melissa—$18,750

    C. Kennedy—$30,000; McKenzie—$30,000; Samantha—$30,000; Tom—$30,000; Melissa—$30,000

    D. Taylor—$37,500; Danielle—$37,500; McKenzie—$37,500; Samantha—$18,750; Melissa—$18,750

28. What are the weighted beta and the weighted geometric mean return of Danielle's investment portfolio over the last five years, based on current market values (excluding bonds and cash)?

	Weighted Beta	**Weighted Geometric Mean**
A.	1.08	7.51
B.	1.05	6.96
C.	5.25	7.51
D.	6.96	1.05

ANSWER SUMMARY

1. C	6. A	11. B	16. D	21. C	26. D
2. D	7. D	12. B	17. C	22. D	27. B
3. B	8. C	13. B	18. A	23. D	28. A
4. C	9. B	14. B	19. C	24. C	
5. B	10. B	15. C	20. C	25. A	

SUMMARY OF TOPICS

1. Fundamentals—Time Value of Money
2. Investments—Asset Allocation
3. Insurance—Coinsurance
4. Investments—Types of Risk
5. Investments—Coefficient of Determination
6. Tax—Installment Sale
7. Tax—Annuities
8. Retirement—Social Security
9. Retirement—Single Life Annuity
10. Tax—Installment Sale
11. Estates—Valuation of Annuities
12. Fundamentals—Time Value of Money/Annuities
13. Estates—Probate Estate
14. Investments—Modified Duration
15. Tax—Sale of Personal Residence
16. Estates—Gifts
17. Insurance—Deficiencies
18. Investments—Risks
19. Investments—Bond Duration
20. Investments—Treasury Bonds
21. Tax—Installment Sale
22. Tax—Section 1244 Stock
23. Investments—Installment Notes
24. Fundamentals—Education Funding
25. Investments—Efficient Market Hypothesis
26. Estates—Planning
27. Estates—Life Insurance
28. Investments—Weighted Beta and Weighted Return

Solutions

Fundamentals—Time Value of Money

1. **C**

They would pay over a period of 120 months at a 15-year fixed rate of 6.75%.

$$n \quad = \quad 120 \, (10 \times 12)$$
$$i \quad \doteq \quad 0.5625 \, (6.75 \div 12)$$
$$PV \quad = \quad -\$120,000$$
$$PMT_{OA} \quad = \quad \$1,377.89$$

Investments—Asset Allocation

2. **D**

Because they need the funds relatively soon, they should invest in assets that are very liquid. The other choices are too aggressive given the Hobarts' risk tolerance and retirement time horizon.

Insurance—Coinsurance

3. **B**

$250,000 × .80 = $200,000

$$\left[\$25,000 \times \left(\frac{\$175,000}{\$200,000} \right) \right] - \$250^* = \$21,625$$

*$250 is the deductible

Investments—Types of Risk

4. **C**

The bond portfolio consists entirely of Treasury securities; therefore, it will have no default risk. Exchange rate risk involves foreign bonds, and financial risk relates to common stock, not bonds. She would certainly be subject to purchasing power risk and reinvestment rate risk.

Investments—Coefficient of Determination

5. **B**

The coefficient of determination is the square of the correlation coefficient. Therefore, because the correlation coefficient is 0.9, the coefficient of determination is 0.81. Thus, 81% of the changes in Danielle's investment portfolio can be explained by changes in the market (systematic risk). As a result, 19% (100% – 81%) of the changes in Danielle's investment portfolio is the result of unsystematic risk.

Tax—Installment Sale

6. **A**

Statement 1 is correct. A portion of the installment payments are included in modified adjusted gross income, which can cause a portion of Billy Joe's Social Security benefits to be taxable when he starts receiving benefits.

Statement 2 is correct.

Statement 3 is incorrect. The note is Danielle's property.

Statement 4 is correct.

Tax—Annuities

7. **D**

Annuity contracts entered into before August 14, 1982, use the FIFO basis recovery rule wherein the basis is recovered first. He may withdraw amounts up to his adjusted tax basis ($25,000) tax free.

Retirement—Social Security

8. **C**

Statements 1, 3, and 4 are correct. Statement 2 is incorrect because the reduction is $1 for every $2 of earnings above a certain threshold.

Retirement—Single Life Annuity

9. **B**

Danielle must waive her marital rights to a survivorship benefit from the pension plan.

Tax—Installment Sale

10. **B**

n	=	120 (10 × 12)	Sale price	$300,000
i	=	0.9167 (11 ÷ 12)	Down payment	(60,000)
PV	=	– $240,000	Balance of installment note	$240,000
PMT_{OA}	=	$3,306		
× 8*	=	$26,448		

*Only 8 payments (May – December) are received next year.
Installment payments are ordinary annuities following the down payment.

Estates—Valuation of Annuities

11. **B**

The annuity will avoid the probate estate because Danielle is the named beneficiary. As an IRD asset, there is not a step-up in basis upon Billy Joe's death. The gain is taxable as ordinary income but Danielle is not subject to a 10% penalty if she receives the annuity proceeds as a lump-sum upon Billy Joe's death.

Fundamentals—Time Value of Money/Annuities

12. B

The lump-sum distribution amount is subject to 20% mandatory withholding. Billy Joe will receive 80% of $400,000, or $320,000.

Set calculator to BEGIN mode

PV $= -\$320,000$

i $= 0.5663 \{[(1.1 \div 1.03) - 1] \times 100\} \div 12$

n $= 300$ (25 years of life expectancy on 10/1 of next year $\times$ 12)

$PMT_{AD} = \$2,207.74$

Estates—Probate Estate

13. B

$20,000

Assets	%	Probate estate
Cash	50%	$0
SPDA	100%	0
IRA investments	100%	0
Defined benefit	100%	0
Residence	50%	0
Vacation home	50%	0
Personal property	50%	0
Auto 1	100%	20,000
Subtotal		$20,000
Life insurance proceeds		0
Total		$20,000

Investments—Modified Duration

14. B

The modified duration of the bonds is equal to the Macaulay duration divided by 1 plus the yield to maturity divided by the number of coupon payments in a year (y). Thus, the modified duration is 3.0389. The calculations are as follows.

Step 1: Calculate the yield to maturity.

	Treasury A	Treasury B	Treasury C
PV	– $929.64	– $1,025.31	– $1,136.14
FV	$1,000	$1,000	$1,000
n	4 (2 × 2)	6 (3 × 2)	10 (5 × 2)
PMT	$25	$50	$62.50
i	8.9188%	9.0183%	9.0544%
Rounded	9%	9%	9%

Notes: i above represents the YTM. Remember to multiply the calculated YTM by 2 to derive the appropriate figure.
All of the bonds have a rounded YTM of 9%.

Step 2: Calculate the duration of the bond portfolio.

FMV	Duration	Weighted duration
$929.64	1.95	$1,812.80
$2,050.62	2.74	$5,618.70
$2,272.28	4.07	$9,248.18
$5,252.54		$16,679.68

The bond portfolio's Macaulay duration = $16,679.68 ÷ $5,252.54 = 3.1756

Step 3: Calculate the bond portfolio's modified duration.

$$\text{Modified duration} = \frac{\text{Macaulay duration}}{1 + y} = \frac{3.1756}{1.045} = 3.0389$$

Tax—Sale of Personal Residence

15. C

Sale price	$300,000
Less: commission	(18,000)
Amount realized	$282,000
Basis	(140,000)
Realized gain	$142,000

Note: They can exclude up to $500,000 of gain from the sale of a personal residence where both the ownership and use requirements are met by both spouses. The Hobarts are not required to reinvest in a new residence to take advantage of the gain exclusion.

Estates—Gifts

16. **D**

This is a term policy. The value of the policy as a gift is equal to the unearned premium at the date of the gift.

Insurance—Deficiencies

17. **C**

Because Billy Joe is retiring and there is no indication that Danielle earns a salary, disability insurance is not necessary. Their net worth is strong, and umbrella liability insurance is sufficient as is their auto insurance coverages. However, the life insurance is insufficient for estate liquidity. Billy Joe's life insurance is payable to his children upon his death, and the statement of financial position shows only $40,000 of liquid assets. Estimated administrative and funeral expenses are $50,000.

Investments—Risks

18. **A**

All risks apply, except default risk, because Treasury bonds are considered default risk free. The other investments are equities and are not subject to default risk.

Investments—Bond Duration

19. **C**

FMV	Duration	Weighted duration
$929.64	1.95	$1,812.80
$2,050.62	2.74	$5,618.70
$2,272.28	4.07	$9,248.18
$5,252.54		$16,679.68

Portfolio duration = $16,679.68 ÷ $5,252.54 = 3.1756.

Because the duration for this portfolio equals 3.1756 years, Danielle should purchase a bond with a duration greater than 3.1756 to increase the duration of the current portfolio. Bond 3 is the only bond with a duration greater than the current portfolio.

Investments—Treasury Bonds

20. **C**

T-notes have semiannual coupon payments.

T-notes are sold in denominations of $100.

Unlike T-bills, T-notes are not issued at a discount.

T-bills do not make coupon payments (they are essentially zero-coupon securities). T-bills are issued at a discount and mature at face value.

Tax—Installment Sale

21. **C**

The down payment does not include ordinary income. The $60,000 down payment is 75% LTCG and 25% return of taxable basis.

Sales price	$300,000	100%	Down payment	$60,000	100%
Basis	(75,000)	(25%)	Return of basis	(15,000)	(25%)
Capital gain	$225,000	75%	LTCG	$45,000	75%

Tax—Section 1244 Stock

22. **D**

Sales price	$100,000
Tax basis	(250,000)
Realized loss	($150,000)
Ordinary portion	(100,000)
Capital loss	($50,000)

Note: Section 1244 stock entitles the owner to receive up to $100,000 (married filing jointly) in ordinary losses instead of capital losses (per year); the remaining $50,000 is a long-term capital loss which can be netted against capital gains in the year of the initial loss. Any remaining capital loss in excess of any capital gains in future years may be deducted at up to $3,000 ($1,500 if MFS) per year until used up.

Investments—Installment Notes

23. **D**

All the identified risks are associated with installment notes. Installment notes have the same basic characteristics as fixed-income securities.

Fundamentals—Educational Funding

24. **C**

A Coverdell account is set up as an individual account for each child. The contributions to a Coverdell account are limited both in the amount of the contribution and the AGI of the donor. Currently, the contribution level for a Coverdell is significantly lower than the amount contemplated by the Hobarts. QTP accounts are also set up as individual accounts. Because of the $14,000 (for 2017) gift tax annual exclusion, the Hobarts could make a $10,000 tax-free gift to a QTP account for each child.

Investments—Efficient Market Hypothesis

25. **A**

Reading an annual report is a type of fundamental analysis. Fundamental analysis is supported only by the weak form of the efficient market hypothesis.

Estates—Planning

26. **D**

A qualified disclaimer has 4 elements.

1. Must be in writing.

2. Must be made within 9 months of when the interest is incurred.

3. The disclaimant cannot have benefited from the interest he is now disclaiming.

4. Disclaimant cannot direct who will receive the interest that is disclaimed.

Estates—Life Insurance

27. **B**

Because the life insurance is to be distributed in equal shares to the surviving children of the insured and to the surviving children of deceased children of the insured, per stirpes, Tom and Melissa will receive Taylor's portion.

Therefore, the $150,000 life insurance payout will be distributed as follows:

- Kennedy—$37,500
- McKenzie—$37,500
- Samantha—$37,500
- Tom—$18,750
- Melissa—$18,750

Investments—Weighted Beta and Weighted Return

28. A

The beta is 1.08, and the weighted return is 7.51%.

Securities	FMV	Portfolio Percentage	Geometric Mean	Weighted Return	Beta	Weighted Beta
ABC Funds	$ 6,000	9%	7.37%	0.66%	1.15	0.10
Tex Oil	10,000	15%	2.89%	0.43%	0.90	0.13
Werner Brothers	10,000	15%	5.74%	0.86%	0.85	0.13
Silicon Graphics	20,000	30%	10.13%	3.04%	1.20	0.36
Growth Fund	21,000	31%	8.12%	2.52%	1.15	0.36
	$67,000	100%		7.51%		1.08

$$\text{geometric mean} = \sqrt[n]{(1+r_1)(1+r_2)(1+r_3)...(1+r_n)} - 1$$

Geometric mean calculation for the ABC fund (use the same methodology to solve for the geometric means of the other securities):

PV = –$1

FV = $1 (1 + 0.10)(1 + 0.15)(1 + 0.12)(1 + 0.06)(1 – 0.05) = $1.4267

N = 5

Solve for I/YR = 7.3659 = 7.37%

Notes: Weighted return = Portfolio percentage × Geometric mean

Weighted beta = Portfolio percentage × Beta

Case Study 11:
Jeff and Rosa Martin

Case Study Facts

Today is December 31, 2017. Jeff and Rosa Martin have come to you, a CFP® professional, for help in developing a plan to accomplish their financial goals. From your initial meeting together, you have gathered the following information.

PERSONAL BACKGROUND AND INFORMATION

Jeff Martin (Age 60)

Jeff is the executive vice president of Postal Accidents, Inc. He has been with the company for 25 years.

Rosa Martin (Age 45)

Jeff's wife Rosa, age 45, taught college courses at State University for 14 years. Three years ago, she retired to devote more time to her family.

The Children

Jeff and Rosa have two children: 13-year-old high school student Steven and 11-year-old Mary, who attends middle school.

Jeff also has a 30-year-old son, Tom, from a previous marriage. Tom is an aspiring actor living in Los Angeles. Two years ago, Tom was arrested for drug possession and is currently on probation.

The Martins

Jeff and Rosa have been married for 19 years.

PERSONAL AND FINANCIAL GOALS

- Save for college tuition
- Pay off all debt by Jeff's retirement
- Retire in six years with 70% of salary at the time of Jeff's retirement
- Prepare a will and estate plan
- Evaluate both investment and insurance risk

ECONOMIC INFORMATION

- They expect inflation to average 4% annually, both currently and long term.
- They expect salaries and net income to increase 4% annually, both currently and long term.
- They believe the S&P 500 Index is a good measure of the market's performance. The index's historical rate of return is 12%.

INCOME TAX INFORMATION

Their marginal income tax bracket has been consistent over the years for federal taxes, and the state income tax rate is a flat 5%.

RETIREMENT INFORMATION

Jeff plans to retire in six years at age 66. The Martins would like to have a standard of living provided by an amount equal to 70% of their preretirement income. They expect to be in retirement for 30 years.

Jeff has a Section 401(k) plan through Postal Accidents, Inc. He has been contributing the maximum allowable amount to the plan. He has named Rosa as sole beneficiary. He has averaged an annual return of 7% over the past eight years. Jeff also has a traditional IRA, for which Rosa is the sole beneficiary. Rosa has a Section 403(b) plan through her former employer, State University.

Jeff expects to collect $29,000 in Social Security benefits at full retirement age (in today's dollars). Rosa expects to collect $14,500 in Social Security benefits at age 67 (in today's dollars). Jeff will begin collecting benefits as soon as he reaches full retirement age. Rosa has been considering the possibility of receiving her Social Security benefits at age 62.

GIFTS, ESTATES, TRUSTS, AND WILL INFORMATION

Gifts

Five years ago, Jeff bought 5,000 shares of stock at $20 per share in Jedco Pharmaceutical Company. He immediately gifted 1,500 shares of the stock to Steven and 1,500 shares to Mary. Today, the stock has a fair market value of $40 per share and is paying a dividend of $2 per share. Jeff feels that the stock and any dividends will appreciate at a rate of 9% per year. They were the only gifts made by Jeff. Rosa has never made any gifts.

Estates

Jeff and Rosa estimate that funeral expenses will be $25,000 each and administrative expenses will be $50,000 each.

Trusts

Jeff is considering creating an irrevocable trust for the benefit of his older son, Tom. Jeff would like income from the trust to be paid to Tom each year and would like for the trustee to have the discretionary power to distribute trust principal to Tom in the case of hardship. Because Tom has experienced drug problems in the recent past, Jeff would like to prevent Tom from having additional access to the trust assets, and he does not want Tom to be able to pledge his interest in the trust as collateral for a loan.

Statement of Cash Flows
Jeff and Rosa Martin
January 1–December 31, 2017

CASH INFLOWS

Salary	Jeff's salary	$260,000	
Unearned income	Rental property loss	(30,000)	
	Dividends	$25,000	
	Interest income	55,000	
	Total unearned income	$50,000	
Total inflows			$310,000

CASH OUTFLOWS

Mortgage payments	Primary residence	$30,000	
Section 401(k) plan contributions	Jeff	$24,000	
Insurance premiums	Homeowners	$2,800	
	Life	8,500	
	Auto	2,400	
	Umbrella liability	800	
	Total insurance premiums	$14,500	
Miscellaneous expenses	Credit card payments	$3,400	
	Entertainment	22,000	
	Food	8,400	
	Clothes	12,000	
	Utilities	6,000	
	Charity	15,000	
	Total miscellaneous expenses	$66,800	
Taxes	Property	$ 19,000	
	Federal and state income tax and FICA	125,000	
	Total taxes	$144,000	
Total outflows			$279,300
Net cash flow			$30,700

Statement of Financial Position
Jeff and Rosa Martin
As of December 31, 2017

ASSETS[1]

Cash/cash equivalents

JT	Savings account	$ 38,000
Jeff	Cash value of universal life policy	25,000
Rosa	Cash value of whole life policy	40,000
	Total cash/cash equivalents	**$103,000**

Invested assets

Jeff	Postal Accidents stock	$600,000
Jeff	Traditional IRA	150,000
Jeff	Section 401(k) plan	550,000
Rosa	Section 403(b) plan	55,000
JT	Investment portfolio	2,000,000
JT	Office building	800,000
	Total investments	**$4,155,000**

Personal-use assets

JT	Primary residence	$450,000
JT	Personal property/furniture	100,000
Jeff	Sports utility vehicle	55,000
Rosa	Sedan	40,000
	Total personal-use assets	**$645,000**
	Total assets	**$4,903,000**

LIABILITIES AND NET WORTH

Liabilities[2]

Current liabilities

Jeff	Credit card A	$6,000
Rosa	Credit card B	10,000
	Total current liabilities	**$16,000**

Long-term liabilities

JT	Mortgage—primary residence	$200,000
	Total long-term liabilities	**$200,000**

Total liabilities	**$216,000**

Net worth	**$4,687,000**

Total liabilities and net worth	**$4,903,000**

Notes to financial statements:

[1] Assets are stated at fair market value (rounded to even dollars).

[2] Liabilities are stated at principal only (rounded to even dollars).

Property Ownership
Client name = Separate property
JT = Joint tenancy with right of survivorship

INSURANCE INFORMATION

Life Insurance

	Universal life	Whole life
Insured	Jeff	Rosa's father
Face amount	$500,000	$300,000
Cash value	$25,000	$40,000
Annual premium	$6,000	$2,500
Premium payer	Jeff	Rosa
Beneficiary	Tom	Rosa
Policyowner	Jeff	Rosa
Comments	Jeff's niece, Janice, is contingent beneficiary.	Rosa purchased this policy from her father for $30,000 and has paid $5,000 in premiums.

Health Insurance

Jeff and Rosa are covered under Jeff's employer plan, which is an indemnity plan with a $500 deductible per person per year and an 80/20 coinsurance clause, with a family annual maximum out-of-pocket amount of $1,500.

Long-Term Disability Insurance

Jeff is covered by an own occupation definition of disability income policy with premiums paid 100% by his employer. The monthly benefit equals 60% of gross pay after a 180-day elimination period payable until age 65. The policy covers both sicknesses and accidents.

Rosa is not covered by disability insurance.

INVESTMENT INFORMATION

Detailed Investment Portfolio

Description	Acquired	Shares	Adjusted basis	Beta	Current FMV
Altria	6/09	14,000	$201,633	0.9	$450,000
Jedco Pharmaceutical	4/10	2,000	$40,000	1.3	$80,000
Tall-Mart	2/11	4,000	$119,000	1.2	$250,000
Nosilla Foods	3/12	22,249	$400,188	1.4	$130,000
T-bills			$1,000,000		$1,090,000
			$1,760,821		$2,000,000

Jeff's Section 401(k) Plan

Jeff currently has a balance of $550,000 in his Section 401(k) plan. This balance is comprised of mutual funds as well as $250,000 of Postal Accidents stock. The stock was contributed to the account by Jeff's employer over his career. The total cost of the contributed stock was $120,000.

Jeff has elected not to participate in his firm's deferred compensation plan. He has the option of deferring up to 30% of his compensation. Any deferred compensation would be paid automatically as an annuity at retirement.

Office Building

Several years ago, Jeff and Rosa purchased an office building for $600,000. They spent $50,000 renovating the building and are currently renting the offices to several doctors. The current value of the building is $800,000. Their annual rental income is $80,000 per year, but they are actually losing money on the property because of taxes, maintenance, and depreciation expenses. For tax purposes, they have taken $65,000 in depreciation deductions over the years.

Questions

1. Jeff and Rosa have decided to begin setting aside funds for their children's educations. Which of the following education funding vehicles could they establish if their goal is to eventually receive tax-free distributions from the account to pay for the education costs?

    1. Roth IRA
    2. Qualified tuition plan
    3. Series EE savings bonds
    4. Coverdell Education Savings Account

    A. 1, 2, and 3
    B. 2 only
    C. 3 and 4
    D. 1, 2, 3, and 4

2. Which of the following education savings vehicles would allow Jeff and Rosa to change the beneficiary from one child to another?

    A. Section 2503(c) trust
    B. UTMA account
    C. Section 529 plan
    D. Series EE savings bonds

3. Which of the following is an income tax ramification of Jeff's employer-sponsored long-term disability coverage?

    A. The benefits would be taxable to Jeff.
    B. The benefits would be income tax free.
    C. The cost of the disability income coverage would be taxable to Jeff.
    D. The cost of the disability income coverage exceeding $50,000 would be taxable to Jeff.

4. When Rosa's father purchased the whole life insurance policy, he elected to include an automatic premium loan provision in the policy. Which of the following statements regarding this provision are CORRECT?

    1. The automatic premium loan provision provides a better option for Rosa's father than reinstatement of a lapsed policy.
    2. The automatic premium loan provision will keep the policy in force, as well as any riders, such as accidental death and disability.
    3. An automatic premium loan will reduce the policy's cash value.
    4. No interest is charged on a loan made under the automatic premium loan provision.

    A. 1, 2, and 3
    B. 1 and 3
    C. 1 and 4
    D. 2, 3, and 4

5. Jeff wants to draft a document that will advise his personal physician of his wishes regarding life-sustaining treatment options if he should ever become terminally ill. Which of the following documents will meet Jeff's needs?

    A. Living will
    B. Durable power of attorney for health care
    C. General power of appointment
    D. Springing power of attorney for property

6. Which of the following statements regarding the Jedco Pharmaceutical stock Jeff gifted to Mary and Steven is CORRECT?

    A. All dividends from Mary's shares will be taxed at her tax rate.
    B. If Steven sold the stock for its fair market value and contributed the proceeds to a qualified tuition plan for Steven's benefit, the gain on the sale of the stock would be income tax free.
    C. If Steven sold the stock for its fair market value, none of the capital gain would be taxed at Jeff's capital gains rate.
    D. A portion of the dividends received by Mary could be taxed at Jeff and Rosa's tax rate.

7. Because Jeff has accumulated a significant amount of his company's stock, which of the following risks should concern him the most?

    A. Interest rate risk
    B. Purchasing power risk
    C. Market risk
    D. Default risk

8. Assuming that Jeff and Rosa actively participate in the management of the office building, how much of the loss could they deduct on their joint income tax return for the current year?

    A. $0
    B. $15,000
    C. $25,000
    D. $30,000

9. Assume Jeff decides to retire next year instead of waiting until he is 66. He has asked you for recommendations on how he should handle the funds in his Section 401(k) plan. Which of the following recommendations would be suitable for Jeff in this scenario?

    1. Rollover the funds into a traditional IRA

    2. Take a lump-sum distribution and elect 10-year forward averaging

    3. Distribute the stock from the Section 401(k) plan as part of a lump-sum distribution and elect net unrealized appreciation (NUA) tax treatment for the stock without immediate income tax consequences

    4. Rollover the funds into a traditional IRA, distribute the stock from the IRA, and elect net unrealized appreciation (NUA) tax treatment for the stock without immediate income tax consequences

    A. 1 and 2

    B. 1 and 3

    C. 2, 3, and 4

    D. 2 and 4

10. Assume that while Jeff and Tom were driving to Texas, they crashed into an 18-wheeler in Oklahoma, killing them both instantly. Under the Uniform Simultaneous Death Act, whom would receive the proceeds of Jeff's universal life insurance policy?

    A. Jeff's estate

    B. Tom's estate

    C. Jeff's children, per stirpes

    D. Janice

11. All of the following would be potential advantages of Jeff's participation in his company's deferred compensation plan EXCEPT

    A. he would reduce his current income tax liability

    B. the earnings within the plan would not be currently taxed to Jeff

    C. the benefit would be income tax free to Jeff when he receives it at retirement

    D. Jeff could defer compensation greater than the defined contribution plan limit

12. Jeff is considering the creation of a charitable remainder annuity trust (CRAT) that would provide him a fixed payment for the rest of his life. If he creates the trust, Jeff would contribute a portion of his Postal Accidents stock. Which of the following statements regarding the trust is CORRECT?

    A. Jeff would be eligible for an immediate charitable contribution deduction equal to the fair market value of the stock transferred to the trust.

    B. Jeff can revoke the trust whenever he chooses.

    C. The trust could sell the stock without recognizing a capital gain.

    D. A private foundation could not be named as the beneficiary of the CRAT.

13. Jeff and Rosa have requested information regarding the characteristics of a Section 2503(c) trust. Which of the following statements concerning such a trust are CORRECT?

    1.   Any remaining trust corpus must be paid to the beneficiary upon attainment of age 21.

    2.   The income earned by the trust assets must be paid out to the beneficiary each year.

    3.   Transfers to the trust will qualify for the gift tax annual exclusion.

    4.   Income accumulated by the trust will be taxed at trust income tax rates.

    A.   1, 3, and 4

    B.   1 and 4

    C.   2 and 3

    D.   2 and 4

14. Which of the stocks in Jeff and Rosa's investment portfolio probably has the most volatile returns over the long term?

    A.   Altria

    B.   Jedco Pharmaceutical

    C.   Nosilla Foods

    D.   Tall-Mart

15. If Rosa's father died today, what would be the income tax ramifications of the life insurance proceeds paid to Rosa?

    A. $260,000 would be taxable as ordinary income, and $40,000 would be income tax free.

    B. $260,000 would be taxable as capital gain, and $40,000 would be taxable as ordinary income.

    C. $265,000 would be taxable as ordinary income, and $35,000 would be income tax free.

    D.   The entire $300,000 would be taxable at ordinary income tax rates.

16. If Jeff died today, how much would be included in his probate estate?

    A. $655,000

    B. $1,355,000

    C. $1,855,000

    D. $3,549,000

17. If Jeff and Rosa elect gift-splitting, what is the maximum amount of gifts they can make to their three children in the current year without exceeding their annual exclusions?

    A. $14,000

    B. $28,000

    C. $42,000

    D. $84,000

18. Jeff and Rosa are considering selling the office building because it is causing administrative headaches and losing money each year. If they sold the office building today for its fair market value, what amount would be taxed at the 25% capital gain rate? (Assume they have owned the building for more than 5 years.)

    A. $150,000
    B. $215,000
    C. $0
    D. $65,000

19. During a meeting with you, Jeff mentions that he would like to protect his gain in the Postal Accidents stock. He is interested in exploring all possible alternatives to achieve this objective short of actually selling the stock. Which of the following recommendations are suitable to help Jeff achieve his objective?

    1. Sell Postal Accidents short
    2. Sell put options on Postal Accidents
    3. Purchase put options on Postal Accidents
    4. Purchase call options on Postal Accidents
    5. Sell call options on Postal Accidents

    A. 1, 2, 3, and 4
    B. 1 and 3
    C. 2, 3, 4, and 5
    D. 2 and 5

20. Rosa is considering the purchase of mortgage-backed securities for her portfolio. These securities are subject to which of the following risks?

    1. Prepayment risk
    2. Inflation risk
    3. Business risk
    4. Interest rate risk

    A. 1, 2, and 4
    B. 2 and 4
    C. 3 only
    D. 1, 2, 3, and 4

21. Which of the following trusts would be the best type of trust for Jeff to establish for the benefit of his son, Tom?

    A. Special needs trust
    B. Section 2503(c) trust
    C. Spendthrift trust
    D. Grantor retained annuity trust

22. The Jedco Pharmaceutical stock is currently trading at $40. If the Martins use the constant growth dividend discount model to value their stocks and their required rate of return is 15%, which of the following statements concerning the current value of the Jedco Pharmaceutical stock is CORRECT?

    A. The stock is overvalued at $40; its intrinsic value is $24.22.
    B. The stock is overvalued at $40; its intrinsic value is $33.33.
    C. The stock is overvalued at $40; its intrinsic value is $36.33.
    D. The stock is correctly valued at $40.

23. Jeff's son, Tom, calls you and asks you several questions about the irrevocable trust agreement Jeff is considering implementing for Tom's benefit. Tom says he is entitled to know the details of the trust because he will be the trust beneficiary. Among other things, Tom wants to know when distributions will be available to him from the trust after the trust is implemented. How should you respond to Tom's request for information?

    A. Answer Tom's questions as completely as possible
    B. Decline to answer Tom's questions over the phone but offer to mail him a copy of the proposed trust document for his review
    C. Tell Tom you will be happy to answer his questions once the trust document is finalized
    D. Decline to answer Tom's questions

24. Assume that as part of your discussions with Jeff about his estate planning goals, Jeff asks you to summarize the consequences that would result if he died today without making any estate planning changes. After reviewing his current estate planning status, you determine which of the following results would occur if Jeff died today?

    1. The Martins' primary residence would pass through probate.
    2. Tom would have to include the $500,000 death benefit from the universal life insurance policy in his gross income.
    3. Jeff's estate would have to liquidate assets to pay his funeral and administrative expenses.
    4. Rosa would have to begin receiving distributions from Tom's traditional IRA beginning next year.

    A. 1, 2, and 3
    B. 2 and 3
    C. 2 and 4
    D. 3 only

ANSWER SUMMARY

1. B	6. D	11. C	16. A	21. C
2. C	7. C	12. C	17. D	22. C
3. A	8. A	13. A	18. D	23. D
4. A	9. B	14. C	19. B	24. D
5. A	10. D	15. C	20. A	

SUMMARY OF TOPICS

1. Fundamentals—Education Savings
2. Fundamentals—Education Savings
3. Insurance—Long-Term Disability
4. Insurance—Policy Provisions
5. Estates—Advance Medical Directives
6. Tax—Kiddie Tax
7. Investments—Risk
8. Tax—Passive Activities
9. Retirement—Plan Distributions
10. Insurance—Life Insurance Provisions
11. Retirement—Deferred Compensation
12. Estates—Charitable Remainder Annuity Trust
13. Estates—2503(c) Trusts
14. Investments—Risk Measurements
15. Tax—Life Insurance Proceeds
16. Estates—Probate Estate
17. Estates—Gift Tax
18. Tax—Section 1250 Property
19. Investments—Options
20. Investments—Risks
21. Estates—Trusts
22. Investments—Constant Growth Dividend Discount Model
23. Fundamentals—Confidentiality
24. Estates—Transfers at Death

Solutions

Fundamentals—Education Savings

1. **B**

   Statement 1 is incorrect. The Martins' modified adjusted gross income (MAGI) precludes them from contributing to a Roth IRA.

   Statement 2 is correct. Distributions from qualified tuition plans used for qualified education costs are income tax free, and qualified tuition plans are available regardless of adjusted gross income.

   Statement 3 is incorrect. At Jeff and Rosa's MAGI level, they will be taxed on earnings when the Series EE savings bonds are redeemed.

   Statement 4 is incorrect. Jeff and Rosa are not eligible to contribute to a Coverdell Education Savings Account because of their MAGI.

Fundamentals—Education Savings

2. **C**

   A Section 2503(c) trust is an irrevocable trust and is considered a completed gift.

   Gifts made to an UTMA account are also completed gifts.

   The owner of the Section 529 plan can change the beneficiary.

   Series EE savings bonds have nontransferable ownership and do not list beneficiaries. Jeff or Rosa could cash in the bonds and use the proceeds for their children's education.

Insurance—Long-Term Disability

3. **A**

   The premiums were paid by the employer, so the disability income benefits will be fully taxable to Jeff.

Insurance—Policy Provisions

4. **A**

   Statement 1 is correct. If the policy should lapse, Rosa's father would be required to show evidence of insurability to reinstate the policy. An automatic premium loan does not require evidence of insurability.

   Statement 2 is correct. Riders would be continued in force with the automatic premium loan provision. Nonforfeiture options in a lapsed policy do not keep the riders in force.

   Statement 3 is correct. The automatic premium loan will reduce the policy's cash value.

   Statement 4 is incorrect. Interest will be charged on a loan made under the automatic premium loan provision.

Estates—Advance Medical Directives

5. **A**

   A living will is used to advise the drafter's personal physician of the drafter's wishes regarding life-sustaining treatment should the drafter ever become terminally ill.

Tax—Kiddie Tax

6. **D**

Mary is under age 19, and as a result, some of her dividend income could be taxed at her parents' rate.

If Steven sold the stock, the gain would still be taxable.

Steven is under age 19, and the kiddie tax rules apply. In a sale, some of the gain could be taxed at Steven's rate.

Investments—Risk

7. **C**

Market risk would be his main concern. He holds equities, so default risk and purchasing power risk are not a primary concern. Interest rate risk could be of concern, but market risk is the most influential.

Tax—Passive Activities

8. **A**

All rental activities are deemed to be passive, and neither Jeff nor Rosa has passive income to offset a passive loss. Therefore, none of the loss would be deductible. The exception allowed for losses on rental real estate of up to $25,000 for married couples does not apply because this loss allowance is phased out at an AGI of $100,000–$150,000 (MFJ). Because Jeff and Rosa's AGI is well above $150,000, none of the loss will be deductible under the real estate exception.

Retirement—Plan Distributions

9. **B**

Statement 1 is correct. Jeff could rollover the Section 401(k) plan into a traditional IRA.

Statement 2 is incorrect. Ten-year averaging is available only for individuals born before January 2, 1936.

Statement 3 is correct. If he receives employer stock in a lump-sum distribution from a qualified plan, only the original cost basis of the stock is taxable at the time of distribution. The net unrealized appreciation (NUA) would not be taxed until the stock was subsequently sold.

Statement 4 is incorrect. Favorable NUA treatment applies only to distributions from a qualified plan, not an IRA.

Insurance—Life Insurance Provisions

10. **D**

Under the Uniform Simultaneous Death Act, the insured (Jeff) is considered to have survived the beneficiary. Therefore, the proceeds would pass automatically to the contingent beneficiary, Janice.

Retirement—Deferred Compensation

11. **C**

Jeff would be taxed on the deferred compensation when he received the money (at retirement).

Estates—Charitable Remainder Annuity Trust

12. C

The amount eligible for the charitable deduction would be equal to the present value of the charitable remainder interest in the trust.

To qualify as a CRAT, the trust must be irrevocable.

A CRAT is a tax-exempt trust. Therefore, the stock could be sold by the trust without a capital gain.

Private foundations can be named as the beneficiary of a CRAT.

Estates—2503(c) Trusts

13. A

Statement 1 is correct. Any remaining trust principal must be distributed to the beneficiary when the beneficiary attains age 21.

Statement 2 is incorrect. Income can be accumulated in the trust until the beneficiary attains age 21.

Statements 3 and 4 are correct.

Investments—Risk Measurements

14. C

Nosilla Foods will probably exhibit the most volatile returns of the stocks in the investment portfolio because it has the highest beta. The company has a beta of 1.4, which means it is 40% more volatile than the market.

Tax—Life Insurance Proceeds

15. C

Because Rosa purchased the policy from her father, a transfer for value has occurred. Therefore, Rosa will be taxed on the life insurance proceeds at ordinary income tax rates. Rosa can reduce the taxable amount by her basis in the policy. Her basis in the policy is the sum of the amount paid for the policy and the premiums she paid after the purchase.

Proceeds:	$300,000
Less basis:	$35,000 ($30,000 paid for policy plus $5,000 of premiums paid)
Taxable amount:	$265,000

Estates—Probate Estate

16. A

Description	Probate estate inclusion
Postal stock	$600,000
SUV	55,000
Total	$655,000

Estates—Gift Tax

17. D

If Jeff and Rosa elect gift-splitting, they can give $28,000 to each of their three children this year, for a total of $84,000, without exceeding their annual exclusions.

Tax—Section 1250 Property

18. D

Because the office building is depreciable real property, it is subject to the Section 1250 recapture rules. The gain on Section 1250 property is taxed at the 25% rate to the extent of depreciation taken.

Proceeds	$800,000
Basis	(585,000) ($650,000 cost less $65,000 accumulated depreciation)
Gain	$215,000

Of the $215,000 gain, only $65,000 would be taxed at the 25% rate. The remaining $150,000 of gain will be taxed at the Martins' long-term capital gains rate.

Investments—Options

19. B

Jeff can either sell the stock short, called *shorting against the box*, or purchase put options. Selling call options will not protect his gain but only limit a loss if the stock price declines. The constructive sale rules have greatly limited the usefulness of the shorting-against-the-box technique for tax purposes.

Investments—Risks

20. A

Choice 3 is incorrect because mortgage-backed securities represent an ownership claim on a pool of mortgages, most commonly on residential property. Business risk is generally not associated with MBSs.

Estates—Trusts

21. C

A spendthrift trust is a trust that restricts the beneficiary from transferring any of his future interest in the corpus or income. This meets Jeff's needs because he wants to prevent Tom from pledging his interest in the trust as collateral for a loan.

A special needs trust is a discretionary trust used for the benefit of a developmentally disabled child.

A Section 2503(c) trust is a minor's trust in which the principal and income must be distributed to the beneficiary upon attainment of age 21.

A GRAT is a trust that pays the grantor an annuity each year for a term of years, at which point the assets in the trust are transferred to the beneficiary.

Investments—Constant Growth Dividend Discount Model

22. **C**

The formula for finding the intrinsic value of a stock using the constant growth dividend discount model is as follows:

$V = D_1 \div (r - g)$

$D_1 = \$2.18\ (\$2.00 \times 1.09)$

$r = 0.15$

$g = 0.09$

Therefore, the intrinsic value of the Jedco stock using the model = $36.33 [$2.18 ÷ (0.15 − 0.09)].

Fundamentals—Confidentiality

23. **D**

You should decline to answer Tom's questions about the trust on the grounds of client confidentiality. Under Rule 3.1 of the Rules of Conduct, a CFP® professional must treat client information as confidential except as required in response to proper legal process, as necessitated by obligations to the professional's employer or partners, as required to defend against charges of wrongdoing, in connection with a civil dispute, or as needed to perform the services. In this case, Jeff and Rosa are your clients and none of the exceptions to client confidentiality are applicable.

Estates—Transfers at Death

24. **D**

Statement 1 is incorrect. The residence is owned jointly by Jeff and Rosa and would pass to Rosa by operation of law outside of probate.

Statement 2 is incorrect because death benefits from a life insurance received as a lump sum are not subject to income tax.

Statement 3 is correct. Jeff's funeral and administrative expenses would total $75,000. Jeff's only liquid asset is the $38,000 savings account, but he owns this asset jointly with Rosa so it would pass to her by right of survivorship at his death and not be part of his probate estate. His estate would need to liquidate other assets to pay the $75,000 in expenses.

Statement 4 is incorrect. Because Rosa is the designated beneficiary of the IRA and is Jeff's surviving spouse, she could defer taking distributions from the IRA until she reaches her own required beginning date.

Case Study 12:
Susan Wood

Case Study Facts

Today is December 31, 2017. Susan Wood has come to you, a CFP® professional, for help in developing a plan to accomplish her financial goals. From your initial meeting together, you have gathered the following information.

PERSONAL BACKGROUND AND INFORMATION

Susan Wood (Age 50)

Susan and her brother, Glen East, along with their mother, Maude, own EastWood Architectural, a C corporation. Susan is divorced with one daughter, Audrey (age 30), and a grandson, Billy (age 2).

Glen East (Age 45)

Glen is Susan's brother and a co-owner of EastWood Architectural, together with Susan and their mother, Maude. He is age 45 and married to Ruth, age 42. Ruth is a stay-at-home mom. They have two children, Matt, age 11, and Sarah, age 8.

Maude East (Age 74)

Maude is 74 years old. Maude's home has a fair market value of $120,000 and no mortgage debt. She receives a modest pension benefit of $12,000 per year from her late husband's employer. She also receives Social Security benefits of $15,000 per year. Her most significant source of income has been interest earned on CDs and government bonds. With the decline in interest rates, her discretionary income has decreased significantly, and she is concerned about having sufficient funds to take care of herself. Her 20% interest in the business is her single largest investment.

EastWood Architectural

Susan, Glen, and Maude own EastWood Architectural (EastWood), a C corporation. Susan and Glen each own 40% of the stock, and Maude owns the remaining 20%. Susan and Glen formed the company 15 years ago with their personal funds and a capital contribution from Maude.

EastWood drafts architectural plans for several different venues, including small office complexes, small- to medium-sized retail centers, and small resorts. Susan and Glen both believe the business has significant growth potential. The firm has been approached for other projects, such as a local government office complex and an upscale retail center.

Today EastWood employs a total of 15 people—Susan, Glen, seven architects, and six administrative office personnel. The firm grossed $3 million last year and had a profit of $700,000. Susan and Glen have not had the firm appraised but believe its reasonable fair market value is $4.5 million. The firm does not pay dividends. Maude has indicated to both Susan and Glen that she would like to start receiving income from the business or sell her stock to Susan and/or Glen.

Susan and Glen each receive a base salary of $250,000 per year. The other seven architects receive salaries ranging from $75,000 to $175,000. Salaries for the remaining office personnel range between $18,000 and $50,000.

Susan and Glen are interested in providing additional benefits that would help them retain their current employees and attract the talent they need to remain competitive. They are also interested in creating a market for their stock. Neither Susan nor Glen is particularly interested in acquiring a bigger stake in the firm, but they do not want to see stock sold to individuals outside the firm. Susan's daughter has no interest in the firm.

SUSAN'S PERSONAL AND FINANCIAL GOALS

- Leave the company within five years and maintain her desired level of income and lifestyle
- Establish an exit strategy for the business
- Ensure that her mother, Maude, has adequate income, possibly through the acquisition of her mother's stock in the company
- Evaluate both investment and insurance risk
- Spend $50,000 on the purchase of new bedroom and living room furniture for her home

ECONOMIC INFORMATION

- Susan expects inflation to average 3.5% annually, both currently and for the long term.
- She expects her salary to increase 10% annually.
- Interest rates are very low and expected to rise in the near future.
- Stocks are expected to appreciate 9.5% annually.

INCOME TAX INFORMATION

Her marginal income tax rate is currently 33% for federal income taxes. The state income tax rate is a flat 5%.

RETIREMENT INFORMATION

Susan plans to retire in five years at age 55. She would like to have a standard of living that can be provided by 80% of her preretirement income. She expects to be in retirement for 35 years.

The company implemented a profit-sharing plan several years ago. Last year, the company contributed 15% of each eligible employee's salary to the plan. The plan initially incorporated a five-year cliff vesting schedule, and employees were eligible to participate after completing one year of service. The plan offers loan provisions, subject to the Tax Code limits. Susan's account has a current balance of $350,000.

Susan expects to collect $24,000 per year in Social Security benefits at her full retirement age. She has been considering the possibility of receiving her Social Security benefits at age 62.

DIVORCE INFORMATION

Susan and her ex-husband Mark were divorced two years ago. Mark works in the marketing department of a Fortune 500 company, and his salary is $75,000. Pursuant to the divorce arrangement, Susan is required to pay Mark alimony in the amount of $45,000 each year for the next seven years. If Susan dies during the next seven years, payments must be made from her estate.

Susan and Mark purchased a house several years ago for $280,000. They owned the house as JTWROS until the divorce. Per the divorce agreement, the house was titled solely in Mark's name. The value of the house at the time of the divorce was $350,000, and today's value of the house is $375,000.

Susan was also required to transfer her $800,000 whole life insurance policy to Mark pursuant to the divorce agreement. The cash value of the policy is currently $40,000, and the divorce agreement requires Susan to pay the annual $10,000 premium as alimony.

GIFTS, ESTATES, TRUSTS, AND WILL INFORMATION

Gifts

Susan has made no taxable gifts.

Estates

Susan's will leaves everything to her ex-husband Mark. She has not updated the will since the divorce.

Statement of Cash Flows
Susan Wood
January 1 – December 31, 2017

CASH INFLOWS

Salary	Salary	$250,000	
	Bonus	100,000	
	Total	$350,000	
Unearned income	Dividends	$2,000	
	Interest income	10,000	
		$12,000	
Total inflows			**$362,000**

CASH OUTFLOWS

Mortgage payments	Primary residence	$50,000	
Insurance premiums	Homeowners	$2,500	
	Auto	3,000	
	Life (policy owned by ex-spouse)	10,000	
	Total insurance premiums	$15,500	
Miscellaneous expenses	Alimony	$45,000	
	Entertainment	20,000	
	Food	8,400	
	Clothes	15,000	
	Utilities	10,000	
	Charity	20,000	
	Total miscellaneous expenses	$118,400	
Taxes	Property	$ 35,000	
	Federal and state income taxes and FICA	135,000	
	Total taxes	$170,000	
Total outflows			**$353,900**
Net cash flow (surplus)			**$8,100**

Statement of Financial Position

Susan Wood

As of December 31, 2017

ASSETS[1]		LIABILITIES AND NET WORTH	
		Liabilities[2]	
Cash/cash equivalents		**Current liabilities**	
S Savings account	$8,000	S Credit card 1	$35,000
S Cash value of universal life policy	20,000	S Credit card 2	$20,000
M Cash value of whole life policy	40,000	**Total current liabilities**	$55,000
Total cash/cash equivalents	$68,000		
		Long-term liabilities	
Invested assets		A Auto loan[3]	$20,000
S EastWood stock	$1,800,000	S Mortgage—primary residence	$600,000
S Profit-sharing plan	350,000	**Total long-term liabilities**	$620,000
S Investment portfolio	900,000	**Total liabilities**	$675,000
Total investments	$3,050,000		
Personal-use assets		**Net worth**	$3,528,000
S Primary residence	$750,000		
S Personal property/furniture	200,000		
S Luxury car	85,000		
S SUV	50,000		
Total personal-use assets	$1,085,000		
Total assets	$4,203,000	**Total liabilities and net worth**	$4,203,000

Notes to financial statements:

[1] Assets are stated at fair market value (rounded to even dollars).

[2] Liabilities are stated at principal only (rounded to even dollars).

[3] The auto loan was used for the purchase of a car by Audrey. Susan is a cosigner on the loan.

Property ownership:

S—Susan's property

M—Mark's property

A—Audrey's property

INSURANCE INFORMATION

Life Insurance

	Universal life	Whole life
Insured	Glen	Susan
Face amount	$500,000	$800,000
Cash value	$20,000	$40,000
Annual premium	$6,000	$10,000
Premium payer	Glen	Susan
Beneficiary	Susan	Mark
Policyowner	Susan	Mark
Comments	Susan is a revocable beneficiary.	Policy was transferred to Mark pursuant to the divorce.

Health Insurance

Susan is covered by the company's health plan, which is an indemnity plan with a $1,000 deductible per person per year and an 80/20 coinsurance clause.

Long-Term Disability Insurance

Susan is covered by an own-occupation policy with premiums paid by the company. The benefits equal 60% of gross income after a 180-day elimination period. The policy covers both sickness and accidents.

INVESTMENT INFORMATION

Detailed Investment Portfolio

Description	Expected return	Current FMV
Taxable zero-coupon bonds	7%	$200,000
Zero-coupon municipal bond fund	6%	$300,000
Long-term municipal bond fund	5%	$200,000
International stocks	10%	$10,000
Precious metals mutual fund	4%	$90,000
Treasury bills	2%	$100,000
Total		$900,000

Susan is willing to take reasonable investment risk if appropriate, but she does not want to invest aggressively.

She is interested in investing in equity securities. She was recently told by a broker that Rett Manufacturing Company stock would be a wise purchase. The stock is currently trading at $45 per share and pays a dividend of $2 per share, with an estimated 4% annual dividend growth rate. The stock has a beta of 1.04.

Questions

1. Susan has told you that Maude wants to divest herself of her interest in EastWood. Because this could affect Susan's financial planning, she has asked you what are the various ways Maude could transfer her interest in the business to Susan and Glen while satisfying her need for income and greater liquidity. Susan wants to assist her mother while also understanding the impact on her own retirement plans. These alternatives could include all the following EXCEPT

    A. a private annuity
    B. an installment sale
    C. an outright gift
    D. company stock redemption

2. Assume that upon your recommendation Susan and Glen implement a private annuity to purchase Maude's business interest. They engage you to monitor the performance of the recommendation and to alert them if any modifications become advisable because of changed circumstances. Which of the following actions would be appropriate in the performance of your monitoring activities?

    1. Once Maude has lived to her full actuarial life expectancy, advise Susan and Glen that they can cease making payments.
    2. When Maude dies, advise Susan and Glen that they can cease making payments.
    3. If Maude ever feels insecure about their ability to make the payments, advise Susan and Glen that they must provide collateral.
    4. If Maude dies, advise Susan and Glen that they receive a stepped-up basis in the business interest.

    A. 1, 2, and 3
    B. 1 and 4
    C. 2 only
    D. 3 and 4

3. Glen is considering converting the business to an S corporation when Susan retires. If this conversion takes place, EastWood may be subject to all of the following EXCEPT

    A. built-in gains tax
    B. LIFO recapture tax
    C. excess net passive income tax
    D. depreciation recapture tax

4. Glen is willing to consider a 10- or 15-year installment sale, but only if Susan will also participate in the purchase of Maude's stock. Is an installment purchase appropriate for Susan's situation?

    A. Yes. It allows her to purchase the stock in small amounts over time.
    B. No. The time frame of the purchase falls within Susan's planned retirement time horizon.
    C. Yes. It allows her to maintain an ownership percentage equal to Glen's.
    D. No. Susan may not be able to fully deduct the interest expense associated with the purchase.

5. What type of plan benefits could EastWood establish that not only would provide a means for Maude to liquidate her stock but eventually could be used to help Susan and Glen liquidate their own holdings?

    A. Restricted stock plan

    B. ESOP

    C. Section 412(e)(3) plan

    D. Corporate-owned life insurance (COLI)

6. Glen and Susan have agreed to implement a cross-purchase buy-sell agreement between the two of them in the event of death or disability. They have chosen not to implement one between them and Maude. Which of the following statements regarding the buy-sell agreement is CORRECT?

    A. Maude could be included in the buy-sell agreement only if she were an active participant in the business.

    B. Life insurance premiums will be deductible by the corporation because the S corporation election was not made.

    C. The cost to insure Maude's life would be significantly more expensive if she were included in the buy-sell agreement.

    D. Provisions in Maude's will could bind Susan and Glen to purchase her shares upon her death.

7. Which of the following items listed on Susan's statement of financial position are examples of tangible personal property?

    1. Primary residence

    2. Luxury car

    3. Savings account

    4. Personal property/furniture

    A. 1 and 2

    B. 1, 2, and 4

    C. 2, 3, and 4

    D. 2 and 4

8. Susan's daughter is married to a wealthy businessman and is financially secure. Susan would prefer that the bulk of her estate go to her grandson after she dies, but she does not want to give up control over her property while she is alive. Which of the following would be the best technique to accomplish her goal?

    A. Make annual gifts to her grandson that do not exceed the annual exclusion amount

    B. Leave assets to the grandson in her will

    C. Title her assets as JTWROS with her grandson

    D. Give her grandson a power of attorney over her property

9. Susan would like to help fund the college education costs for her grandson. Assuming she does not want to give up control of the assets and wants tax deferral, which of the following would be an appropriate vehicle to consider?

   A.   Section 2503(b) trust
   B.   Roth IRA
   C.   UGMA
   D.   Section 529 plan

10. Which of the following investments would be appropriate to diversify Susan's investment portfolio?

   1.   Zero-coupon municipal bond fund
   2.   International stocks
   3.   S&P 500 Index fund
   4.   Leveraged commercial real estate

   A.   1 and 4
   B.   2 and 3
   C.   2, 3, and 4
   D.   1, 2, 3, and 4

11. Assume Susan has retained you to monitor the performance of her investment portfolio. If the economic expectations outlined in this case regarding interest rates are accurate, which of the following strategies would you recommend for Susan?

   A.   Sell the Treasury bills
   B.   Buy convertible bonds
   C.   Sell the long-term municipal bond fund
   D.   Buy intermediate-term bonds

12. Assuming that Susan has a required rate of return of 7%, would the purchase of Rett Manufacturing Company stock be advisable for her portfolio?

   A.   Yes, because the stock is undervalued
   B.   No, because the stock is overvalued
   C.   Yes, because the required rate of return is greater than the expected growth rate
   D.   No, because the stock is not within her risk tolerance

13. Which of the following benefits could EastWood install on a discriminatory basis without adverse tax consequences for covered individuals?

   1.   A group term life insurance plan that provides up to $50,000 of coverage
   2.   A supplemental executive retirement plan (SERP)
   3.   Section 125 cafeteria plan

   A.   1, 2, and 3
   B.   1 and 3
   C.   2 only
   D.   3 only

14. If Susan and Glen entered into a stock redemption buy-sell agreement with EastWood, which of the following would be a disadvantage?

A. A transfer-for-value problem could occur if either Susan or Glen transfers a life insurance policy to EastWood to fund the agreement.

B. More policies will be required with a stock-redemption agreement than with a cross-purchase agreement.

C. The owner who survives will be required to come up with sufficient cash to purchase the interest of the deceased owner.

D. The insurance proceeds to EastWood upon the death of Susan or Glen could be subject to income taxation.

15. Maude is covered by Medicare Parts A and B. Which of the following expenses is NOT covered under Medicare?

A. Hospice costs for terminally ill patients

B. Mammograms

C. Annual flu shots

D. Coverage for long-term custodial care

16. Marvin, a long-time employee at EastWood Architectural, resigned during the year to pursue other opportunities. How many months of medical insurance COBRA continuation coverage will be available to Marvin?

A. 0 months

B. 18 months

C. 29 months

D. 36 months

17. Per the divorce agreement, Susan and Mark's house was transferred to Mark. Which of the following statements regarding the income tax consequences of the transfer is CORRECT?

A. Because the transfer occurred after the couple was no longer married, a gift occurred from Susan to Mark.

B. Mark will have a basis in the home of $280,000.

C. Mark's basis in the home will be increased by gift tax paid upon the transfer.

D. Mark will have a basis in the home of $350,000.

18. Which of the following statements regarding the whole life insurance policy on Susan's life is(are) CORRECT?

    1. If Susan died today, the entire $800,000 death benefit would be included in her probate estate.
    2. The cash value of the policy, less the annual exclusion, was considered a taxable gift from Susan to Mark.
    3. Susan is entitled to an income tax deduction for the premiums paid on the life insurance policy.
    4. A transfer of a life insurance policy pursuant to a divorce agreement is considered a transfer for value for income tax purposes; therefore, the death benefit will be taxable to Mark when Susan dies.

    A. 1, 3, and 4
    B. 2 and 4
    C. 3 only
    D. 1, 2, 3, and 4

19. Which of the following statements regarding Susan's financial statements are CORRECT?

    I. Susan should not include the whole life insurance policy on her statement of financial position.
    II. If Susan purchases new bedroom and living room furniture for her home, this purchase would appear as a variable outflow on her cash flow statement.

    A. I only
    B. II only
    C. Both I and II
    D. Neither I nor II

20. Susan has inquired about the possibility of taking a loan from the profit-sharing plan to pay some general expenses. Which of the following statements regarding loans from qualified plans is CORRECT?

    A. Because the plan is a Keogh plan, loans to Susan, a businessowner, will be limited to 20% of her gross salary.
    B. The interest paid on the loan will be deductible for income tax purposes to the extent Susan has taxable investment income.
    C. Susan is not permitted to take a loan from the plan because she is a more than 10% owner.
    D. The maximum loan Susan can take from the plan is $50,000.

21. Glen and Susan use the same CFP® professional for financial planning advice. Maude, however, does not have a financial planner, believing it is too late in her life to engage one. The siblings approach you, their CFP® professional, and tell you they will be bringing in Maude for financial planning services, especially her ongoing retirement planning and estate planning so they can be assured they know what is happening with their mother financially, assuming you will keep them informed. Which of the following actions can you do while remaining in compliance with CFP® Board's Code of Ethics?

   1. You can disclose the details of Maude's financial status to Glen and Susan because they are members of Maude's immediate family.

   2. You can disclose the details of Maude's financial status to Glen and Susan only if the siblings benefit from her will.

   3. You can disclose the details of Maude's financial status to Glen and Susan with Maude's authorization.

   4. You can disclose the details of Maude's financial status if the records are subpoenaed for a court proceeding.

   A. 1 and 3
   B. 3 and 4
   C. 1, 2, and 3
   D. 2, 3, and 4

ANSWER SUMMARY

1. C	6. C	11. C	16. A	21. B
2. C	7. D	12. A	17. B	
3. D	8. B	13. C	18. C	
4. B	9. D	14. D	19. C	
5. B	10. B	15. D	20. D	

SUMMARY OF TOPICS

1. Estates—Business Continuation
2. Estates—Private Annuity
3. Tax—Taxation of Business Entities
4. Estates—Business Succession Planning
5. Retirement—Qualified Plans
6. Estates—Buy-Sell Agreement
7. Fundamentals—Financial Statements
8. Estates—Gifting Techniques
9. Fundamentals—Education Funding
10. Investments—Diversification
11. Investments—Portfolio Management
12. Investments—Constant Growth Dividend Discount Model
13. Insurance—Employee Benefits
14. Estates—Buy-Sell Agreement
15. Insurance—Medicare
16. Insurance—COBRA
17. Tax—Property Transfer
18. Tax—Life Insurance
19. Fundamentals—Financial Statements
20. Retirement—Qualified Plan Rules
21. Fundamentals—Code of Ethics

Solutions

Estates—Business Continuation

1. **C**

   Susan and Glen could purchase Maude's interest in EastWood using either a private annuity or an installment sale, or EastWood could repurchase Maude's stock in the company. Each would affect Susan's retirement planning, and further scenario analysis would be needed by Susan's CFP® professional to develop a recommendation on which would satisfy Susan's needs and also her mother's. An outright gift of her business interest would not satisfy Maude's desire for income or need for greater liquidity.

Estates—Private Annuity

2. **C**

   Statement 1 is incorrect. Payments under a private annuity continue for as long as the seller lives, even if that is longer than her actuarial life expectancy.

   Statement 2 is correct.

   Statement 3 is incorrect. A private annuity cannot be secured by collateral.

   Statement is incorrect. The buyers under a private annuity do not receive a stepped-up basis when the seller dies. Their basis is the total amount of the payments made under the annuity.

Tax—Taxation of Business Entities

3. **D**

   S corporations may be subject to built-in gains tax, LIFO recapture tax, and excess net passive income tax if they were previously C corporations.

Estates—Business Succession Planning

4. **B**

   Susan is planning on retiring in five years. Therefore, a 10- to 15-year payable installment note is not the best choice. All of the stock is purchased at one time. Only the payments are made over time. Susan wishes to retire soon. Interest expense is deductible in installment sales.

Retirement—Qualified Plans

5. **B**

   A restricted stock plan would provide more shares to the owners. This plan would not help in the liquidation of the owners' interests.

   An employee stock ownership plan (ESOP) may be appropriate. This plan, which is a qualified plan, could purchase the stock from the shareholders. ESOPs have other tax advantages as well.

   A Section 412(e)(3) plan is a defined benefit plan that is funded with life insurance.

   COLI is a good planning strategy but will not solve their liquidation goals.

Estates—Buy-Sell Agreement

6. **C**

Maude is older; therefore, premiums on a life insurance policy on her life would be more expensive. Buy-sell agreements are not limited to active participants. The premiums are not deductible. Maude's will cannot require Susan and Glen to purchase her shares.

Fundamentals—Financial Statements

7. **D**

Tangible personal property is personal property that is moveable and subject to physical possession, such as furniture and automobiles. Structures on land, such as a residence, are real property. A savings account is an example of intangible personal property.

Estates—Gifting Techniques

8. **B**

Although most of the strategies have merit, Susan should leave the property to her grandson in her will. All of the other choices involve giving up some current control over the assets.

Fundamentals—Education Funding

9. **D**

A Section 2503(b) trust would cause Susan to give up control of the assets and does not provide tax deferral.

Susan does not qualify for a Roth IRA because of her income.

An UGMA account would cause Susan to give up control of the assets and does not provide tax deferral.

A Section 529 plan is the best choice for Susan. A college savings plan can permit the contributor to select among different investment strategies designed exclusively for the program when the initial contribution is made to establish the account.

Investments—Diversification

10. **B**

Investment options 2 and 3 would provide additional diversification because Susan has relatively no equity exposure in her portfolio other than the stock in the closely held company.

Investment option 1 is incorrect. The municipal bond fund would not provide the needed growth component.

Investment option 4 is incorrect. Leveraged commercial real estate is outside her risk tolerance.

Investments—Portfolio Management

11. **C**

When interest rates are expected to rise, an investor should sell long-term bonds and reinvest the proceeds at a future higher coupon rate.

Investments—Constant Growth Dividend Discount Model

12. A

The formula for finding the value of a stock using this model is as follows:

$V = D_1 \div (r - g)$

V = the intrinsic value of the stock

D_1 = the dividend paid at the end of period 1

r = the investor's required rate of return

g = the dividend growth rate

Intrinsic value = $[\$2 \times (1.00 + .04)] \div (0.07 - 0.04) = \$69.33$

The stock is undervalued at $45 per share.

Insurance—Employee Benefits

13. C

Statement 1 is incorrect. If a group term life insurance plan is discriminatory, the key employees will lose the $50,000 income tax exclusion.

Statement 2 is correct. A SERP is a nonqualified plan and can be discriminatory.

Statement 3 is incorrect. If a cafeteria plan is discriminatory, key employees will have adverse tax consequences.

Estates—Buy-Sell Agreement

14. D

A transfer of a life insurance policy from a shareholder to a corporation will not be considered a transfer for value.

A cross-purchase agreement will typically require the purchase of more policies.

Under a stock redemption buy-sell agreement, the corporation (not the surviving owner) buys the shares of a deceased owner.

Life insurance proceeds received by a corporation may be subject to corporate alternative minimum tax.

Insurance—Medicare

15. D

Custodial care is not covered under Medicare.

Insurance—COBRA

16. A

COBRA coverage applies only to employers with 20 or more employees.

Tax—Property Transfer

17. B

When a spouse receives property pursuant to a divorce, the basis in the property will always be carryover basis from the transferor spouse.

Tax—Life Insurance

18. C

Statement 1 is incorrect. The death benefit is not included in Susan's probate estate because Susan is not the owner of the policy and the proceeds are not payable to her estate.

Statement 2 is incorrect. A transfer of a life insurance policy pursuant to a divorce is not subject to gift tax.

Statement 3 is correct. Susan transferred ownership of the policy and she is required to pay premiums on the life insurance policy, so the premium payments will be considered deductible alimony. Note that Mark will be required to include the amount of the premium payments in his gross income.

Statement 4 is incorrect. Transfers incident to a divorce are not subject to the transfer-for-value rule.

Fundamentals—Financial Statements

19. C

Both statements I and II are correct. Statement I is correct because Susan is not the owner of the policy. Statement II is correct because this purchase is a variable outflow. This purchase would also appear as a personal-use asset on her net worth statement.

Retirement—Qualified Plan Rules

20. D

The plan is not a Keogh plan because the company is a C Corporation. In addition, there is no such rule for loans.

Interest on loans for other than the acquisition of a principal residence from qualified plans is considered personal interest and is not deductible for income tax purposes.

Although there previously were restrictions on loans for businessowners, those restrictions have been eliminated. The previous restrictions applied only to Keogh plans.

The maximum loan that can be taken from a profit-sharing plan is $50,000.

Fundamentals—Code of Ethics

21. B

Statement 3 is correct. The Code of Ethics' Principle 5—Confidentiality requires certificants to ensure that clients' information is accessible only to those authorized to have access. Statement 4 is also correct. Rule of Conduct 3.1 compels certificants to treat information as confidential except as required in response to proper legal process, as necessitated by obligations to a certificant's employer or partners, to defend against charges of wrongdoing; in connection with a civil dispute; or as needed to perform the services.

Item Set and
Mini-Case Questions

ITEM SET 1

Al and Irma have resided in New Orleans for several years. During the current year, a fire damaged their home, automobiles, and personal property:

Description	FMV before fire	FMV after fire
Dwelling	$200,000*	$120,000
Personal property	$ 50,000	$ 25,000
Auto #1	$ 18,000	$ 14,500
Auto #2	$ 20,000	$ 18,000

* Replacement cost on the dwelling = fair market value (FMV) before the fire

The couple had insurance on the home, automobiles, and personal property.

Homeowners insurance	
Policy type	HO-3
Coverage limit	$150,000
Deductible	$500
Annual premium	$1,025
Liability limit	$100,000
Medical payments limit	$1,000
Coinsurance requirement	80%

Automobile insurance		
	Auto #1	Auto #2
Annual premium	$1,200	$950
Coverage limit	$50,000/$100,000	$50,000/$100,000
Comprehensive deductible	$250	$500
Collision deductible	$500	$1,000

The homeowners policy contains an endorsement for personal property to be valued at replacement cost value.

1. How much will the insurance company pay to repair the dwelling?

    A. $80,000
    B. $75,000
    C. $74,500
    D. $64,000

2. How much will Al and Irma have to pay to fix the automobiles?

    A. $4,750
    B. $4,650
    C. $850
    D. $750

3. Assume Al and Irma have an adjusted gross income for the current year of $60,000, and they receive the following amounts of insurance proceeds:

Dwelling	$74,500
Personal property	$25,000
Auto #1	$1,000
Auto #2	$1,000

How much of a casualty loss can Al and Irma deduct on their current federal income tax return?

A. $2,900
B. $9,000
C. $3,000
D. $8,500

ITEM SET 2

Harold is a 55-year-old corporate executive employed by a Fortune 500 company. He is planning to retire at age 65 and then expects to live for another 25 years. He has accumulated a stock portfolio and a bond portfolio as shown below. Harold is willing to accept enough risk to meet his goals, but he neither wants to accept additional risk, nor wants to die with less than $1 million (in today's dollars) in his brokerage account (i.e., he hopes to have at least this much in his estate at the end of the 25-year retirement period).

	Stock portfolio	Bond portfolio
Current market value	$572,160	$143,040
Average historic return	12%	7%
Standard deviation	15%	9%
Current YTM	N/A	7%
Duration	N/A	5 years
Correlation to the stock market	77.5%	N/A

Note: The correlation coefficient between Harold's stock portfolio and bond portfolio is +0.40.

1. Harold is concerned about the volatility of his portfolio and would like help in assessing the risk. Based on his current allocation between his stock portfolio and his bond portfolio, what is the standard deviation of his total portfolio?

   A. 12.0%
   B. 12.4%
   C. 12.8%
   D. 13.8%

2. Harold has taken an active role in developing his financial goals by reading *Investors Magazine*. After reading about diversification, he has become concerned about the diversity of his stock portfolio. What portion of the risk in his stock portfolio is inherent to a specific business or industry?

   A. 20%
   B. 40%
   C. 60%
   D. 80%

3. What would be the approximate decline in the value of Harold's bond portfolio if interest rates increase to 7.43%?

   A. 1.0%
   B. 2.0%
   C. 3.0%
   D. 5.8%

4. Harold knows that the bond market has been performing well. What is the probability of having a return of at least 16% from his bond portfolio?

   A. 9%
   B. 16%
   C. 22%
   D. 34%

5. Harold's previous financial planner told him that he should allocate 45% of his portfolio to stocks and 55% to bonds. How much would his portfolio be worth when he retired if he followed this advice? Assume the portfolio retains this 45%/55% asset allocation until his retirement.

   A. $1,732,375
   B. $1,772,428
   C. $1,773,385
   D. $1,813,313

ITEM SET 3

During 2017, Smallco, Inc., has 3 employees as indicated below:

Employee	Age	Status	Section 401(k) plan deferral	Compensation	Health plan coverage
Aaron	30	Single	$3,000	$34,000	Single coverage
Barbara	65	Married	$6,000	$60,000	Family coverage
Charlie	45	Married	$4,000	$47,500	Family coverage

Smallco has a group health insurance plan with the following annual deductibles:

■ Individual: $2,000
■ Family: $4,000

Smallco pays 100% of the premiums.

Barbara is also employed by ABC Corporation, where she is covered under a major medical health plan as an employee with individual coverage. The employer pays the entire premium, and the annual deductible for individual coverage is $500.

1. What is the maximum amount that Aaron can contribute to a health savings account (HSA) for 2017?

   A. $1,000
   B. $1,300
   C. $2,900
   D. $3,400

2. Assume that in 2016 and 2017, Aaron made contributions to an HSA. In 2017, he married Doris, who is employed with XYZ Corporation and covered under the XYZ health care plan. In late 2017, Doris became sick and Aaron took a distribution from his HSA to cover the deductible and coinsurance amounts under her health plan. What are the tax consequences to Aaron regarding this transaction?

   A. The withdrawal was used for qualified medical expenses; therefore, no tax consequences.
   B. The withdrawal was used for qualified medical expenses; therefore, the withdrawal is treated as ordinary income, but there is no penalty.
   C. The withdrawal is treated as ordinary income and is subject to a 20% penalty.
   D. The withdrawal is treated as a qualified plan distribution subject to capital gains taxation and a 10% penalty.

3. Barbara would like to open her own HSA. How much can she deduct from her taxes and contribute to the HSA for 2017?

   A. $0
   B. $1,300
   C. $3,400
   D. $6,750

4. Assume Charlie establishes an HSA in 2017, contributes $7,000, and makes no withdrawals. What are Charlie's tax consequences for 2017 related to the establishment and funding of his HSA?

   A. He may take a tax deduction of $7,000.
   B. He may take a tax deduction of $6,750 but must pay an excise penalty of $15.
   C. He may take a tax deduction of $6,750 but must pay an excise penalty of $25.
   D. He may take a tax deduction of $7,000 but must pay an excise penalty of $25.

5. Barbara has a working spouse who is 61 years old and is not an active participant in a qualified plan. What is the maximum deductible traditional IRA contribution that Barbara's husband can make for 2017, assuming he earns $50,000 in compensation?

   A. $0
   B. $4,000
   C. $5,500
   D. $6,500

6. Charlie has a 42-year-old, nonworking spouse and wishes to establish an IRA for her. What is the maximum deductible IRA contribution that Charlie can make for himself and his wife for 2017?

   A. $0
   B. $5,500
   C. $6,500
   D. $11,000

ITEM SET 4

Anna Bartoromo, age 64, died on September 8, 2017. She had been employed with XYZ Corporation, where she had a vested qualified retirement plan account and a completely vested Section 401(k) plan account. In addition, she had an IRA and the other property listed below. She had not started any distributions by the date of her death. Anna was married to Zack and they have a son, Carl, and a daughter, Marie.

Valuation of Her Interest				
Asset	9/08/17	Date of disposition 1/1/18	Adjusted cost basis	Titling or beneficiary*
Qualified plan account	$1,000,000		$0	Beneficiary M
Section 401(k) plan	750,000		0	Beneficiary C
IRA	2,000,000		0	Beneficiary Z
½ personal residence	400,000		280,000	JTWROS with Z
Annuity (10-year certain)	300,000		200,000	Beneficiary Z
Installment note (5-year/9%)	200,000		160,000	Willed to Z
Other property	250,000	$300,000	80,000	Willed to Z

*Z = Zack
 C = Carl
 M = Marie

1. What is the approximate value of Anna Bartoromo's probate estate?

    A. $450,000
    B. $750,000
    C. $1,150,000
    D. $2,150,000

2. Zack Bartoromo consults a CFP® professional for advice regarding Anna's individual retirement account (IRA). Which of the following is(are) permissible options for Zack when taking distributions from the IRA?

   1. He can roll over her balance into his IRA account and begin distributions when he attains age 70½.
   2. He can maintain the same account and begin distributions when Anna would have attained age 70½.
   3. He can take a distribution from the account immediately and will not be subject to the 10% early withdrawal penalty, even if he is under age 59½.

   A. 1 and 2
   B. 1 and 3
   C. 2 only
   D. 1, 2, and 3

3. Anna's 35-year-old son, Carl, is the beneficiary of her Section 401(k) plan. He consults his CFP® professional for advice about his options for taking distributions from the plan. Which of the following options could the CFP® professional appropriately suggest to Carl?

   1. Carl could leave the balance in Anna's name and take a distribution from the account immediately. He will not be subject to the 10% early withdrawal penalty.
   2. Carl could leave the balance in Anna's name and begin distribution over the son's life expectancy in the year following the year of death.
   3. Carl could transfer the Section 401(k) plan to an inherited-titled IRA and delay distributions until he is age 70½.

   A. 1 and 2
   B. 1 and 3
   C. 2 only
   D. 1, 2, and 3

ITEM SET 5

Keri Mayer, age 64, died September 8, 2017. She had been employed with Reed Corporation, where she had a vested retirement account and a completely vested Section 401(k) plan account. In addition, she had an IRA and the other property listed below. She had not started any distributions. Keri was married to Arthur and they have a son, Walter, and a daughter, Celeste.

	Valuation of Her Interest			
Asset	9/08/17	Date of disposition 1/1/18	Adjusted cost basis	Titling or beneficiary*
Qualified retirement account	$1,000,000		$0	Beneficiary A
Section 401(k) plan	750,000		0	Beneficiary W
IRA	2,000,000		0	Beneficiary C
Personal residence (½ interest)	400,000**		280,000***	JTWROS with A
Annuity (10-year certain)	300,000		200,000	Beneficiary A
Installment note (5-year/9%)	200,000		160,000	Willed to A
Other property	250,000	$300,000	80,000	Willed to A

*A = Arthur   ** Represents 50% of value of personal residence
 W = Walter   *** Represents 50% of total basis
 C = Celeste

1. What is Arthur's adjusted tax basis in the installment note?

    A. $0
    B. $160,000
    C. $183,789
    D. $200,000

2. What is Arthur's adjusted tax basis in the assets listed as other property?

    A. $0
    B. $80,000
    C. $250,000
    D. $300,000

3. What is Arthur's adjusted tax basis in the annuity?

    A. $0
    B. $200,000
    C. $290,000
    D. $300,000

4. What is Arthur's adjusted tax basis in the personal residence?

    A. $400,000
    B. $540,000
    C. $680,000
    D. $800,000

5. What is Walter's adjusted tax basis in the Section 401(k) plan?

    A. $0
    B. $300,000
    C. $600,000
    D. $350,000

ITEM SET 6

On August 23, 2017, Fred, a single taxpayer, gave his son, Sammy, a gift of ABC stock with a fair market value of $100,000, as of the date of the gift. Fred made only this gift this year. Fred had an adjusted tax basis (cost) in the ABC stock of $160,000 and acquired the stock on July 31, 2009. Fred has a remaining net worth of $1.3 million.

1. What are Fred's taxable gifts for 2017?

   A. $46,000
   B. $86,000
   C. $100,000
   D. $160,000

2. Assume that on December 31, 2017, Sammy sold the ABC stock for $140,000. What are the income tax consequences to Sammy for this sale?

   A. No gain or loss
   B. Short-term capital gain of $40,000
   C. Long-term capital gain of $40,000
   D. Short-term capital loss of $20,000

3. Assume that Sammy sold the ABC stock on December 31, 2017, for $90,000. What are the income tax consequences to Sammy for this sale?

   A. No gain or loss
   B. Short-term capital loss of $10,000
   C. Long-term capital loss of $10,000
   D. Short-term capital loss of $70,000

4. Regardless of what Sammy does with the stock, what are the income tax consequences to Fred in 2017 regarding the gift of ABC stock?

   A. No gain or loss
   B. Short-term capital loss of $60,000, fully deductible
   C. Long-term capital loss of $60,000, fully deductible
   D. Short-term capital loss of $60,000, limited to $3,000 deductible

ITEM SET 7

Bob invested $5 million in investment A, which had a fair market value of $6.5 million at the end of year 1. He also invested $8 million in investment B, which had a fair market value of $10 million at the end of year 1. Bob's required rate of return is 10%.

1. Which of the following investments has a net present value of $909,090.90?

    A. Investment A
    B. Investment B
    C. Both investment A and investment B
    D. Neither investment A nor investment B

2. Which of the following investments has an IRR of 25%?

    A. Investment A
    B. Investment B
    C. Both investment A and investment B
    D. Neither investment A nor investment B

3. Which of the following investments has an IRR of 30%?

    A. Investment A
    B. Investment B
    C. Both investment A and investment B
    D. Neither investment A nor investment B

4. Which of the following investments has a net present value of $1,909,090.09?

    A. Investment A
    B. Investment B
    C. Both investment A and investment B
    D. Neither investment A nor investment B

▌ ITEM SET 8

Doris buys 1,000 shares of ABC stock for $100 per share, with an initial margin of 55% and a maintenance margin of 30%.

1. At what price will Doris receive a margin call?

   A. $45.00
   B. $55.00
   C. $64.29
   D. $69.23

2. If the stock drops to $70 per share, how much cash per share will Doris be required to deposit in her brokerage account to meet a margin call?

   A. $0.00
   B. $6.00
   C. $6.54
   D. $8.57

3. If the stock drops to $50 per share, how much cash will Doris be required to deposit to cover the margin call?

   A. $2,000
   B. $5,000
   C. $10,000
   D. $19,220

ITEM SET 9

You have a 2-asset portfolio with equal weighting and the following characteristics:

	Return	Risk (σ)
Asset A	5%	20%
Asset B	15%	40%

1. If the correlation coefficient between assets A and B is 0.6, what is the standard deviation of the 2-asset portfolio?

    A. Below 15%
    B. 15–30%
    C. 30–50%
    D. Over 50%

2. If the correlation coefficient between assets A and B is 1.0, what is the standard deviation of the 2-asset portfolio?

    A. 15–29%
    B. 30%
    C. 31–50%
    D. Cannot be determined

ITEM SET 10

Diana, a U.S. citizen, has a portfolio of $1 million and an AGI of $200,000 per year. She is 40 years old and is very concerned about her disabled child, Kevin, who is 8 years old. Diana wants to provide an inflation-protected lifetime income for Kevin when he reaches age 21. In addition, Diana wants to leave the principal of her portfolio to the New Orleans Museum of Art. She has a cost basis in the portfolio of $800,000. Her AGI is expected to remain constant for the next 10 years. If sold, the portfolio would result in long-term capital gains.

1. Which of the following parties could Diana name as a replacement remainder beneficiary for the New Orleans Museum of Art, assuming that she no longer wanted to benefit the museum and that she had a properly drafted charitable remainder trust to benefit Kevin during his life?

    1. Loyola University
    2. Kevin himself
    3. Diana herself
    4. Buffy, the friend of Diana's husband

    A. 1 only
    B. 2 only because he is already the beneficiary
    C. 3 only because she is the grantor
    D. 1, 2, 3, and 4

2. Suppose that Diana changes her mind and considers donating the entire portfolio directly to the charity with no income to Kevin. What is the maximum charitable deduction she can take in the current year?

    A. $60,000
    B. $100,000
    C. $800,000
    D. $1 million

3. What is the maximum total amount of charitable contributions Diana can deduct over the next 10 years from this contribution if Kevin is not a beneficiary and if this is a straight charitable contribution of the $1 million portfolio? Assume Diana makes no other charitable contributions.

    A. $360,000
    B. $500,000
    C. $600,000
    D. $1 million

ITEM SET 11

1. The Guffins refinanced their home exactly 2 years ago at a 30-year interest rate of 7.5%. If the remaining mortgage balance at the time of refinancing was $104,000, how much do they owe today? (Assume they made all payments as agreed, including today's payment.)

    A. $103,922
    B. $102,008
    C. $105,160
    D. $106,133

2. The Guffins refinanced their home 2 years ago on January 1 at a 30-year interest rate of 7.5%. The initial 30-year loan was for $112,820 and was paid as agreed until refinancing. The balance at refinancing was $104,200, with a remaining term of exactly 22 years. Closing costs of 3% were paid separately. Assuming the old loan was at an interest rate of 9%, how much total cash will they save if they pay equal monthly payments over the remaining life of the old loan?

    A. $20,204
    B. $26,596
    C. $32,109
    D. $36,400

ITEM SET 12

Ingrid, a CFP® professional, is meeting with her client, Humphrey, after he called her to ask questions about stock options. Humphrey is a successful programmer who develops hand-held games and apps for cell phones. His employer granted him enough stock options today to purchase 1,000 shares of the company stock with an exercise price of $22.00 when the fair market value of his employer's stock is also $22.00. He is uncertain as to the value of owning the stock options but does know the company is growing and that the stock should significantly appreciate in value.

1. During the meeting, Humphrey inquired about how stock options work. What should Ingrid do next to assist Humphrey in understanding his stock options?

   A. Ingrid should tell him these are incentive stock options (ISOs) that he must exercise within 2 years.

   B. Ingrid should identify the options as nonqualified stock options (NQSOs) in which he has a basis of $22 per share.

   C. Ingrid should ask Humphrey to bring her all of the documentation regarding the options, including any corporate information given to employees on the stock option plan.

   D. Ingrid should tell Humphrey he will have alternative minimum tax consequences in the year he exercises the options.

2. After analyzing the documentation on the stock options, Ingrid determined Humphrey has been issued incentive stock options (ISOs). What information should Ingrid give to Humphrey about his ISOs?

   A. Ingrid should tell Humphrey that in order to maintain ISO treatment of the stock options, he must not sell any stock he purchases with the options within 1 year from the grant date or 2 years from the date the options were exercised.

   B. Ingrid should assure Humphrey there is no alternative minimum tax (AMT) issue associated with ISOs at exercise.

   C. Ingrid should inform Humphrey the ISOs are not taxable for federal income tax at the grant date but are taxable for alternative minimum tax at the grant date.

   D. Ingrid should tell Humphrey that the ISOs must be exercised before the options expire and that he cannot transfer the ISOs to anyone else during his life.

3. Because Ingrid determined the stock was a good value, she recommended that Humphrey exercise the ISOs immediately. What should Ingrid do next?

   A. Ingrid should continue to monitor the stock for the best time to sell the shares in a qualified disposition.

   B. Because Humphrey has been informed of the rules for a disqualifying disposition of the stock, Ingrid need not monitor his ISOs.

   C. When Humphrey sells the shares, Ingrid should make certain the bargain element is added back as a positive adjustment to calculate alternative minimum taxable income (AMTI) in the year of sale.

   D. Ingrid should tell Humphrey that the gain on the sale of the shares will be ordinary income in a qualified disposition of the shares.

ITEM SET 13

Matching: You may use an answer more than once or not at all.

A.   Charitable remainder annuity trust (CRAT)

B.   Charitable remainder unitrust (CRUT)

C.   Both CRAT and CRUT

D.   Neither CRAT nor CRUT

1.   ____ Charitable deduction; fixed amount of annuity payment regardless of the value of the trust assets

2.   ____ Charitable deduction; revocable

3.   ____ Variable amount of annuity payment depending on annual revaluation of trust assets

4.   ____ Charitable deduction; remainder interest passes to charity

ITEM SET 14

Brett has invested 40% in Portfolio A and 60% in Portfolio B. The correlation coefficient between Portfolio A and Portfolio B is 0.4, and the respective portfolio standard deviations are 15.5% and 13.5%.

1. What is the combined standard deviation of Portfolios A and B?

    A.   11.0%
    B.   12.0%
    C.   14.3%
    D.   14.5%

2. What would be the answer to the above question if Portfolios A and B had no correlation?

    A.   10.2%
    B.   11.0%
    C.   12.0%
    D.   14.3%

ITEM SET 15

Marleen, who turned age 70½ on June 30, 2017 owns 12% of ABC Company. She has amassed $5 million in her qualified plan account as of December 31 of the previous year and $5.5 million as of December 31 of the current year. Distribution periods per IRS tables are as follows:

Age	Distribution period
70	27.4
71	26.5
72	25.6

1. What is Marleen's required minimum distribution for the current tax year?

    A. $0
    B. $182,482
    C. $188,680
    D. $195,313

2. If Marleen receives a distribution of $150,000 during the current year, how much is her income tax penalty when she files her income tax return for the current year?

    A. $0
    B. $3,868
    C. $15,000
    D. $19,340

3. Which of the following statements regarding Marleen is(are) CORRECT?

    1. If Marleen continues to work for ABC Company, she is permitted to defer her required minimum distribution until after she retires.
    2. Marleen can roll over her account balance into an IRA rollover account if she is no longer employed by ABC Company.
    3. Marleen is unable to roll over her account balance into a Roth IRA because she is over age 70½.
    4. If Marleen leaves ABC Company and chooses to roll over her plan balance to an IRA via a direct trustee-to-trustee rollover, she will be subject to 20% withholding on the plan balance.

    A. 1 and 2
    B. 2 only
    C. 2 and 4
    D. 3 and 4

ITEM SET 16

Bob, the CEO of Tango, Inc., was awarded the following stock options from his company:

Stock option	Grant date	Type	Exercise price	Number of shares
A	February 1, 2014	ISO	$20	100
B	July 1, 2015	NQSO	$25	100
C	August 1, 2016	ISO	$30	100
D	May 1, 2017	NQSO	$30	100

During 2017, Bob had the following transactions regarding the above stock options:

Stock option	Date	Action	Number of shares	Market price on action date
A	2/1	Exercised	100	$42
A	2/1	Sold	100	$42
B	2/14	Exercised	100	$45
C	2/14	Exercised	100	$45
D	5/1	Exercised	100	$50
D	6/1	Sold	100	$60

1. Which of the following statements regarding stock option A for 2017 is CORRECT?

    A. Bob has a long-term capital gain of $2,200.
    B. Bob has a short-term capital gain of $2,200.
    C. Bob has W-2 compensation income, subject to payroll taxes, of $4,200.
    D. Bob has W-2 compensation income, not subject to payroll taxes, of $2,200.

2. Which of the following consequences regarding stock option B for 2017 is CORRECT?

    A. No tax consequences to exercising stock option B in 2017 because it was not sold
    B. $2,000 of LTCG
    C. $2,000 of STCG
    D. $2,000 of W-2 compensation income subject to payroll taxes

3. Which of the following statements regarding stock option C for 2017 is CORRECT?

    A. Bob has LTCG of $1,500.
    B. Bob has a positive AMT adjustment of $1,500 but no regular taxable income.
    C. Bob has STCG of $1,500.
    D. Bob has W-2 compensation income, subject to payroll taxes, of $1,500.

4. Which of the following statements regarding stock option D for 2017 is CORRECT?

   A. Bob must recognize $3,000 of STCG and $2,000 LTCG.

   B. Bob must recognize $3,000 of LTCG and no STCG.

   C. Bob must recognize $3,000 of W-2 compensation income, and the $3,000 gain will be subject to payroll taxes.

   D. Bob must recognize $1,000 of STCG and $2,000 of W-2 compensation income, and the income will be subject to payroll taxes.

ITEM SET 17

Kirk, a CFP® professional, is meeting with Jane, who with her husband George, has been a long-time client. George died in May 2017. Jane is executrix of George's estate. Jane has brought documentation on the estate assets as of George's date of death to Kirk and has several questions for Kirk. She would like to become comfortable with the information before she begins discussions with estate lawyers. Kirk already has much of this documentation in his files regarding the couple. She is not seeking legal advice. The following are the assets George owned on his date of death:

Asset	Title	Basis	FMV
Personal residence	JT[1]	$375,000	$725,000
ABC stock	JT[2]	$80,000	$210,000
DEF stock	JT[1]	$160,000	$420,000
Traditional IRA	G[3]	$50,000	$1,000,000
Personal auto 1	JT[1]	$56,000	$40,000
Personal auto 2	JT[1]	$40,000	$26,000
Partner's share of XYZ partnership	G[4]	$1,200,000	$2,750,000
Vacation home	G[5]	$675,000	$460,000
Cash in checking and savings accounts	POD[6]	$2,300,000	$2,300,000

[1] Held as JTWROS with his wife, Jane.
[2] The ABC stock is owned as JTWROS with his brother, Marcus.
[3] Beneficiary is Jane. George's basis consists of nondeductible contributions he has made.
[4] George is a general partner with 3 other partners. There is a cross-purchase buy-sell agreement covering George's share of the partnership. The fair market value of each partner's interest is reflected in the agreement and is used in the calculation of the gross estate.
[5] George inherited the vacation home in 2013 when it had a FMV of $675,000.
[6] The designated beneficiary is Jane.
For all jointly-owned assets, George provided 100% of the purchase price.

In his will, George left his probate assets to Jane. The couple was childless. The will indicates that any disclaimed assets go to his alma mater, Louisiana State University.

1. What should Kirk tell Jane is the value of George's gross estate?

    A. $5,510,000
    B. $7,220,500
    C. $7,325,500
    D. $7,921,000

2. What should Kirk tell Jane is the value of the assets that must be included in George's probate estate?

    A. $3,210,000
    B. $5,510,000
    C. $7,220,500
    D. $7,325,000

3. What is Marcus's basis in the ABC stock after George's death?

    A. $0
    B. $80,000
    C. $105,000
    D. $210,000

4. What is Jane's basis in the DEF stock after George's death?

    A. $80,000
    B. $160,000
    C. $290,000
    D. $420,000

5. Jane has questions regarding the XYZ partnership. She is not sure she wants to be involved in the partnership since George had died. What should Kirk tell Jane regarding George's interest in the partnership?

    A. The partnership will purchase George's partnership interest at his death.
    B. The surviving partners will purchase George's partnership interest at his death.
    C. Jane should look for someone to purchase George's partnership interest.
    D. Because of the cross-purchase agreement, the surviving partners inherit George's partnership interest by operation of law.

ITEM SET 18

Smith invests in a limited partnership that requires an immediate cash outlay of $9,200. At the end of years 1 through 5, he will receive the cash inflows shown below. The partnership will be liquidated at the end of the fifth year, and Smith expects to recover his initial investment upon liquidation. Smith's required rate of return is 9%.

Years	End of year cash inflows
1	$600
2	$2,300
3	$2,200
4	$6,800
5	$300

1. The IRR of this investment is

   A. 17.41%

   B. 19.20%

   C. 24.18%

   D. 28.00%

2. Which of the following statements is(are) CORRECT?

   1. The IRR is the discount rate that equates the present value of an investment's expected costs to the present value of the expected cash inflows.

   2. The net present value of the investment's expected cash inflows is $5,976.77.

   3. For Smith to actually realize this rate of return, the investment's cash inflows will have to be reinvested at the IRR.

   4. Because Smith's required rate of return for this investment is 9%, the investment should be rejected.

   A. 1 only

   B. 1, 2, and 3

   C. 2 and 3

   D. 2 and 4

ITEM SET 19

Bob and Ann are both age 62. Bob is retiring from his employer of 40 years. He is soon to receive a $300,000 lump-sum distribution from a profit-sharing plan maintained by his employer. He has come to you for assistance in establishing an IRA into which the lump-sum distribution will be deposited. He anticipates receiving the check for the lump-sum distribution in the next month and wants to have the IRA established prior to receiving the check. There are no plans to draw an income from the rollover or the Roth IRA at this time, as they can live comfortably on his Social Security retirement income and craft sale income. He plans on claiming his Social Security retirement benefits now that he is age 62. Bob is also covered by an old defined benefit plan that pays QJSA benefit of $1,000 ($1,250 if single life only) with a survivor lifetime benefit of 50% to Ann at Bob's death. The survivor income is important to Ann.

There are 2 old participating paid-up whole life insurance policies on Bob's life. One policy has a $250,000 face amount and a cash value of $50,000. The second policy has a $50,000 face amount and a cash value of $10,000. Bob believes final expenses will not exceed $50,000, so he intends to surrender the larger policy and use the cash value. He mentions he has always taken policy dividends in cash, but in recent years, the full dividend has become taxable and he wonders if the tax treatment of policy dividends has changed.

Bob and Ann are avid craft artisans—they plan on traveling the Midwest selling handmade crafts at festivals and craft shows. They are generally able to generate a net income of $2,000 per month from craft sales.

In answering the following questions, also consider the following information.

- Bob believes his life expectancy to be 20–25 years.
- The couple files their income tax returns as married filing jointly.
- There is $60,000 in a Roth IRA established 10 years ago and funded with regular contributions.
- Social Security at FRA (age 66) = $1,600.
- The retirement income need is approximately $4,000 per month.
- The $300,000 lump-sum distribution from the profit-sharing plan consists 100% of employer contributions and earnings attributable to employer contributions.
- Bob and Ann are comfortable assuming a 5% annual return for any retirement calculations.

1. Under Bob's plan, which of the following statements regarding his Social Security retirement benefits in his first year of retirement is CORRECT?

   A. In his first year of retirement, instead of receiving the FRA amount, Bob's Social Security retirement benefits will be reduced by $8,340.

   B. In his first year of retirement, instead of receiving the FRA amount, Bob's Social Security retirement benefits will be reduced by $4,800.

   C. In his first year of retirement, instead of receiving the FRA amount, Bob's Social Security retirement benefits will be reduced by $3,540.

   D. In his first year of retirement, instead of receiving the FRA amount, Bob's Social Security retirement benefits will be reduced by $5,760.

2. Under Bob's plan as described, which of the following statements regarding the income tax aspects for the first year of Bob's retirement is CORRECT?

   A. No more than 50% of Bob's Social Security retirement benefits will be subject to taxation in his first year of retirement because his earned income plus one half of his Social Security benefit falls between the threshold of $32,000 to $44,000 for MFJ taxpayers.

   B. None of Bob's Social Security retirement benefits will be subject to income tax because his earned income is less than $32,000.

   C. 100% of Bob's Social Security retirement benefits will be subject to taxation in his first year of retirement because his earned income in retirement is greater than his Social Security retirement benefit.

   D. Up to 85% of Bob's Social Security retirement benefits may be subject to taxation in his first year of retirement.

3. Based on Bob's plan as described, which of the following statements is(are) accurate observations a planner could make in discussing the plan with Bob?

   1. Bob and Ann could consider waving the QJSA.

   2. Bob should execute a direct transfer of his profit-sharing lump-sum distribution to avoid current taxes on $60,000.

   3. A surrender of the $250,000 whole life policy will result in $50,000 taxable income.

   4. Bob should consider waiting until his FRA (age 66) to claim his Social Security retirement benefits.

   A. 2 only

   B. 3 and 4

   C. 4 only

   D. 1, 2, 3, and 4

ITEM SET 20

Clark, a CFP® professional, is meeting with his clients, Vivien and Lawrence. The couple are both executives with Golden Metro Corporation and have each been granted enough nonqualified stock options (NQSOs) to purchase 10,000 shares of the company stock. The options have an exercise price of $170.00 per share and will not be vested if an identified sales goal is not met or exceeded by the end of the current fiscal year. The market price per share of Golden Metro was $170.00 per share on the date of grant. The couple would like to know what their options are regarding the NQSOs. Vivien has stated she wishes to donate some of her options to a charity she favors and gift the rest to family members. Lawrence states that he will probably exercise his options, but only after he understands all of the tax ramifications for a sale as well as gifting Vivien's options.

1. What should Clark tell the couple regarding Lawrence's concerns of the tax implications on the proposed disposition of the NQSOs?

   1. NQSOs cannot be transferred to another during Vivien's lifetime, but she can bequeath them to family members and charities through her will.
   2. Both Lawrence and Vivien will recognize ordinary income on the value of the NQSOs on the date of grant.
   3. The difference between the exercise price and the fair market value of the stock when the options are exercised is taxed as W-2 compensation income, subject to payroll taxes, in the year of exercise.
   4. The bargain element will be reported as W-2 compensation income, subject to payroll taxes, upon the exercise of the NQSOs.

   A. 1 only
   B. 1 and 2
   C. 2 and 3
   D. 3 and 4

2. Vivien is very interested in gifting her NQSOs. She wants to know how the gift will impact her taxes if she gives some or all of her NQSOs to a charity. What should Clark tell her?

   A. There is no completed gift for gift tax purposes until the charity exercises the stock options.
   B. If Vivien dies within 3 years after the charity exercised the options, the value the options would have had on her date of death will be included in her gross estate.
   C. Vivien will not have to recognize any compensation income when the charity exercises the options.
   D. If the charity exercises the NQSOs after her death, the estate is not entitled to a charitable deduction because the NQSOs were never included in Vivien's income during life.

3. Six months later, Clark is in another meeting with Vivien and Lawrence. Clark has analyzed the couple's current financial position before the meeting with a stated goal of possibly exercising Lawrence's NQSOs. The current stock price is $180.00 per share. Vivien's and Lawrence's cash liquidity is more than ample to fund the stock exercise. What should Clark tell Vivien and Lawrence regarding the effects of the option exercise on their financial position?

   A. Their assets on their Statement of Financial Position will decrease by $1.7 million dollars at the exercise date.

   B. Lawrence will have $100,000 of compensation income that is subject to payroll taxes on his W-2 in the year of exercise.

   C. The bargain element of the exercise is a positive adjustment for the alternative minimum taxable income (AMTI) calculation.

   D. Lawrence's basis in the shares will be different for income tax purposes than for alternative minimum tax purposes.

ITEM SET 21

Matching: You may use an answer more than once or not at all.

A. Subrogation
B. Assumption of risk
C. Collateral source rule
D. Vicarious liability

1. _____ Scott owns a delivery business. He is held liable for damages caused by one of his employees who was involved in an automobile accident while on company business.

2. _____ John is injured and has health insurance that pays for his injuries, but he can still sue Jack, the negligent party who caused his injuries.

3. _____ Mary was hit in the head and injured by a foul ball at a baseball game.

4. _____ A contractual provision designed to prevent the insured from profiting from an insured loss.

ITEM SET 22

Matching: You may use an answer more than once or not at all.

A. FIFO tax treatment
B. LIFO tax treatment
C. Specific identification
D. Either FIFO or specific identification
E. None of these

1. _____ Loan from a modified endowment contract (MEC)
2. _____ Nonqualified distribution from a Roth IRA
3. _____ Sale of 300 shares of ABC stock
4. _____ Distribution from a nondeductible traditional IRA

ITEM SET 23

Aaron, age 62, is preparing to retire. He has 3 adult children who are named as equal beneficiaries of his whole life insurance policy. He has asked you to help him determine the implications of transferring, surrendering, or borrowing from this contract. The contract's latest values are posted below. Aaron has also received $10,000 in dividends from the policy.

Description	Amount
Death benefit of policy	$1 million
Cash value of policy	$90,000
Outstanding loan on policy	$35,000
Net premiums paid	$58,000

1. If Aaron surrenders the policy, how much cash will he receive from the insurance company?

   A. $32,000
   B. $35,000
   C. $58,000
   D. $55,000

2. How much will be included in Aaron's taxable income if he surrenders his policy?

   A. $42,000
   B. $35,000
   C. $58,000
   D. $55,000

ITEM SET 24

Garrick, a CFP® professional, is meeting with a married couple, Marshall and Annette. Both are age 58. Marshall has been an employee of ABC Company for 1 year. Marshall and Annette have a 30-year-old son, Jake. Garrick's review of the couple's statement of financial position reveals that Marshall owns the following retirement plans:

Description	Current value	Beneficiary
Section 401(k) plan from ABC Company (Marshall's current employer)	$1,000,000	Annette
Section 401(k) plan from Johnson Industries (Marshall's former employer—separated from service 10 years ago)	$90,000	Annette
Roth IRA (established several years ago with a $2,000 initial contribution; no additional contributions made)	$10,000	Annette
Traditional IRA (established several years ago with $10,000 of after-tax contributions)	$58,000	Jake

1. Marshall plans on retiring in March of this year, and he and Annette would like to take a vacation to the Bahamas in November. He would like to pay for the $10,000 of travel and hotel costs of the vacation by taking a distribution from one of his retirement plans. Which of the following plans would allow Marshall to take a penalty-free withdrawal to fund his vacation (ignoring mandatory tax withholding)?

    A. Section 401(k) plan from ABC Company
    B. Section 401(k) plan from Johnson Industries
    C. Roth IRA
    D. Traditional IRA

2. Which statement regarding the beneficiary designations of Marshall's retirement plans is NOT correct?

    A. Marshall can change the beneficiary designation of his Roth IRA without obtaining prior consent from Annette.
    B. If Marshall changes the beneficiary designation of his traditional IRA to his grandson, his minimum required distributions at age 70½ will not be affected.
    C. Marshall must have Annette's consent to change the beneficiary of his Johnson Industries Section 401(k) plan.
    D. Marshall can change the beneficiary designation of his ABC Company Section 401(k) plan to Jake without obtaining prior consent from Annette.

ITEM SET 25

Use the following client information to answer the questions below.

Description	Amount
Bank loan balance	$30,000
Alimony payment	$10,000
Dividend income	$2,000
Wages (W-2)	$60,000
Federal income taxes owed (<3 years old)	$18,000
Government student loans (<5 years old)	$22,000
Monthly mortgage payments	$2,000
Municipal bonds	$20,000
Tax-exempt interest from municipal bonds	$1,000
Auto loan balance	$12,000

1. Which of the following items would NOT be included in the client's statement of cash flows?

   A. Mortgage payments
   B. Alimony payment
   C. Tax-exempt interest
   D. Auto loan balance

2. If the client filed for bankruptcy under Chapter 7, how much can be discharged?

   A. $42,000
   B. $44,000
   C. $52,000
   D. $60,000

3. Assume the client borrowed money on margin to purchase the municipal bonds. The client paid $1,500 of margin interest expense during the current year. How much of the margin interest expense is deductible for federal income tax purposes?

   A. $0
   B. $1,000
   C. $1,500
   D. $2,000

ITEM SET 26

On August 30, the SmoothCo December $55 call option has a premium of $6.50. The stock's market price is currently $58 per share. The stock is publicly traded and has a current P/E ratio of 15.

1. What is the intrinsic value of the call option?

    A. $0.00
    B. $2.00
    C. $3.00
    D. $3.50

2. What is the time value of the call option?

    A. $0.00
    B. $2.00
    C. $3.00
    D. $3.50

3. A financial analyst used the Black-Scholes option valuation model to value the call option. Which of the following factors will cause the value of the option to increase?

    A. A decrease in the volatility of the stock
    B. A decrease in the price of the stock
    C. A decrease in market interest rates
    D. A decrease in the exercise price of the option

ITEM SET 27

Matching: You may use an answer more than once or not at all.

A. Capital asset
B. Ordinary asset
C. Section 1231 asset
D. None of the above

1. _____ Copyright held by the person who applied for and received it
2. _____ Welding machinery used by Roche Welding
3. _____ Personal automobile
4. _____ Electric razors sold and manufactured by the Razor Company

ITEM SET 28

Mary has become very wealthy as a result of her business dealings. In 2017, she established an irrevocable trust with Crummey provisions for her 33-year-old daughter, Rianna. The trust document provides that the income from the trust will be paid to Rianna each year, and the remainder will pass to Mary's granddaughter, Erin, at Rianna's death. In 2017, Mary contributed $100,000 of non-dividend-paying stock to the trust.

1. If Rianna exercises her Crummey right, how much can she withdraw from the trust during 2017?

   A. $14,000
   B. $5,000
   C. $100,000
   D. 5% of the trust value

2. If no other property is gifted to the trust, how much can Rianna withdraw in 2018?

   A. $0
   B. $5,000
   C. $100,000
   D. 5% of the trust value

3. If Mary dies 2 years after making the gift, can Rianna change the remainder beneficiary of the trust to her husband Jack, instead of Mary's granddaughter, Erin?

   A. No, the trust terms name the beneficiary and Rianna has no control over the remainder beneficiary of the trust.
   B. As the income beneficiary of the trust, Rianna can change the remainder beneficiary after Mary's death.
   C. The Crummey provision gives Rianna the right to change the remainder beneficiary within 30 days of Mary's death.
   D. Rianna can change the beneficiary to Jack if Erin consents.

ITEM SET 29

Today is March 2, 2017. Denise, a CFP® professional, is meeting with her client, Roger. In a previous meeting, Roger told Denise he needs $22,000 in cash to pay for a new car. Roger's objective is to minimize the income tax that will result from the sale of one of the assets listed below to finance the car purchase. Denise has analyzed Roger's financial status, including the listed assets. Roger is age 35 and single. He is taxed in the 25% marginal income tax bracket. He has the following assets in his investment portfolio:

Description	Holding period	Fair market value	Basis
Rare stamp collection	18 months	$25,000	$10,000
Section 1202 qualified small business stock	10 years	$25,000	$7,000
ABC common stock	11 months	$25,000	$13,000
Investment land	3 years	$25,000	$3,000

1. Which of the assets listed above should Denise recommend that Roger sell to both raise the needed cash but also minimize the income tax on the sale?

   A. Rare stamp collection
   B. Section 1202 qualified small business stock
   C. Common stock
   D. Investment land

2. If Roger decided to donate the rare stamp collection to the Boy Scouts, which of the following statements made by Denise is CORRECT (ignore AGI limits)?

   A. He will receive a charitable deduction of $10,000 because the stamp collection is considered a collectible.
   B. He will receive a charitable deduction of $25,000 because the stamp collection is capital gain property.
   C. He will receive a charitable deduction of $10,000 because the property is use unrelated.
   D. He will receive a charitable deduction of $25,000 because the stamp was held long term.

3. Denise has further comments on Roger's investments. Which of the following statements regarding Roger's investments is CORRECT?

   A. The Section 1202 qualified small business stock receives favorable income tax treatment, so the stock will not receive a step-up in basis at the owner's death.
   B. A portion of the excluded gain on the sale of Roger's Section 1202 qualified small business stock is a tax preference item for purposes of alternative minimum tax.
   C. If Roger transfers his rare stamps to his traditional IRA, he could sell the stamps and pay no income tax until amounts are withdrawn from the IRA.
   D. If Roger exchanges his investment land for his friend's principal residence, which he plans on using for his own personal use, Roger will be eligible for like-kind exchange treatment.

ITEM SET 30

Cathy is 55 years old and in the distribution/gifting phase of her life. She wants to gift some of her assets and is seeking the professional advice of Cliff, a CFP® professional, to determine to which donees she should gift certain assets. The assets she is currently considering gifting have all been held for more than one year and are as follows:

Asset	Type	Fair market value	Yield	Adjusted tax basis	Expected future appreciation
A	Stock	$25,000	1%	$5,000	2%
B	Bond	$25,000	8%	$25,000	0%
C	Stock	$25,000	2%	$20,000	6%
D	Stock	$25,000	4%	$32,500	2%
E	Stock	$25,000	0%	$21,000	12%

1. Cathy wants to assist her mother, who is in need of current income, by gifting her one of the listed assets. Which of these assets should Cliff recommend as the most appropriate choice?

    A. Stock A
    B. Bond B
    C. Stock C
    D. Stock E

2. Cathy's son is 32 years old and is established in his career as a public television program director. Cathy wants to gift either Stock A or Stock E to her son because she is concerned with the tax consequences of asset appreciation. Which of the following of Cliff's recommendations would be best for Cathy?

    1. Stock A should be gifted to Cathy's son so she can avoid the tax consequences associated with the stock's large capital appreciation.
    2. Considering the expected future appreciation for Stock E, Cathy should gift this stock to her son.
    3. Because Stock E currently has a 0% yield, appreciation of this stock would not be a concern for Cathy.

    A. 1 only
    B. 2 only
    C. 3 only
    D. None of these

3. Cathy wants to gift one of her assets to her favorite public charity. Ignoring the choices made in the previous questions, which of the following assets should Cliff recommend she gift to this charity?

    A. Stock A
    B. Bond B
    C. Stock D
    D. Stock E

4. If Cathy is planning on selling one of the assets, which asset should Cliff recommend she sell? Assume her objective is based on income tax benefits and she is also making gifts to her mother, son, friend, and charity.

   A. Stock A
   B. Bond B
   C. Stock C
   D. Stock D

ITEM SET 31

Your client made the following stock purchases on January 1 of the current year:

Stock	Number of shares purchased on January 1 of current year	Original purchase price per share	Ending price on 12/31 of current year	Dividends paid per share on 12/31 of current year
ABC	200	$16	$8	None
XYZ	200	$18	$15	$.75
THE	200	$14	$16	$1.00

On July 1 of the current year, the XYZ stock split 2 for 1. On December 31, XYZ stock declared earnings per share of $1.50. Use this information to answer the following questions.

1. What would be the total value of the stocks on the client's statement of financial position on December 31, assuming the client did not sell any of the stock this year?

   A. $6,300
   B. $7,800
   C. $9,600
   D. $10,800

2. What is the net cash flow from the stock for the current year, assuming the client did not sell any of the stock this year?

   A. $9,100 net cash inflow
   B. $9,100 net cash outflow
   C. $9,600 net cash inflow
   D. $9,600 net cash outflow

3. What is the P/E ratio of XYZ stock on December 31 of the current year?

   A. 1
   B. 2
   C. 5
   D. 10

ITEM SET 32

Tom, age 48, is single and is an active participant in his employer's Section 401(k) plan. He has the following income and loss items for the current year:

- $85,000 salary as an investment adviser from Bank of Texas Capital Management
- $800 of preferred stock dividends from XYZ company preferred stock
- $300 of interest income from a corporate B rated bond
- $1,000 of interest income from a qualified private activity bond issued and acquired by Tom in 2007
- $3,000 loss from an 8% limited partnership interest in Realty Capital Partners, a limited partnership
- $5,000 loss from a 25% interest in ABC Partnership (he does not materially participate in the partnership)
- $2,000 loss from an interest in an S corporation in which he materially participates
- Mortgage interest expense of $8,000
- Margin interest expense of $4,000

Use the above information to answer the following questions.

1. What is Tom's adjusted gross income (AGI)?

   A. $64,000
   B. $64,100
   C. $78,100
   D. $84,100

2. Assuming Tom itemizes his deductions this year, how much of his margin interest expense will be deductible if he wants to make the maximum possible deduction?

   A. $0
   B. $300
   C. $1,100
   D. $2,100

3. Tom consults a CFP® professional for advice concerning his retirement planning options. Which of the following recommendations is(are) suitable for Tom's situation?

    1. Tom should contribute to a Roth IRA for the current year.
    2. Tom should contribute to a deductible traditional IRA this year.
    3. Tom should contribute to a nondeductible traditional IRA this year.
    4. Tom should convert his existing traditional IRA to a Roth IRA this year.

    A. 1, 3, and 4
    B. 1 and 4
    C. 2 and 3
    D. 2, 3, and 4

4. What is Tom's passive loss carryforward to next year?

    A. $0
    B. $3,000
    C. $5,000
    D. $8,000

MINI-CASE 1

Scott, a successful young professional, has been married to Nicole for 3 years. He and Nicole are your clients and they meet with you each year to discuss specific goals. During your meeting with Scott today, he informs you that he and Nicole had their first child, Julia, last week and, because of their new addition to their family, their financial goals have changed. Last month, Scott and Nicole had been looking for a new home with the intention of purchasing one for $175,000 with a 20% down payment and financing the balance over 30 years at 8%. The couple have had to put their house hunting on hold as Nicole delivered Julia last week earlier than expected. Known for being financially prudent, Scott would like to start saving for Julia's education today so that she can start college at age 18 without the financial burdens that Scott and Nicole had when they went to school. Scott would like to make the first payment for Julia's education today and assume that she will start college 18 years from today.

Julia will attend college for 4 years, and the annual payment will be due at the beginning of the school year. The current cost of the state college education is $25,000 per year. The cost of a college education is expected to increase at an average rate of 7% per year during the projection period and the general rate of inflation will be 4%. Julia has the option of investing in the following funds: (1) a stock mutual fund expected to earn 12% during the projection period and (2) a bond fund expected to earn 8.5% during the projection period.

1. What is the sum of the projected withdrawals for Julia's college education? (Round to the nearest dollar.)

    A. $350,623
    B. $375,168
    C. $401,429
    D. $206,792

2. Which of the following is the annual payment that will be required to fund the cost of college education assuming Scott and Nicole invest in the bond fund and make deposits on every birthday, exclusive of Julia's 18th birthday? (Round to the nearest dollar.)

    A. $9,373
    B. $7,759
    C. $8,419
    D. $8,793

3. If Scott and Nicole make a contribution to a qualified tuition plan, which of the following statements is CORRECT?

    A.   The plan is not subject to market risk.
    B.   Gifts to the qualified tuition plan are subject to the gift tax rules.
    C.   A portion of the interest and dividends that the plan earns will be taxed at the parents' highest marginal tax rate.
    D.   Making similar periodic contributions to the plan is considered an active investment strategy.

4. If Scott and Nicole purchase a home at the terms Scott has communicated to you, what would be their monthly payments?

    A. $1,020.47
    B. $1,027.27
    C. $1,275.58
    D. $1,284.09

5. Assume Scott and Nicole purchase the house on January 1 of the current year. If payments are due the first of each month, how much qualified residence interest may they deduct on their IRS Form 1040 this year if they itemize deductions?

    A. $10,266.67
    B. $10,231.52
    C. $11,157.74
    D. $11,299.97

6. If Scott and Nicole financed the house over 15 years instead of 30, how much interest would they save over the life of the loan, assuming the same interest rate?

    A. $0
    B. $55,915.20
    C. $89,175.60
    D. $128,993.40

7. Based on your discussion with Scott, what is the best step to take next?

    A. Determine the best investment vehicle for the college funding plan
    B. Advise Scott that he and Nicole should purchase their home before saving for Julia's college expenses
    C. Arrange to speak with Nicole to discuss the couple's goals
    D. Suggest that Scott and Nicole use any equity in their home at the time Julia starts college to pay for her college expenses

MINI-CASE 2

Joe, age 50, Kim, age 55, and Rick, age 58, founded JKR, Inc., 15 years ago. Each invested $100,000 to start the company, and they are all officers in the corporation. Ten years ago, the corporation was valued at $3 million, at which time Joe, Kim, and Rick executed a cross-purchase buy-sell agreement. In the event of death of a shareholder, each shareholder has agreed to purchase one-half of the deceased shareholder's interest in the company, at a price based on the most recent professional valuation of the business. The agreement calls for a professional valuation every 5 years.

Each shareholder applied for, owns, and pays the premium for a $500,000 variable universal life insurance policy insuring the lives of each of the other 2 shareholders. Each of the policies was issued with the election of a level death benefit, and each policyowner has elected to allocate the policies' cash value in growth stock subaccounts. The owners pay a level premium each year. The most recent professional valuation of the corporation is $6 million.

Joe and Kim are personal financial planning clients of Sue, a CFP® professional. Sue was the insurance broker in establishing the insurance contracts for the buy-sell agreement.

Rick is starting to plan for retirement and has approached Sue to seek financial planning advice. In the initial meeting with Sue, Rick states he invested an additional $50,000 lump sum into the policy he owns on Joe's life in the second year of the policy and the policy was deemed a modified endowment contract (MEC). Rick has paid a total of $100,000 in premiums into the policy. Currently, the policy has a cash surrender value of $125,000, and Rick is interested in withdrawing the extra $50,000 he paid into the policy.

1. If each shareholder's sole heir is an adult child, in the event of death of a shareholder, what is the income tax treatment to the heir if the heir sells the decedent's business interest to the surviving shareholders for its fair market value on the date of death?

    A. The heir will pay income taxes on a $1.9 million long-term capital gain.
    B. The heir will pay income taxes on a $900,000 long-term capital gain.
    C. The heir will not incur any income taxes on the sale.
    D. The heir will pay income taxes on a $1.9 million short-term capital gain.

2. If Rick takes a policy loan of $50,000 from his policy covering Joe this year, how much income tax, if any, will Rick pay on the distribution? Assume Rick's marginal tax bracket is 28%.

    A. $14,000
    B. $7,000
    C. $0
    D. $9,500

3. Rick sends Sue an email asking the current cash surrender value of the life insurance policies held by Joe and Kim insuring Rick's life and also asks if they have any outstanding loans on the policies. How should Sue respond?

   A. Because Rick is the insured on these policies, Sue should secure the requested information and send it to Rick.

   B. Sue should inform Rick she may not disclose the requested information without express consent from Joe and Kim.

   C. Sue should inform Rick the values would be approximately the same as the policies he owns because they were issued at the same time.

   D. Sue should provide the information to Rick but copy Joe and Kim on the correspondence so they will be aware of the request.

4. If a shareholder dies today and the buy-sell agreement is carried out at the agreed-upon terms, what is the basis in JKR, Inc., of each surviving shareholder?

   A. $1.1 million

   B. $3 million

   C. $600,000

   D. $100,000

5. If after the death of a shareholder the 2 surviving shareholders decide to change the buy-sell agreement to an entity purchase agreement and sell the life insurance policies they own on one another to JKR, Inc., which of the following is(are) CORRECT regarding the income tax treatment of the transfer?

   1. Ultimately, at the subsequent death of the insured, the death proceeds received by JKR., Inc., will be subject to regular income tax to the extent the proceeds exceed the amount paid in the transfer plus premiums paid after the transfer.

   2. Any amount received by the shareholder in the transfer in excess of the shareholder's basis in the contract is taxable.

   3. Ultimately, at the subsequent death of the insured, the death proceeds received by JKR., Inc., will not be subject to regular income tax.

   4. After the transfer, JKR, Inc., is allowed a tax deduction for premiums paid as a business expense.

   A. 1 and 2

   B. 1 and 4

   C. 2 and 3

   D. 3 and 4

6. Which of the following statements regarding the life insurance policies owned by the shareholders is(are) CORRECT?

1. The subaccounts into which each policy's cash value has been allocated may generate market-based returns but offer the security of a minimum guaranteed return.

2. As long as the policyowners continue to pay a level premium, the death benefit of the policies is guaranteed at the issued face amount.

3. The death benefit Rick will receive in the event of Joe's death will be fully taxable.

4. A total of 6 policies have been issued to insure the lives of the shareholders.

A. 1 and 2

B. 3 and 4

C. 4 only

D. 1, 2, 3, and 4

MINI-CASE 3

Walter is single and age 65. He has one child, Shelby, from a previous marriage. Walter is planning to retire and wants to transfer his 100% ownership interest in Walco, his construction company, to his daughter, Shelby. Shelby is age 32 and works full time as the vice president of Walco. The current fair market value of Walco is $1 million. Walter's adjusted basis in the property is $300,000. Walter is in excellent health and has a family history of long life. His mortality table life expectancy is 17 years. Any installment sale to Shelby would be for 12 years. An appropriate market interest rate is 9%. Assume interest rates remain stable.

Walter is also in need of advice regarding the tax treatment of various stock transactions he was involved in during 2017:

1. Sold 1,000 shares of Graham, Inc., for $15,000 on June 1, 2017. The stock was originally purchased on January 1, 2017, for $12,000.

2. Purchased 500 shares of Graham, Inc., on June 15, 2017, for $16 per share.

3. Sold 200 shares of Laconde Corp. stock (Section 1244 stock) for $35,000 on September 1, 2017. The stock was originally purchased for $125,000 on December 15, 2010.

4. Sold 500 shares of Ferris, Inc., on June 1, 2017, for $12,000. The stock was inherited from his uncle, who died on March 1, 2017. His uncle's basis was $2,000, and the fair market value on the uncle's date of death was $11,000.

5. Shares of Marsh, Inc., became worthless on September 1, 2017. He originally purchased the stock on October 1, 2016, for $5,000.

6. On July 15, 2017, Walter sold 200 shares of Energy Enterprises for $3,000. Walter had received the stock on December 31, 2016, in exchange for 300 shares of Princeton Power, Inc., stock (Princeton Power, Inc., FMV at date of exchange was $3,700). Walter originally purchased Princeton Power, Inc., on June 15, 2015, for $3,000.

1. Walter has decided to use a traditional installment sale to transfer the property to Shelby. The terms of the sale are 20% down on July 31 of the current year, and the balance is to be paid in equal monthly installments beginning August 31 of the current year, over a period of 12 years at 9% interest. How much cash does Walter expect to receive in the current year?

    A. $236,417
    B. $245,521
    C. $254,625
    D. $309,251

2. Including the amount received from the down payment and the periodic payments, how much ordinary income does Walter have in the current year? (Assume the same installment sale terms listed in question 1.)

    A. $14,195
    B. $17,743
    C. $21,292
    D. $29,765

3. If Walter dies after receiving 48 installment note payments, what will be the remaining unpaid principal balance on the note? (Assume the same installment sale terms listed in question 1.)

    A. $0
    B. $365,852
    C. $621,442
    D. $636,845

4. What amount of the down payment under the installment note represents capital gain to Walter? (Assume the same installment sale terms listed in question 1.)

    A. $0
    B. $60,000
    C. $140,000
    D. $200,000

5. What is the capital gain on the sale of Graham, Inc.?

    A. $3,000 LTCG
    B. $3,000 STCG
    C. $4,500 LTCG
    D. $2,500 STCG

6. Regarding all of the stock sales, which of the following statements is(are) NOT correct?

    1. Walter's maximum deductible capital loss for the current year is $3,000.
    2. How Walter's uncle acquired Ferris stock is irrelevant for the purpose of determining Walter's capital gain/loss from sale of the stock.
    3. The sale of Graham, Inc., (Transaction #1) falls under the wash sale rules.
    4. Walter's basis in Energy Enterprises stock was $3,700.

    A. 1 and 4
    B. 2 only
    C. 2 and 3
    D. 2, 3, and 4

7. What are Walter's combined long-term capital gains/losses for the current year (before netting with short-term gains/losses)? (Assume the same installment sale terms listed in question 1 for the sale of Walco.)

    A. $4,071 LTCL
    B. $38,071 LTCL
    C. $51,029 LTCG
    D. $107,029 LTCG

8. What is Walter's short-term capital gain/loss for the current year (before netting with long-term gains/losses)?

    A. No short-term gains or losses

    B. $2,800 STCL

    C. $2,300 STCG

    D. $3,000 STCG

MINI-CASE 4

Charles and Marie are planning to retire on January 1 of next year. They share the same birthdate and will attain age 65 and claim Social Security retirement benefits on that date. They have approached Todd, a CFP® professional, for financial planning advice related to their pending retirement.

Both will enroll in Medicare upon attaining age 65. Until then, they are covered under a high-deductible health plan with a $3,000 per year deductible. The couple's Social Security full retirement age (FRA) is 66.

Charles and Marie are considering the purchase of tax-qualified partnership long-term care (LTC) insurance. Charles's father and Marie's mother each developed Alzheimer's disease after age 70. Charles and Marie are concerned they may one day develop Alzheimer's disease as well. They have been researching various options available for long-term care (LTC) insurance and believe they would like to purchase a policy with the following benefit structure, although they are not certain they can afford the premiums:

> Initial maximum daily benefit of $250; 1,095-day benefit period; pool of money structure ($273,750); 30-day elimination period

Charles and Marie have a health savings account (HSA) with a balance in excess of $100,000. Both have been healthy the past 10 years since establishing the HSA and have made only small distributions from the HSA. They have always made the maximum contributions to the HSA, but have yet to make a contribution for the current tax year.

There are 2 paid-up whole life insurance policies insuring Charles. One policy has a death benefit of $250,000 with a cash surrender value of $75,000. The second policy has a face amount of $100,000 with a cash surrender value of $30,000. There is also a universal life policy insuring Marie with a death benefit of $100,000 and a cash surrender value of $20,000. Charles and Marie believe life insurance in the amount of $50,000 each will suffice to pay for final expenses.

Marie has a traditional IRA with an account balance of $50,000. Charles has a tax-deferred annuity with an account balance of $30,000.

1. Which of the following should Todd do next in assisting Charles and Marie?

A. Todd should meet with Charles and Marie to submit an application for long-term care (LTC) insurance before January 1.

B. Todd should gather information to determine Charles and Marie's retirement income needs, income sources, and net cash surplus or deficit and perform a retirement needs analysis.

C. Todd should recommend a 90-day elimination period for the long-term care (LTC) insurance to reduce the premium.

D. Todd should recommend Charles surrender his $250,000 life insurance policy and apply the cash surrender value of $75,000 to their retirement income needs.

2. Which of the following statements regarding either Charles and Marie's Social Security retirement benefits or Medicare benefits is CORRECT?

   A. Because Charles and Marie will claim Social Security retirement benefits prior to attaining age 66, their benefit will be reduced by 30%.

   B. Because Charles has accumulated 40 Social Security credits, his Medicare Part A and Part B coverage will not require payment of a premium.

   C. Charles and Marie should consider delaying enrollment in Medicare until attaining age 66, so there will be no reduction in benefits for enrolling prior to full retirement age (FRA).

   D. If Marie and Charles claim reduced Social Security retirement benefits at age 65, the benefit will not be increased upon attaining full retirement age (FRA).

3. Which of the following statements regarding either long-term care insurance (LTC) insurance or a health savings account (HSA) is(are) CORRECT?

   1. Regarding long-term care insurance, Todd should advise Charles and Marie they will have to secure a 90-day elimination period, rather than a 30-day elimination period because benefits may not be paid from a tax-qualified partnership long-term care insurance policy prior to 90 days.

   2. Distributions may be taken tax free from a health savings account to pay for long-term care services during the elimination period of a long-term care insurance policy.

   3. Distributions may be taken tax free from a health savings account to pay premiums on a qualified long-term care insurance policy.

   4. Charles could elect to make a tax-free exchange of a life insurance policy for a qualified long-term care insurance policy.

   A. 1, 2, and 3

   B. 2 and 3

   C. 2, 3, and 4

   D. 1, 2, 3, and 4

4. Which of the following statements regarding the tax-qualified partnership long-term care insurance Charles and Marie are considering is(are) CORRECT?

   1. Tax-qualified long-term care insurance premiums (up to a specified limit) may be included as a qualified medical expense in calculating one's itemized deduction for medical expenses on Schedule A of the tax return.

   2. When an insured files a claim for long-term care insurance benefits due to cognitive impairment, a physician must certify the condition is expected to last at least 90 days.

   3. In the event an insured exhausts the benefits of a tax-qualified partnership long-term insurance policy, prior to qualifying for Medicaid long-term care benefits, the insured must spend-down assets to approximately $2,000.

   4. Charles could execute a tax-free exchange of her tax-deferred annuity for a tax-qualified long-term care insurance policy.

   A. 1 and 2

   B. 1 and 4

   C. 3 and 4

   D. 1, 2, 3, and 4

Item Set and
Mini-Case Solutions

ANSWER SUMMARY

Item Set 1	Item Set 2	Item Set 3	Item Set 4	Item Set 5
1. C	1. C	1. D	1. A	1. B
2. D	2. B	2. A	2. D	2. C
3. A	3. B	3. A	3. A	3. B
	4. B	4. B		4. C
	5. A	5. D		5. A
		6. D		

Item Set 6	Item Set 7	Item Set 8	Item Set 9	Item Set 10
1. B	1. A	1. C	1. B	1. A
2. A	2. B	2. A	2. B	2. B
3. B	3. A	3. C		3. C
4. A	4. D			

Item Set 11	Item Set 12	Item Set 13	Item Set 14	Item Set 15
1. B	1. C	1. A	1. B	1. C
2. B	2. D	2. D	2. A	2. A
	3. A	3. B		3. B
		4. C		

Item Set 16	Item Set 17	Item Set 18	Item Set 19	Item Set 20
1. D	1. C	1. C	1. A	1. D
2. D	2. A	2. B	2. D	2. B
3. B	3. D		3. D	3. B
4. D	4. C			
	5. B			

Item Set 21	Item Set 22	Item Set 23	Item Set 24	Item Set 25
1. D	1. B	1. D	1. A	1. D
2. C	2. A	2. A	2. D	2. A
3. B	3. D			3. A
4. A	4. E			

Item Set 26	Item Set 27	Item Set 28	Item Set 29	Item Set 30
1. C	1. B	1. A	1. B	1. B
2. D	2. C	2. A	2. C	2. B
3. D	3. A	3. A	3. B	3. A
	4. B			4. D

Item Set 31	Item Set 32	Mini-Case 1	Mini-Case 2	Mini-Case 3
1. D	1. D	1. B	1. C	1. B
2. B	2. C	2. B	2. D	2. D
3. D	3. A	3. B	3. B	3. C
	4. D	4. B	4. A	4. C
		5. B	5. C	5. B
		6. D	6. C	6. C
		7. C		7. D
				8. C

Mini-Case 4				
1. B				
2. D				
3. C				
4. B				

ITEM SET 1 SOLUTIONS

Insurance—Homeowners Insurance

1. **C**

80% of replacement cost is the coinsurance requirement for partial losses.

80% of $200,000 = $160,000. Because they only have $150,000 of coverage, they are subject to coinsurance.

$$\frac{\$150,000}{\$160,000} = 93.75\% \text{ (insurer's portion)}$$

Loss	$80,000	($200,000 – $120,000)
Insurer %	0.9375	
	$75,000	Rounded
Deductible	(500)	
	$74,500	Will be paid by the insurance company

Insurance—Automobile Insurance

2. **D**

	Auto #1	Auto #2	Total
Loss	$3,500	$2,000	$5,500
Less comprehensive deductible	(250)	(500)	(750)
Loss payable by insurance company	$3,250	$1,500	$4,750

Al and Irma will pay a total of $750 for the 2 deductibles.
Note: This loss is indemnified under comprehensive coverage.

Tax—Itemized Deductions

3. **A**

Total loss	$110,500	(80,000 + 25,000 + 3,500 + 2,000)
Less insurance proceeds	(101,500)	(74,500 + 25,000 + 1,000 + 1,000)
Unreimbursed loss	$9,000	
Less 10% AGI floor	(6,000)	(60,000 × 10%)
Less $100	(100)	(casualty loss reduction = $100 per occurrence)
Deductible loss	$2,900	

ITEM SET 2 SOLUTIONS

Investments—Standard Deviation of a Two-Asset Portfolio

1. C

Percentage of stock = 80%

Percentage of bonds = 20%

$$\sigma_p = \sqrt{W_s^2\sigma_s^2 + W_b^2\sigma_b^2 + 2W_sW_b\left[COV_{sb}\right]}$$

$$\sigma_p = \sqrt{(.80)^2(.15)^2 + (.20)^2(.09)^2 + 2(.80)(.20)\left[(.40)(.15)(.09)\right]}$$

$$\sigma_p = \sqrt{(.64)(.0225) + (.04)(.0081) + (.32)(.0054)}$$

$$\sigma_p = \sqrt{.0144 + .0003 + .0017}$$

$$\sigma_p = \sqrt{.0164}$$

$$\sigma_p = .1281, \text{ or } 12.81\%$$

Investments—Coefficient of Determination

2. B

Correlation coefficient = 0.775

Coefficient of determination = $(0.775)^2$ = 0.60

Thus, 60% of the performance of Harold's stock portfolio is directly attributable to the performance of the market (systematic risk), and 40% of the returns are related to risk of a particular stock or industry (unsystematic risk).

Investments—Percentage Change in the Price of a Bond

3. B

Harold's bond portfolio experiences a 2% decline in value if interest rates increase to 7.43%.

$$\frac{\Delta P}{P} = -D\left[\frac{\Delta y}{1+y}\right]$$

$$\frac{\Delta P}{P} = -5\left[\frac{(.0743-.07)}{1.07}\right]$$

$$\frac{\Delta P}{P} = -5 \times .0040$$

$$\frac{\Delta P}{P} = -.02, \text{ or } -2\%$$

Investments—Normal Distribution

4. **B**

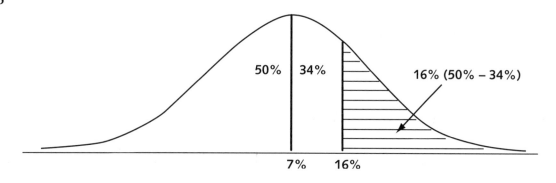

The probability of a return falling within 1 standard deviation (in this case, −2% to 16%) is 68%. Thus, the probability of a return between 7% and 16% must be 34% (one-half of 68%). Because 50% of returns will fall below and above the mean of 7%, it follows that the probability of a return above 16% is 16% (50% − 34%).

Investments—Investment Returns

5. **A**

Weighted return = (0.45)(0.12) + (0.55)(0.07) = 0.0925, or 9.25%

The weighted return represents the return for a set of securities, such as a portfolio, where each return is weighted by the proportion of the security to the entire group or portfolio. The weighted return must be used instead of determining the FV of stocks and bonds separately because of the assumption that the 45%/55% allocation will be maintained throughout the holding period.

PV   = (−715,200)
n = 10 years
i = 9.25
PMT   = 0
FV   = 1,732,375, or $1,732,375

ITEM SET 3 SOLUTIONS

Employee Benefits—Health Savings Account

1. **D**

   The maximum HSA contribution for 2017 for a self-only eligible individual is $3,400.

Employee Benefits—Health Savings Account

2. **A**

   Because Aaron used his HSA distribution for the qualified medical expenses of his spouse, there are no tax consequences.

Employee Benefits—Health Savings Account

3. **A**

   Barbara is not eligible for an HSA because she is covered under a health plan that is not a high deductible health plan.

Employee Benefits—Health Savings Account

4. **B**

   There is a 6% excise tax penalty for overfunding an HSA. The maximum contribution for family coverage in 2017 is $6,750. The HSA has been overfunded in the amount of $250. The excess contribution has a penalty of 6% × $250 = $15.

Retirement—Traditional IRA

5. **D**

   Barbara is an active participant in a Section 401(k) plan, which is a qualified plan. The couple's AGI is under the threshold that applies when one spouse is an active participant. Therefore, her husband is eligible for a deductible IRA contribution of $6,500 ($5,500 + $1,000 catch-up for individuals who have attained the age of 50 by the close of the tax year).

Retirement—Traditional IRA

6. **D**

   The maximum deductible contribution is a total of $11,000 for both spouses for 2017. Charlie is an active participant in a Section 401(k) plan, which is a qualified plan, but his income is less than the deduction phaseout threshold for 2017. In 2017, the maximum IRA contribution is $5,500 ($6,500 for individuals who have attained the age of 50 by the close of the tax year).

ITEM SET 4 SOLUTIONS

Estates—Probate Estate

1. A

Probate assets are valued at the date of death (includes the note and the other property); $200,000 + $250,000 = $450,000. All other assets are nonprobate assets.

The qualified plan, Section 401(k) plan, IRA, and annuity all have a designated beneficiary and will avoid probate. The personal residence is titled as joint tenancy with rights of survivorship (JTWROS) with her husband, Zack. Therefore, her share of the residence will automatically pass to her husband by operation of law at her death and avoid probate.

Retirement—Traditional IRA

2. D

All of the options are available for a spouse beneficiary of an individual retirement account (IRA).

Retirement—Section 401(k) Plan

3. A

A nonspouse beneficiary can transfer a qualified plan or IRA into an inherited-titled IRA; however, the nonspouse must begin taking minimum distributions from that amount beginning in the year following the decedent's death.

ITEM SET 5 SOLUTIONS

Tax—Basis of Inherited Property

1. **B**

   $160,000—The installment notes are income in respect of a decedent (IRD), so there is not a stepped-up basis at death.

Tax—Basis of Inherited Property

2. **C**

   $250,000—The fair market value on the date of death.

Tax—Basis of Inherited Property

3. **B**

   $200,000—The carryover basis. There is no step-up to FMV for annuities because annuities are income in respect of a decedent (IRD).

Tax—Basis of Inherited Property

4. **C**

   Arthur owned one-half already ($280,000 + $400,000 = $680,000). The decedent's half receives a step-up to FMV on the date of death.

Tax—Basis of Inherited Property

5. **A**

   Walter has a zero basis in the Section 401(k) plan because it is a qualified retirement plan. There is no step-up to FMV at death for qualified retirement plans. Note: There is also no step-up to FMV for IRAs.

ITEM SET 6 SOLUTIONS

Estates—Gift Tax Calculation

1. **B**

The amount of the gift is the fair market value of the gifted property on the date of the gift ($100,000). The gift is a present interest, so it qualifies for the annual exclusion ($14,000 in 2017). The taxable gift is $86,000.

Tax—Basis of Property Received by Gift

2. **A**

Sammy's adjusted tax basis for gain is $160,000. His basis for losses is $100,000. The sale price was between the gain basis and the loss basis; therefore, there is no recognized gain or loss. Note: The double-basis rule applies to this gift because the fair market value was less than the donor's adjusted tax basis on the date of the gift (loss property).

Tax—Basis of Property Received by Gift

3. **B**

The basis for loss is $100,000. Because this sale results in a loss (i.e., the loss basis of $100,000 is used), the holding period starts on the date of the gift. Therefore, this is a short-term capital loss of $10,000. Sammy's holding period would tack on to Fred's holding period only if the gain basis was used.

Estates—Tax Implication of Gifting

4. **A**

This is a gift. There are no income tax consequences to Fred.

ITEM SET 7 SOLUTIONS

Solutions to Questions 1–4.

		Investment A	Investment B
IRR:	PV	(5,000,000)	(8,000,000)
	n	1	1
	PMT	0	0
	FV	6,500,000	10,000,000
	IRR(i)	30	25
NPV:	CF_0	(5,000,000)	(8,000,000)
	CF_1	6,500,000	10,000,000
	i	10	10
	NPV	909,090.90	1,090,909.09

Fundamentals—TVM

1. A

Fundamentals—TVM

2. B

Fundamentals—TVM

3. A

Fundamentals—TVM

4. D

ITEM SET 8 SOLUTIONS

Investments—Use of Leverage

1.   C

$$\frac{\text{debit balance}}{(1 - \text{maintenance margin})} = \text{margin call}$$

Debit balance (per share) = $(0.45) \times \$100 = \$45$

Therefore, a margin call will occur at $64.29 ($45 ÷ 0.7).

Investments—Use of Leverage

2.   A

	Current equity		Required equity
Stock price	$70	Stock price	$70
Loan	(45)	Equity %	× .30
Equity	$25	Equity	$21

No margin call will occur because the current equity of $25 is greater than the required equity of $21.

Investments—Use of Leverage

3.   C

	Current equity		Required equity
Stock price	$50	Stock price	$50
Loan	(45)	Equity %	× .30
Equity	$5	Equity	$15

Difference between required equity and current equity = $10 per share × 1,000 shares = $10,000 cash deposit required to cover margin call

Alternative method

  $64.29

($50.00)

  $14.29

× .70

$10.00 per share × 1,000 shares = $10,000 cash deposit required to cover margin call

ITEM SET 9 SOLUTIONS

Investments—Standard Deviation of a Two-Asset Portfolio

1. **B**

$$\sigma_p = \sqrt{W_A^2\,\sigma_A^2 + W_B^2\,\sigma_B^2 + 2W_A W_B[COV_{AB}]}$$

$$\sigma_p = \sqrt{(0.5^2)(0.2^2) + (0.5^2)(0.4^2) + 2(0.5)(0.5)(0.6)(0.2)(0.4)}$$

$$\sigma_p = \sqrt{0.01 + 0.04 + 0.024}$$

$$\sigma_p = \sqrt{0.074}$$

$$\sigma_p = 27.2\%$$

Note: The weighting is 50% for A and B.

$$COV_{AB} = \rho_{AB}\,\sigma_A\sigma_B$$

Investments—Standard Deviation of a Two-Asset Portfolio

2. **B**

$$\sigma_p = \sqrt{W_A^2\,\sigma_A^2 + W_B^2\,\sigma_B^2 + 2W_A W_B[COV_{AB}]}$$

$$\sigma_p = \sqrt{(0.5^2)(0.2^2) + (0.5^2)(0.4^2) + 2(0.5)(0.5)(1.0)(0.2)(0.4)}$$

$$\sigma_p = \sqrt{0.01 + 0.04 + 0.04}$$

$$\sigma_p = \sqrt{0.09}$$

$$\sigma_p = 30\%$$

Note: The weighting is 50% for A and B.

$$COV_{AB} = \rho_{AB}\,\sigma_A\sigma_B$$

ITEM SET 10 SOLUTIONS

Estates—Charitable Transfers

1. A

Diana can reserve the right to change the name of the charitable remainder beneficiary to some other charitable remainder beneficiary. She cannot name 2, 3, or 4, nor can she reserve the right to change the beneficiary to a noncharitable beneficiary and still have the trust qualify as an irrevocable charitable remainder trust.

Tax—Charitable Deduction

2. B

Diana can elect to deduct the basis and is then limited to 50% of AGI or $100,000. If she elects to deduct the FMV, she is limited to 30% of AGI or $60,000 in the current year.

Tax—Charitable Deduction

3. C

Diana gets the deduction this year and a carryover for 5 years (total 6 years × $100,000 or $600,000 if she elects to deduct the basis, as opposed to the FMV). If the FMV were chosen, she would get to deduct a total of $360,000.

ITEM SET 11 SOLUTIONS

Fundamentals—TVM

1. **B**

PV	=	(104,000)		PV	=	(104,000)
n	=	360		n	=	24 (2 × 12)
i	=	0.625 (7.5 ÷ 12)		PMT_{OA}	=	727.18
PMT_{OA}	=	727.18, or $727.18		i	=	0.625 (7.5 ÷ 12)
				FV	=	102,008, or $102,008

Fundamentals—TVM

2. **B**

	Old payment			New payment	
n	= 360		n	= 264 (22 × 12)	
PV	= (112,820)		PV	= (104,200)	
i	= 0.75 (9 ÷ 12)		i	= 0.625 (7.5 ÷ 12)	
FV	= 0		FV	= 0	
PMT	= 907.78		PMT	= 807.04	

Old payment	$907.78 × 22 × 12	=	$239,654
New payment	$807.04 × 22 × 12	=	$213,058
			$26,596

ITEM SET 12 SOLUTIONS

Fundamentals—Domain 2 - Gathering the Information Necessary to Fulfill the Engagement

1. **C**

Ingrid needs the documentation on the stock options to determine whether the options are ISOs or NQSOs. Once she analyzes the documents, Ingrid can explain what kind of options he has been granted and what the rules are for benefiting from the options.

Insurance and Employee Benefits—Incentive Stock Options

2. **D**

ISOs have an expiration date for exercise that cannot exceed 10 years from the date of grant. ISOs are not transferable by the employee during life but may be transferred at death by will. ISOs must not be sold within 2 years from the date of grant and 1 year from the date of exercise in order to maintain the favorable ISO tax treatment. There is no income tax liability on the date of exercise of the ISOs, but the bargain element (difference between the exercise price and the fair market value of the stock at exercise) is an AMT adjustment.

Fundamentals—Domain 7 - Monitoring the Recommendations

3. **A**

Ingrid should continue to monitor the situation with the ISOs and help her client to determine the best time to sell his shares, if he wishes, and make certain any sale is not a disqualifying disposition so as to retain the favorable tax treatment of the ISOs. The bargain element for the ISOs at exercise was a positive preference item for AMT in the year of exercise, not the year of sale. In a qualified disposition of the shares purchased with ISOs, the gain is a capital gain and Humphrey will be taxed at his long-term capital gains rate.

ITEM SET 13 SOLUTIONS

Estates—Charitable Remainder Trusts

1. **A**

   CRATs pay a fixed annuity, while CRUTs pay an amount that can vary each year based on the valuation of the assets in the trust.

Estates—Charitable Remainder Trusts

2. **D**

   Both CRUTs and CRATs are irrevocable trusts.

Estates—Charitable Remainder Trusts

3. **B**

   Only CRUTs provide a variable annuity payment.

Estates—Charitable Remainder Trusts

4. **C**

   Both CRATs and CRUTs provide for the remaining property (remainder interest) to pass to charity.

ITEM SET 14 SOLUTIONS

Investments—Standard Deviation of a Two-Asset Portfolio

1. **B**

Based on a correlation coefficient of 0.4, the standard deviation of the 2 portfolios is approximately 12%.

$$\sigma_p = \sqrt{W_A^2\,\sigma_A^2 + W_B^2\,\sigma_B^2 + 2W_A W_B[COV_{AB}]}$$

$$\sigma_p = \sqrt{(0.4)^2(0.155)^2 + (0.6)^2(0.135)^2 + 2(0.4)(0.6)(0.4)(0.155)(0.135)}$$

$$\sigma_p = \sqrt{0.00384 + 0.00656 + 0.00402}$$

$$\sigma_p = \sqrt{0.01442}$$

$$\sigma_p = 12.01\%$$

Investments—Standard Deviation of a Two-Asset Portfolio

2. **A**

Recall the correlation between 2 assets that have no relationship is zero. The correlation coefficient of zero is then used in the formula for the standard deviation of a two-asset portfolio.

$$\sigma_p = \sqrt{W_A^2\,\sigma_A^2 + W_B^2\,\sigma_B^2 + 2W_A W_B[COV_{AB}]}$$

$$\sigma_p = \sqrt{(0.4)^2(0.155)^2 + (0.6)^2(0.135)^2 + 2(0.4)(0.6)(0)(0.155)(0.135)}$$

$$\sigma_p = \sqrt{0.00384 + 0.00656 + 0}$$

$$\sigma_p = \sqrt{0.01040}$$

$$\sigma_p = 10.2\%$$

ITEM SET 15 SOLUTIONS

Retirement—Required Minimum Distributions

1. C

The required minimum distribution for the current tax year is found by dividing the balance on December 31 of the previous year by the distribution factor for age 71 (because Marleen will be age 71 by December 31 of the current year). The result is $188,680 ($5,000,000 ÷ 26.5). The required minimum distribution does not have to be received until April 1 of the year *after* Marleen turns 70½.

Retirement—Distribution Rules

2. A

No penalties will be assessed for the current year because Marleen has until April 1 of next year to make the RMD for the current year. In this case, she will need to withdraw an additional $38,680 by April 1 of next year to comply with the RMD of $188,680 for the current year.

Retirement—Distribution Rules

3. B

Statement 1 is incorrect. Because Marleen is a greater than 5% owner, she is not allowed to defer her required minimum distribution until April 1 of the year following the year she retires.

Statement 2 is correct. Marleen is permitted to roll her account balance into an IRA rollover account.

Statement 3 is incorrect. There is no age limit for establishing a Roth IRA.

Statement 4 is incorrect. The 20% withholding does not apply to direct trustee-to-trustee rollovers.

ITEM SET 16 SOLUTIONS

Employee Benefits—ISOs

1. **D**

Bob has W-2 compensation income, not subject to payroll taxes, of $2,200, the difference between the exercise price ($20 per share) and the sale price ($42 per share). This option is an ISO, and while he has held it for longer than 2 years from the grant date, he has not held it for more than 1 year from the exercise date, resulting in the recognition of ordinary income. Because Bob has sold the stock within the same year as he exercised it, the ordinary income is reportable on the W-2 as compensation income, but it is not subject to payroll taxes.

Employee Benefits—NQSOs

2. **D**

Bob must recognize $2,000 of W-2 compensation income, subject to payroll taxes, upon exercising the NQSO (100 shares × $20 per share).

Employee Benefits—ISOs

3. **B**

Bob recognizes a positive $1,500 AMT adjustment at the exercise date but does not recognize any regular taxable income until he sells the stock.

Employee Benefits—NQSOs

4. **D**

Bob must recognize $2,000 as W-2 compensation income, subject to payroll taxes, on the exercise date, then $1,000 of STCG on the sale date.

ITEM SET 17 SOLUTIONS

Estates—Gross Estate

1. **C**

George's gross estate is $7,325,500. His gross estate includes 50% of the value of the assets he owned as JTWROS with Jane, 100% of the value of the assets he owned as JTWROS with Marcus, and 100% of the value of the assets he owned individually.

Asset	Gross Estate Inclusion
Personal residence	$362,500
ABC stock	210,000
DEF stock	210,000
Traditional IRA	1,000,000
Personal auto 1	20,000
Personal auto 2	13,000
Partner's share of XYZ partnership	2,750,000
Vacation home	460,000
Cash in checking and savings accounts	2,300,000
Total gross estate	**$7,325,500**

Estates—Probate Estate

2. **A**

The value of George's probate estate is $3,210,000, consisting of his interest in the XYZ partnership ($2,750,000) and the vacation home ($460,000). The assets owned as JTWROS pass to the surviving joint tenant by operation of law, and the assets with designated beneficiaries pass to the beneficiaries by contract.

Estates—Basis of Inherited Assets

3. **D**

Because George provided 100% of the purchase price for the ABC stock and 100% of the value of the stock is included in his gross estate, Marcus receives a stepped-up basis in 100% of the stock. His basis is the fair market value of the stock on George's date of death.

Estates—Basis of Inherited Assets

4. **C**

Jane's basis in the one-half of the DEF stock that was included in George's gross estate is stepped up to its fair market value on the date of death ($210,000). Because the stock is a qualified joint interest, Jane also has a basis of $80,000 in the one-half of the stock that was not included in George's gross estate, for a total basis of $290,000.

Estates—Cross-Purchase Buy-Sell Arrangements

5. **B**

Kirk should tell Jane that the cross-purchase buy-sell arrangement between George and his partners represents a commitment on the part of the surviving partners to purchase George's interest upon his death. Because of the existence of the agreement, Jane will not need to find a purchaser for George's interest.

ITEM SET 18 SOLUTIONS

Fundamentals—Uneven Cash Flows

1. **C**

(9,200)	CF_o
600	CF_1
2,300	CF_2
2,200	CF_3
6,800	CF_4
9,500	CF_5 (year 5 cash flow of $300 plus the liquidation value of $9,200)
	IRR = 24.18%

Fundamentals—Uneven Cash Flows

2. **B**

   Only Statement 4 is incorrect. If the cost of capital is less than the IRR, then the project should be accepted (NPV > $0).

ITEM SET 19 SOLUTIONS

Retirement—Social Security Benefits—Domain 3 - Analyzing and Evaluating the Client's Current Financial Status

1. **A**

Bob's plan, as described, will cause his Social Security retirement benefits to be reduced under two separate rules. First, because Bob plans to claim his benefit at age 62, which is 4 years prior to his Full Retirement Age (age 66), the benefits will be reduced. Under this rule, his benefit is reduced as follows:

5/9 of 1% for the first 36 months under FRA [(5/9 × 36) ÷ 100] = .20 (20%) + 5/12 of 1% for each month over 36 months prior to FRA [(5/12 × 12) ÷ 100] = .05 (5%). The total reduction is 25%. (1,600 × .25 × 12 = $4,800)

Additionally, because Bob will have earned income prior to attaining FRA, his Social Security retirement benefit will be further reduced under the earnings limitation rules. In 2017, the earnings limitation prior to FRA is $16,920. Bob's benefit will be reduced in the first year $1 for every $2 his earned income exceeds the threshold. ($24,000 – $16,920) ÷ 2 = $3,540

The total reduction under the separate rules is $8,340.

Tax—Taxation of Social Security Benefits—Domain 3 - Analyzing and Evaluating the Client's Current Financial Status

2. **D**

As much as 85% of Bob's Social Security retirement benefit may be subject to taxation. Considering provisional income consisting only of Bob and Ann's earned income, one-half of Bob's Social Security retirement benefit and the defined benefit pension plan income, an 85% inclusion amount is not reached. However, Bob's plan, as described, will also cause a portion of the profit-sharing lump-sum distribution to be included in income, thus causing the Social Security benefit to reach the 85% inclusion level. When Bob receives the profit-sharing plan lump-sum distribution check, it will be net of a 20% withholding for federal income taxes ($60,000). That $60,000 is considered a distribution from the plan and is included in Bob's gross income in the year of distribution. The only way to avoid including the tax withholding in his income is for Bob to deposit both the check he receives for the distribution and an additional $60,000 from other funds to bring the total rolled over (within 60 days of distribution) back to $300,000. There is no evidence in the facts that Bob will be adding to the check when he deposits it in the IRA. The maximum amount of Social Security benefits that may be included in income for the year is 85%.

Retirement—Retirement Planning Alternatives—Domain 4 - Analyzing and Evaluating the Client's Current Financial Status

3. **D**

Each of these observations is accurate and present alternatives that could enhance Bob's retirement plan.

Bob and Ann could consider waiving the QJSA payout from the defined benefit plan. Doing so will increase the pension payments during Bob's life by 25%, to $1,250. Rather than surrendering the paid-up $250,000 whole life policy, the policy should be earmarked as Ann's survivor income vehicle. The life insurance policy can provide a much larger survivor income than the 50% QJSA through the defined benefit plan. The QJSA survivor benefit is $500 per month. Annuitized at the 5% assumed rate of return, it would only require approximately $214,000 of the life insurance proceeds to provide a survivor income of $1,250 per month (same as during Bob's life).

1,250 PMT; 0 FV; 300 N; .4167 I/YR(5 ÷ 12); solve for PV (213,825), or $213,825

Bob should, indeed, execute a direct-transfer of his profit-sharing lump-sum distribution to avoid current taxes on $60,000. Bob's current plan is to take possession of the lump-sum distribution with a subsequent rollover into an IRA. This plan will require mandatory 20% withholding of $60,000. Additionally, if Bob does not replace the $60,000 with other funds, the $60,000 withheld is considered a distribution, subject to taxation.

A cash surrender of the $250,000 whole life policy will result in $50,000 taxable income. Bob mentioned the full dividend has been taxable in recent years, causing him to think the tax law has changed. The reason the dividend is fully taxable is because cumulative dividends over the years now exceed Bob's basis in the policy. Therefore, the entire $50,000 cash value will be taxable upon surrender.

On the surface, it appears Bob could not wait until FRA, age 66, to claim his Social Security retirement benefit and still reach his income goal. However, by annuitizing the Roth IRA over the next 4 years, to age 66, Bob can replace the $1,200 per month he would get from Social Security at age 62 and enable him to receive his full PIA of $1,600 per month at FRA of 66.

1,200 PMT; 0 FV; 48 N; .4167 I/YR(5 ÷ 12); solve for PV (52,108), or $52,108

The Roth IRA is the best choice to annuitize over 4 years because the income will be tax free. If he uses the rollover IRA to provide the income payments, it will be taxable.

ITEM SET 20 SOLUTIONS

Insurance and Employee Benefits—Gifting NQSOs

1. **D**

NQSOs can be transferred to charities, family members, and other persons during the employee's lifetime. Because there is a substantial risk of forfeiture of the NQSOs (failure to meet the sales goal), the NQSOs are not taxed on the grant date, but on the exercise date. The difference between the exercise price and the fair market value of the stock when the options are exercised (bargain element) is taxed as W-2 compensation income, subject to payroll taxes, in the year of exercise.

Insurance and Employee Benefits—Gifting NQSOs

2. **B**

Clark should tell Vivien that if she dies within 3 years after the charity exercised the options, the value the options would have had on her date of death will be included in her gross estate. When Vivien transfers the NQSOs to the charity, the gift is a completed gift for gift tax purposes. If the charity exercises the NQSOs during Vivien's lifetime, she will have to recognize the bargain element as W-2 compensation income, subject to payroll taxes, on the exercise date. If the charity exercises the options after Vivien's death, her estate is entitled to a charitable deduction.

Tax—NQSOs

3. **B**

Lawrence will have W-2 compensation income, subject to payroll taxes, and taxed at his ordinary income tax rate in the amount of the bargain element, $100,000 ($180 − $170 × 10,000 shares). This increases Lawrence's basis in the shares to $180 per share, making his basis in the share for both regular income tax and the alternative income tax the same. Because Lawrence used $1.7 million of cash plus the $100,000 of reported compensation to purchase the shares, his assets on his financial statement will reflect $1.8 million in Golden Metro shares. Because the bargain element is taxed as ordinary income in the year of exercise, it is not an alternative minimum tax (AMT) adjustment.

ITEM SET 21 SOLUTIONS

Insurance—Legal Aspects

1. **D**

   Vicarious liability occurs when one person is held liable for the torts of someone else.

Insurance—Legal Aspects

2. **C**

   Under the collateral source rule, damages assessed against the negligent party are not reduced just because the injured party is insured.

Insurance—Legal Aspects

3. **B**

   Mary assumed the risk of being hit by a foul ball by attending the baseball game. If Mary sues the baseball team, the team may use the defense of assumption of risk to shield itself from liability.

Insurance—Legal Aspects

4. **A**

   Subrogation means that if the insured party collects from the insurer, the insured party relinquishes the right to collect damages from the negligent party (the insurer can collect from the negligent party).

ITEM SET 22 SOLUTIONS

Tax—Cost Recovery

1. **B**

   Loans (or distributions) from a MEC are always taxed as though the earnings are distributed first. Therefore, basis is recovered last resulting in LIFO (last in, first out) tax treatment.

Retirement—Roth IRA Distributions

2. **A**

   Nonqualified distributions from a Roth IRA are first treated as a return of basis. Therefore, FIFO tax treatment would apply.

   Note: Qualified distributions from a Roth IRA are income tax free.

Tax—Cost Recovery

3. **D**

   When selling stock, the seller can use either the specific identification or FIFO (first shares purchased are the first shares sold) to determine basis in the shares sold.

Retirement—Traditional IRA Distributions

4. **E**

   Basis (after-tax contributions) in a traditional IRA is recovered pro rata when the owner receives a distribution from the IRA.

ITEM SET 23 SOLUTIONS

Insurance—Life Insurance

1. **D**

    Aaron will receive $55,000 from the insurance company ($90,000 cash value less $35,000 outstanding loan).

Insurance—Income Taxation of Life Insurance

2. **A**

    Aaron must include $42,000 in his taxable income ($90,000 cash value minus basis of $48,000). The premiums paid minus the dividends received represent Aaron's basis in the policy ($58,000 – $10,000 = $48,000).

ITEM SET 24 SOLUTIONS

Retirement—Distribution Rules

1. **A**

The Section 401(k) plan from ABC company will be exempt from the 10% early withdrawal penalty. If a participant separates from service after the attainment of age 55, he can take a penalty-free withdrawal from the employer's qualified plan without incurring the early withdrawal penalty.

Marshall is younger than age 59½ and separated from service from Johnson Industries at the age of 48 (10 years ago). Therefore, he had not attained age 55 and will be subject to the penalty.

The exception to the penalty for separation from service after attainment of age 55 does not apply to IRAs.

Retirement—Beneficiary Considerations

2. **D**

Spousal consent is not required when changing the beneficiary of an IRA.

The required minimum distribution is calculated using a prescribed IRS table. The table must always be used to calculate the minimum required distribution, unless the beneficiary is the spouse and the spouse is more than 10 years younger than the participant. If the beneficiary is Marshall's son or grandson, the IRS table must be used, and, therefore, the required minimum distribution will be the same in either case.

A participant of a qualified plan must have spousal consent to change the beneficiary.

ITEM SET 25 SOLUTIONS

Fundamentals—Statements of Cash Flows

1. **D**

Only the auto loan balance would not be included in the client's statement of cash flows because it is neither income nor a cash outflow; rather, it is a liability listed on the statement of financial position.

Fundamentals—Bankruptcy

2. **A**

The federal income taxes (less than 3 years old), alimony, monthly mortgage payments (secured debt), and government student loans cannot be discharged. Student loans can only be discharged if paying them would cause an undue hardship. Personal debt, such as bank loans ($30,000) and auto loan debt ($12,000), may be discharged. Thus, $42,000 is the total amount that may be discharged.

Tax—Itemized Deductions

3. **A**

Because the amounts borrowed were used to purchase tax-exempt securities, none of the margin interest expense is deductible.

ITEM SET 26 SOLUTIONS

Investments—Derivatives

1. C

The intrinsic value of a call option is the excess (if any) of the stock's fair market value over the exercise price of the option. The intrinsic value of this option is $3 ($58 stock value − $55 option price).

Investments—Derivatives

2. D

The time value of a call option is the excess of the option's price over the option's intrinsic value. The time value of this option is $3.50 ($6.50 option price − $3 intrinsic value).

Investments—Black-Scholes Option Valuation Model

3. D

A decrease in the exercise price of a call option will increase the option's value under the Black-Scholes option valuation model.

ITEM SET 27 SOLUTIONS

Tax—Classification of Assets

1. **B**

   A copyright held by the person who applied for and received it is considered an ordinary asset.

Tax—Classification of Assets

2. **C**

   Machinery used in a trade or business is depreciable Section 1231 property.

Tax—Classification of Assets

3. **A**

   A personal auto not used in a trade or business is considered a capital asset.

Tax—Classification of Assets

4. **B**

   Razors sold by a company that manufactures razors would be considered inventory, which is an ordinary asset.

ITEM SET 28 SOLUTIONS

Estates—Crummey Powers

1. **A**

Rianna can withdraw $14,000, the gift tax annual exclusion amount for 2017.

The Crummey provision provides a right of withdrawal equal to the lesser of (1) the gift tax annual exclusion amount or (2) the value of the gift transferred.

Estates—Crummey Powers

2. **A**

Because there was no additional contribution to the trust, Rianna cannot withdraw any amounts from the trust in the second year.

The Crummey provision provides a right of withdrawal equal to the lesser of (1) the gift tax annual exclusion amount or (2) the value of the gift transferred.

Estates—Irrevocable Trust

3. **A**

Unless specifically given the ability to change the remainder beneficiary by the terms of the trust, the income beneficiary does not have an inherent right to control who that beneficiary will be. The facts of the question state that the only right given to the income beneficiary was a Crummey provision for Rianna.

ITEM SET 29 SOLUTIONS

Tax—Capital Assets

1. **B**

   Rare stamps are collectibles and are taxed at a maximum capital gains rate of 28%. However, because his marginal rate is 25%, that is the maximum he will be taxed on the collectible. The total tax on the gain would be $3,750 ($15,000 gain × 25% tax rate), resulting in only $21,250 ($25,000 − $3,750) of after-tax proceeds.

   The Section 1202 qualified small business stock is the correct choice. If Section 1202 qualified small business stock is held for more than 5 years, only 50% of the gain is taxed. Roger has held the stock for 10 years. The remaining gain is taxed at a flat 28% rate (making the effective tax rate 14% because half the gain is excluded). Therefore, the tax due will be $2,520 ($18,000 gain × 50% × 28% tax rate). Roger will have $22,480 ($25,000 − $2,520) cash remaining after taxes, which is more than enough to fund the purchase.

   Because the common stock was held short term, the gain on the common stock will be taxed at Roger's 25% ordinary income tax rate. Therefore, the tax on the gain will be $3,000 ($12,000 gain × 25% tax rate), resulting in only $22,000 ($25,000 − $3,000) of after-tax proceeds.

   The investment land was held long term, resulting in a 15% capital gain rate. However, the basis is so low that the tax on the gain will be $3,300 ($22,000 gain × 15% tax rate). Roger will only have $21,700 ($25,000 − $3,300) of cash remaining.

Tax—Charitable Contribution

2. **C**

   Roger will only be allowed a charitable deduction for his tax basis in the stamps because the property is use-unrelated.

Tax—Tax Consequences

3. **B**

   Section 1202 qualified small business stock receives a step-up in basis at Roger's death.

   Roger may exclude 50% to 75% or even 100% of the gain on the sale of Section 1202 qualified small business stock, if certain conditions are met. However, a portion of the excluded gain is a tax preference item for purposes of alternative minimum tax (except for Section 1202 qualified small business stock acquired after 9/27/10 where 100% of the gain is excluded for both regular income tax and AMT).

   Collectibles (such as Roger's rare stamp collection) are prohibited investments in IRAs.

   Personal use assets, such as a principal residence, are not considered like-kind property. Therefore, Roger would be required to recognize gain on the exchange. If Roger converted the personal residence for use as a rental (investment) property, then the transaction could qualify for like-kind treatment.

ITEM SET 30 SOLUTIONS

Estates—Gifting Strategies

1. **B**

   Bond B is the best choice because Cathy's mother would benefit from the coupon (interest) payments from the bond.

Estates—Gifting Strategies

2. **B**

   Stock E is the best choice because Cathy can remove the stock from her assets and ultimately her estate before large appreciation becomes an issue. Her son is young, and he will be able to take advantage of appreciating property. Stock A is not the best choice because it has appreciated the most and her son would be responsible for the capital gains tax when he sells the stock. The son would receive a carryover basis as a result of the lifetime gift.

Estates—Gifting Strategies

3. **A**

   By selecting Stock A, Cathy can remove this highly appreciated asset from her estate, have no capital gain consequences, and take a charitable income tax deduction based on the fair market value of the asset.

Estates—Gifting Strategies

4. **D**

   Cathy should sell Stock D because it is currently valued at a loss. Assets that have an FMV lower than the owner's basis at the time of gift are subject to the double-basis rule. The recipient gets the FMV basis for losses and the adjusted basis for gains. Thus, the current loss on the asset would be lost. If she wanted to gift this property, she should first sell it for the loss, claim the loss deduction (subject to the applicable limits) herself, and then gift the proceeds.

ITEM SET 31 SOLUTIONS

Fundamentals—Statement of Financial Position

1. **D**

Stock	Number of shares owned on 12/31 of current year	Ending price on 12/31 of current year	Total value of stock on statement of financial position
ABC	200	$8	$1,600
XYZ	400 (split)	$15	$6,000
THE	200	$16	$3,200
			$10,800

The total value reported is $10,800.

Fundamentals—Statement of Cash Flows

2. **B**

Stock	Number of shares owned on 12/31	Dividends paid per share on 12/31	Total dividends paid
ABC	200	$0	$0
XYZ	400 (split)	$0.75	$300
THE	200	$1.00	$200
			$500

The total dividends received this year were $500.

Stock	Number of shares purchased on 1/1 of current year	Original purchase price per share	Total purchase price
ABC	200	$16	$3,200
XYZ	200	$18	$3,600
THE	200	$14	$2,800
			$9,600

The total cash paid for the shares on January 1 was $9,600. Therefore, the net cash outflow was $9,100 ($9,600 − $500).

Investments—P/E Ratio

3. **D**

P/E ratio = market price per share ÷ earnings per share

Therefore, the P/E ratio for XYZ stock on December 31 of the current year equals 10 ($15 ÷ $1.50).

ITEM SET 32 SOLUTIONS

Tax—AGI

1. **D**

Description	Amount
Salary	$85,000
XYZ Company preferred stock dividend	$800
Interest income from corporate bond	$300
S corporation loss	($2,000)
Adjusted gross income (AGI)	$84,100

The interest income from the qualified private activity bond is not taxable.

Because Tom is a limited partner in Realty Capital Partners, he is not a material participant; therefore, his passive loss from this activity is not deductible (Tom has no passive activity income).

Because Tom is not a material participant in ABC partnership, his passive loss from this activity is not deductible (Tom has no passive activity income).

The mortgage interest expense and margin interest expense are itemized deductions and are not deductible in arriving at adjusted gross income.

Tax—Itemized Deductions

2. **C**

Investment interest expense (margin interest) is deductible only to the extent of taxable investment income. Tom has taxable investment income of $300 if the preferred stock dividends are qualified dividends taxable at capital gains tax rates. If the $800 of preferred stock dividends are taxed at his ordinary income tax rate, those dividends also qualify when calculating taxable investment income for purposes of determining the investment interest expense and will allow Tom the maximum deduction for margin interest expense. The private activity bond interest income is not taxable.

Retirement Planning—IRAs

3. **A**

Statement 1 is correct. Tom's AGI is less than $118,000, which is the 2017 AGI phaseout for single taxpayers. Therefore, he can contribute to a Roth IRA.

Statement 2 is incorrect. Tom is an active participant in the Section 401(k) plan. His AGI exceeds the phaseout limit ($72,000 for 2017), and, therefore, he cannot deduct his contributions to a traditional IRA.

Statement 3 is correct. Tom could contribute to a nondeductible traditional IRA. Anyone with earned income can contribute to a nondeductible IRA.

Statement 4 is correct. Tom can convert an existing traditional IRA to a Roth IRA regardless of his AGI.

Tax—Passive Loss Activity

4. **D**

The loss from the S corporation is deductible this year because Tom is a material participant. The passive losses from Realty Capital Partners ($3,000) and ABC Partnership ($5,000) are disallowed because Tom does not have any passive activity income to offset this year and the losses must be carried forward.

MINI-CASE 1 SOLUTIONS

Fundamentals—Future Value

1. **B**

		Tuition Yr. 1	Tuition Yr. 2	Tuition Yr. 3	Tuition Yr. 4
PV	=	(25,000)	(25,000)	(25,000)	(25,000)
n	=	18	19	20	21
i	=	7	7	7	7
PMT	=	0	0	0	0
FV	=	84,498.31	90,413.19	96,742.11	103,514.06
Total	=	$375,167.67	($84,498.31 + $90,413.19 + $96,742.11 + $103,514.06)		

Fundamentals—Education Planning and Time Value of Money

2. **B**

Step 1:
25,000 +/PV
18 N
7 I/YR
Solve for FV = 84,498.3069

Step 2:
BEG mode
84,498.3069 +/PMT
1.4019 I/YR
4 N
Solve for PV = 331,048.3787

Step 3:
BEG mode
331,048.3787 FV
18 N
8.5 I/YR
Solve for PMT = 7,759.1676

Fundamentals—Education Funding

3. **B**

Gifts to a qualified tuition plan (Section 529) are subject to the gift tax rules. For example, in 2017, a contributor is permitted to make one $70,000 contribution (the gift tax annual exclusion of $14,000 multiplied by 5) and treat the contribution as if made ratably over the current year and the next 4 years (a total of 5 years). In addition, if the contributor splits that gift with a spouse, a one-time contribution (every 5 years) of $140,000 may be made to any beneficiary, including the account owner if so desired.

Market risk is a systematic risk and inherent to all investment markets. Qualified tuition plan earnings grow tax deferred, and distributions are tax free for qualified education expenses. Active investment strategies involve security selection and market timing. Dollar cost averaging is the process of purchasing securities over time by investing a predetermined amount at regular intervals.

Fundamentals—TVM

4. **B**

FMV	=	$175,000
20% down payment	=	$35,000
Financed balance	=	$140,000

FV	=	0
n	=	360 (12 × 30)
i	=	0.6667 (8 ÷ 12)
PV	=	(140,000) (175,000 × 80%)
PMT_{OA}	=	1,027.27, or $1,027.27

Fundamentals—TVM

5. **B**

PV	=	(140,000)
n	=	11
i	=	0.6667 (8 ÷ 12)
PMT_{OA}	=	1,027.27
FV	=	138,931.55

Principal reduction $140,000 − $138,931.55 = $1,068.45

Total payments ($1,027.27 × 11) − $1,068.45 = $10,231.52 interest expense

Note: If you arrive at a figure that is slightly off, it may be due to a failure to round to a monthly payment of $1,027.27

Fundamentals—TVM

6. **D**

FV	=	0
n	=	180 (12 × 15)
i	=	0.6667 (8 ÷ 12)
PV	=	(140,000)
PMT_{OA}	=	1,337.91

$1,027.27 × 360	=	$369,817.20
$1,337.91 × 180	=	−240,823.80
		$128,993.40 Savings

Fundamentals—Scope of Engagement

7. C

Because both Scott and Nicole are your clients, it is important to confirm that her goals are the same as Scott's goals. This can be done informally through a congratulatory phone call to her. Under the Practice Standards 100 Series, the scope of the engagement is mutually defined. This includes defining the parties. In this case, Nicole is a party to the client-planner engagement and, as such, should be aware of any actions taken.

MINI-CASE 2 SOLUTIONS

Estates—Basis of Inherited Property

1. **C**

   The heir will not incur any income tax on the sale of the business interest to the surviving shareholders. When a beneficiary receives property from a decedent, the basis of the inherited property is the FMV at the date of death (or the FMV 6 months later if alternate valuation date is selected).

Tax—Taxation of Modified Endowment Contracts

2. **D**

   Assuming a 28% marginal income tax bracket, Rick will pay total taxes of $9,500. The policy Rick owns insuring Joe is a MEC. Therefore, the loan will be subject to LIFO tax treatment and will be taxable to the extent the loan distribution is in excess of Rick's basis in the contract. The policy has a basis of $100,000 and a cash value of $125,000, resulting in a taxable distribution of $25,000. Because the distribution is from a MEC and prior to age 59 ½, a penalty tax of 10% is paid in addition to the marginal tax of 28% (38% × $25,000 = $9,500).

Fundamentals—Principle of Confidentiality

3. **B**

   Sue should inform Rick that she may not disclose the requested information without express consent from Joe and Kim. Although Rick is the insured, he does not own the policies insuring his life and is not authorized to be provided with the information requested. Under the Principle of Confidentiality contained in the CFP® Board Standards of Professional Conduct, Sue must ensure that client information is accessible only to those authorized to have access.

Estates—Buy-Sell Agreements

4. **A**

   The buy-sell agreement states the surviving shareholders will each purchase one-half of the deceased shareholder's interest in the company based on the most recent professional valuation of the company. The most recent valuation of JKR, Inc., was $6 million and therefore, each shareholder's interest is $2 million. The surviving 2 shareholders would each purchase one-half of the deceased's interest in the company at a price of $1 million. The purchase price is added to the shareholder's original basis of $100,000, for a total basis of $1.1 million.

Tax—Transfer-For-Value Rules

5. **C**

   Statements 2 and 3 are correct. An amount received by the shareholder in excess of basis in the transfer is taxable. The sale of the policies to the corporation is not considered transfer for value because a transfer to a corporation in which the insured is a shareholder is an exception to the transfer for value rules. Therefore, the death proceeds received by JKR, Inc., will not be subject to regular income tax. After the transfer, JKR, Inc., will not be allowed a deduction for premiums paid because JKR, Inc., will be the owner and beneficiary of the policies.

Insurance—Variable Universal Life Insurance

6. C

Only Statement 4 is correct. Each shareholder owns 2 policies for a total of 6 policies. Variable life growth stock subaccounts offer no minimum guaranteed return. A level premium does not guarantee the death benefit in a variable universal life policy allocating 100% of the cash value into growth stock subaccounts. The subaccount may go to zero, causing the policy to lapse. Although the policy Rick owns insuring Joe is a modified endowment contract, the death benefit remains tax free to Rick.

MINI-CASE 3 SOLUTIONS

Fundamentals—Time Value of Money

1. **B**

$1,000,000	Sale price	PV		=	(800,000)
(200,000)	Down payment	FV		=	0
$800,000	Present value	n		=	144 months
		i		=	0.75 (9 ÷ 12)
		PMT_{OA}		=	9,104.25

$245,521 = $200,000 + 45,521 [$9,104.25 (PMT) × 5]

Tax—Installment Notes

2. **D**

Walter's adjusted basis in the business is $300,000. The interest is considered ordinary income.

n	=	5 months
PV	=	800,000
PMT	=	(9,104.25)
i	=	0.75 (9 ÷ 12)
FV	=	784,244.18

Total payments $45,521 = ($9,104.25 × 5) less principal reduction

Original debt	$800,000	Total payment	$45,521
Remaining debt at 12/31	(784,244)	Principal reduction	(15,756)
Principal reduction	$15,756	Ordinary income from interest	$29,765

Fundamentals—Time Value of Money

3. **C**

The remaining unpaid principal balance if Walter dies after receiving 48 payments will be $621,442.

n	=	96 (144 months − 48 months)
FV	=	0
PMT_{OA}	=	9,104.25
i	=	0.75 (9 ÷ 12)
PV	=	621,442, or $621,442

Tax—Installment Notes

4. **C**

Because the total sales price is $1 million and Walter's adjusted basis is $300,000, 30% of the down payment is considered a return of basis and 70% is considered capital gain. Therefore, 70% of the $200,000 down payment ($140,000) is considered capital gain.

Tax—Capital Assets

5. **B**

The gain on the stock is $3,000. The gain is short term (held for 5 months).

Tax—Tax Consequences of the Disposition of Property

6. **C**

Statement 2 is incorrect. If the uncle received Ferris stock as a gift from Walter within a year of his death, Walter would not have a stepped up basis in the stock. Thus, it is relevant how the uncle acquired the stock. Statement 3 is incorrect because the wash sale rules apply only to losses, not gains, so the repurchase in Transaction #2 within 30 days has no effect on Transaction #1. Walter's basis in Energy Enterprises is $3,700. Transaction #6 cannot be a like-kind exchange (securities do not qualify for like-kind exchange treatment), thus the basis of the shares acquired is equal to the FMV at the date of acquisition.

Tax—Capital Assets

7. **D**

$40,000 LTCL (Transaction #3).

$1,000 LTCG (Transaction #4).

$5,000 LTCL (Transaction #5).

$151,029 LTCG (capital gain portion of installment sale downpayment and the five 2017 installment payments [$15,756 principal reduction x 70% capital gain on the sale]).

Net $107,029 LTCG.

Regarding Transaction #3, Walter is single and his maximum available Section 1244 loss deduction is $50,000 in 2017. The remaining $40,000 is treated as a LTCL.

Regarding Transaction #4, Walter's basis in the inherited stock is the FMV at the date of death ($11,000). Walter has a gain of $1,000 on the transaction ($12,000 − $11,000). Inherited property automatically gets a long-term holding period.

Regarding Transaction #5, worthless securities are deemed to have become worthless on the last day of the year; in this case, December 31, 2017. Therefore, Walter will have a long-term capital loss of $5,000.

Tax—Capital Assets

8. **C**

$3,000 STCG (Transaction #1).

$700 STCL (Transaction #6).

Net $2,300 STCG.

Regarding Transaction #6, securities do not qualify as a like-kind exchange.

When Walter exchanged his Princeton Power, Inc., stock, it had an adjusted basis of $3,000 plus a long-term gain of $700. The new basis for Energy Enterprises was $3,700, but Walter sold it for $3,000. This resulted in a short-term capital loss of $700.

MINI-CASE 4 SOLUTIONS

Retirement—Needs Analysis

1. **B**

   While each of the choices may ultimately be recommended, the next step Todd should take is to provide a retirement needs analysis. The other recommendations would be premature if executed prior to having a clearer picture of the couple's retirement income needs and what resources are available to meet those needs.

Retirement—Social Security Benefits

2. **D**

   A beneficiary's retirement benefit is not increased at FRA if initially claimed prior to FRA. Charles and Marie are claiming Social Security retirement benefits 12 months prior to FRA, so the benefit will be reduced 5/9ths of 1% times 12 months. In this case, the reduction is approximately 6.7%, not 30%. Charles's Medicare Part A coverage will not require a premium, but Medicare Part B coverage does require a premium. Medicare benefits are linked to age 65, not a taxpayer's FRA under Social Security.

Insurance—Long-Term Care

3. **C**

   Statements 2, 3, and 4 are correct. Statement 1 is incorrect because benefits may be received prior to 90 days. For a chronic illness claim (2 of 6 ADLs) for long-term insurance benefits, a doctor must certify the condition is expected to last at least 90 days, but with such certification benefits may commence prior to 90 days if the elimination period is shorter.

Insurance—Tax-Qualified Long-Term Care Insurance Policy

4. **B**

   Statements 1 and 4 are correct. Tax-qualified long-term care insurance premiums (up to a specified limit) may be included as a medical expense in calculating the itemized deduction for medical expenses on the tax return for a taxpayer who itemizes. A tax-free exchange of a tax-deferred annuity for a tax-qualified long-term care insurance policy is possible. Statement 2 is incorrect because a physician must certify the condition is expected to last at least 90 days if the claim is being made due to the inability to perform 2 of 6 activities of daily living (ADLs), not for cognitive impairment. Statement 3 is incorrect because a partnership long-term care insurance policy allows an insured to protect a higher asset level without completely spending down to qualify for Medicaid.

Appendix

Appendix 1: CFP Board-Provided Information Online

CFP Board provides the Investment Formulas and Tax Tables online at the class site.

(The formula sheet below was current at press time. Please refer to CFP Board's website, **http://www.cfp.net/become-a-cfp-professional/cfp-certification-requirements/applications-resources.**

CFP BOARD

CERTIFIED FINANCIAL PLANNER BOARD OF STANDARDS, INC.

Provided Formulas

These formulas are available to exam candidates when taking the CFP® Certification Examination:

$$V = \frac{D_1}{r-g}$$

$$\alpha_p = \overline{r_p} - \left[\overline{r_f} + \left(\overline{r_m} - \overline{r_f} \right) \beta_p \right]$$

$$r = \frac{D_1}{P} + g$$

$$T_p = \frac{\overline{r_p} - \overline{r_f}}{\beta_p}$$

$$COV_{ij} = \rho_{ij} \sigma_i \sigma_j$$

$$D = \frac{1+y}{y} - \frac{(1+y)+t(c-y)}{c\left[(1+y)^t - 1\right] + y}$$

$$\sigma_p = \sqrt{W_i^2 \sigma_i^2 + W_j^2 \sigma_j^2 + 2 W_i W_j COV_{ij}}$$

$$\frac{\Delta P}{P} = -D \left[\frac{\Delta y}{1+y} \right]$$

$$\beta_i = \frac{COV_{im}}{\sigma_m^2} = \frac{\rho_{im} \sigma_i}{\sigma_m}$$

$$IR = \frac{R_P - R_B}{\sigma_A}$$

$$\sigma_r = \sqrt{\frac{\sum_{t=1}^{n} (r_t - \overline{r})^2}{n}}$$

$$EAR = \left(1 + \frac{i}{n}\right)^n - 1$$

$$S_r = \sqrt{\frac{\sum_{t=1}^{n} (r_t - \overline{r})^2}{n-1}}$$

$$TEY = r/(1-t)$$

$$r_i = r_f + (r_m - r_f)\beta_i$$

$$AM = \frac{a_1 + a_2 + a_3 + \cdots + a_n}{n}$$

Provided Formulas (cont.)

$$S_p = \frac{\overline{r}_p - \overline{r}_f}{\sigma_p}$$

$$\sqrt[n]{(1 + r_1) \times (1 + r_2) \times ... (1 + r_n)} - 1$$

$$_1R_N = [(1 + {}_1R_1)(1 + E({}_2r_1))...(1 + E({}_Nr_1))]^{1/N} - 1$$

$$HPR = [(1 + r_1) \times (1 + r_2) \times ...(1 + r_n)] - 1$$

2017 CFP Board-Provided Tax Tables

The income and estate tax tables provided by CFP Board for the 2017 examinations were unavailable at press time. Once released by CFP Board, you will be able to find them on the Board's website at http://www.cfp.net/become-a-cfp-professional/cfp-certification-requirements/cfp-exam-requirement/exam-resources/provided-exam-tax-tables. A copy of these tax tables will also be posted on your Exam Prep Review course dashboard in the folder titled *EPR Announcements and Supplemental Documents*.

Appendix 2:

CFP Board Investment Formulas with Titles and Explanations

These formulas will be provided to all candidates taking the CFP© Certification Examination; however, they will appear without titles indicating the meaning and use of each formula. Note CFP Board's Formula Page appears as Appendix 1 in this volume.

Constant Growth Dividend Discount Model $$V = \frac{D_1}{r - g}$$	**Capital Asset Pricing Model** $$r_i = r_f + \left(r_m - r_f\right)\beta_i$$
Expected Return Form of Dividend Discount Model $$r = \frac{D_1}{P} + g$$	**Effective Annual Rate of Return** $$EAR = \left(1 + \frac{i}{n}\right)^n - 1$$
Covariance Between Two Sample Assets $$COV_{ij} = \rho_{ij}\sigma_i\sigma_j$$ **Standard Deviation of a Two-Asset Portfolio** $$\sigma_p = \sqrt{W_i^2\sigma_i^2 + W_j^2\sigma_j^2 + 2W_iW_j\,COV_{ij}}$$	**Sharpe Ratio of Portfolio Performance** $$S_p = \frac{\overline{r_p} - \overline{r_f}}{\sigma_p}$$ **Jensen's Alpha of Portfolio Performance** $$\alpha_p = \overline{r_p} - \left[\overline{r_f} + \left(\overline{r_m} - \overline{r_f}\right)\beta_p\right]$$
Beta Coefficient of Sample Asset $$\beta_i = \frac{COV_{im}}{\sigma_m^2} = \frac{\rho_{im}\sigma_i}{\sigma_m}$$	**Treynor Ratio of Portfolio Performance** $$T_p = \frac{\overline{r_p} - \overline{r_f}}{\beta_p}$$
Population for Standard Deviation of a Single Asset $$\sigma_r = \sqrt{\frac{\sum_{t=1}^{n}\left(r_t - \overline{r}\right)^2}{n}}$$	**Taxable Equivalent Yield** $$TEY = r / (1 - t)$$ **Arithmetic Mean** $$AM = \frac{a_1 + a_2 + a_3 + \dots + a_n}{n}$$
Sample for Standard Deviation of a Single Asset $$S_r = \sqrt{\frac{\sum_{t=1}^{n}\left(r_t - \overline{r}\right)^2}{n-1}}$$	**Estimate Change in Price of a Bond** $$\frac{\Delta P}{P} = -D\left[\frac{\Delta y}{1+y}\right]$$
Geometric Mean $$\sqrt[n]{(1+r_1)\times(1+r_2)\times\dots\times(1+r_n)} - 1$$	**Information Ratio** $$IR = \frac{P - R_B}{\sigma_A}$$
Unbiased Expectations Theory $$_1R_N = [(1 +_1 R_1)(1 + E(_2r_1))\dots(1 + E(_Nr_1))]^{1/N} - 1$$ **Holding Period Return** $$HPR = [(1 + r_1)\times(1 + r_2)\times\dots\times(1 + r_n)] - 1$$	

Definitions of variables and symbols used in CFP Board formula page:

V = intrinsic value of stock as used in constant growth dividend discount model
D_1 = next year's dividend payable by stock in constant growth dividend discount model
r = required rate of return in constant growth dividend discount model; also used to mean expected rate of return in expected return form of dividend discount model
g = growth rate of dividends in constant growth dividend discount model
P = purchase price of targeted stock using expected return form of dividend discount model
COV_{ij} or COV_{im} = covariance between two sample assets ($_{ij}$) or covariance between one sample asset and market or market index ($_{im}$)
P_{ij} or P_{im} = correlation coefficient between two sample assets ($_{ij}$) or correlation coefficient between one sample index and market or market index ($_{im}$)
σ_i = standard deviation of first sample asset
σ_j = standard deviation of second sample asset
σ_p = standard deviation of a portfolio
W_i = weighting percentage of first sample asset in standard deviation of a portfolio formula
W_j = weighting percentage of second sample asset in standard deviation of a portfolio formula
2 = number of sample assets in standard deviation of a portfolio formula
β_i = beta coefficient of sample asset
r_m = market rate of return in capital asset pricing model
β_i = beta coefficient of sample stock or asset in capital asset pricing model
r_p = portfolio rate of return in capital market line theory, Sharpe ratio, Jensen's alpha, and Treynor ratio measures of portfolio performance
S_p = Sharpe ratio measure of portfolio performance
α_p = Jensen's alpha measure of portfolio performance
β_p = beta coefficient of sample portfolio in Jensen's alpha and Treynor ratio measures
T_p = Treynor ratio measure of portfolio performance
D = Macauley duration of a bond
ΔP = change in bond price given a respective change in market interest rates (Δy)
σ_m = standard deviation of market or market line
σ_r = population for standard deviation of a single asset
Σ = Greek sigma meaning multiple number (n) of actual returns
r = average or mean return among multiple number of actual returns (in standard deviation formulas)
s_r = sample for standard deviation of single asset
y = Yield to Maturity
t = Term to Maturity

2

c = Coupon Rate
r_i = required rate of return in capital asset pricing model
r_f = risk-free rate of return in capital asset pricing model, capital market line theory, Sharpe ratio, Jensen's alpha, and Treynor ratio measures of portfolio performance
EAR = effective annual return
TEY = taxable equivalent yield
t = tax rate (as a decimal) in TEY calculation
AM = arithmetic
a = rate of return for given period
$_1R_N$ = rate of return for period N
N = number of periods
$_1R_1$ = interest rate for period 1
$E(_2r_1)$ = expected interest rate for period 2
$E(_Nr_1)$ = expected interest rate for given period
HPR = holding period return

Appendix 3:

Asset Pricing Models

Security Market Line (SML)

$$r_s = r_f + (r_m - r_f)\beta_\iota$$

r_s	= the portfolio expected return
r_f	= the risk-free rate of return
r_m	= the market rate of return
β_ι	= beta, measures the systematic risk associated with a particular portfolio
$(r_m - r_f)$	= market risk premium (the return from the market that exceeds the risk-free rate of return)
$(r_m - r_f)\beta_i$	= the stock risk premium

Characteristic line (CL)

$$r_j = \alpha_j + \beta_j r_m + e$$

r_j	= expected return for asset j
α_j	= y-intercept or constant term
β_j	= the slope of the line (beta)
r_m	= rate of return for the market
e	= error term from the analysis

Multiple Factors or Variables

Arbitrage pricing theory (APT)

$$r_i = a_0 + b_1F_1 + b_2F_2 + \ldots + b_nF_n + e$$

r_i	= expected return from the security
a_0	= risk-free rate of return
b_n	= the sensitivity of the security to factor F_n
F_n	= the factor that affects the security, such as GDP of 3%
e	= the return that is unique to the security. It is also called an error term in some cases. **Note:** This error term should drop out if all relevant factors are captured by the equation.

Measures of Risk

Weighted-average beta

$$\beta_w = \sum_{i=1}^{n}(\beta_i \times \%_i)$$

β_w	= weighted-average beta
β_i	= beta return for security i
$\%_i$	= portion of security i to total portfolio
n	= number of securities

Expected rate of return

$$E(r) = P_1(R_1) + P_2(R_2) + \ldots + P_t(R_t)$$

$E(r)$	= the expected return
P_1	= the probability assigned to the first rate of return
R_1	= the first rate of return
t	= the number of events being examined

Standard deviation of forecasted returns

$$\sigma = \{P_1[r_1 - E(r)]^2 + P_2[r_2 - E(r)]^2 + \ldots + P_t[r_t - E(r)]^2\}^{1/2}$$

$E(r)$	= expected return (calculated)
r_t	= forecasted return for outcome t
P_t	= probability of outcome t

Performance Measures
Summary of Financial Ratios

Liquidity Ratios

Current ratio
$$\frac{\text{Current assets}}{\text{Current liabilities}}$$

Acid test or quick ratio
$$\frac{\text{Current assets} - \text{inventory}}{\text{Current liabilities}}$$

Activity Ratios

Inventory turnover ratio
$$\frac{\text{Cost of goods sold}}{\text{Average inventory}}$$

Average collection period
$$\frac{\text{Receivables}}{\text{Credit sales per day}}$$

Fixed asset turnover
$$\frac{\text{Annual sales}}{\text{Fixed assets}}$$

Profitability Ratios

Operating profit margin
$$\frac{\text{Earnings before interest and taxes}}{\text{Sales}}$$

Net profit margin
$$\frac{\text{Earnings after taxes}}{\text{Sales}}$$

Return on assets (ROA)
$$\frac{\text{Earnings after taxes}}{\text{Total assets}}$$

Return on equity (ROE)
$$\frac{\text{Earnings after taxes}}{\text{Equity}}$$

Leverage Ratios

Debt ratio
$$\frac{\text{Total debt}}{\text{Total assets}}$$

Debt-equity ratio
$$\frac{\text{Total debt}}{\text{Total equity}}$$

Ratios for Bond Analysis*

Times interest earned
$$\frac{\text{Earnings before interest and taxes}}{\text{Annual interest charges}}$$

*Also see inventory turnover and accounts receivables turnover

Ratios for Stock Analysis**

Payout ratio
$$\frac{\text{Dividends}}{\text{Earnings}}$$

Price-to-earnings ratio (basic calculation)
$$\frac{\text{Market price per share}}{\text{Earnings per share}}$$

**Also see ROE, ROA, and gross profit margin

Rates of Return

Holding period return (HPR)

$$\text{HPR} = \frac{\text{ending value of investment} - \text{beginning value of investment} +/- \text{cash flows}}{\text{beginning value of investment}}$$

Internal rate of return (IRR)

$$\text{PV} = \frac{CF_1}{(1+y)^1} + \frac{CF_2}{(1+y)^2} + \ldots + \frac{CF_t}{(1+y)^t}$$

PV   = the present value of the security

CF_t = the cash flow for a particular period

y   = the internal rate of return (discount rate or earnings rate)

t   = the number of cash flows to be evaluated

Yield to maturity (YTM)

$$\text{PV} = \frac{CF_1}{(1+y)^1} + \frac{CF_2}{(1+y)^2} + \ldots + \frac{\text{par value}}{(1+y)^t}$$

PV   = the present value of the security

CF_t = the cash flow for a particular period

y   = discount rate per period—yield to maturity

t   = the number of cash flows to be evaluated

Yield to call (YTC)

$$\text{PV} = \frac{CF_1}{(1+y)^1} + \frac{CF_2}{(1+y)^2} + \ldots + \frac{\text{call price}}{(1+y)^t}$$

PV   = the present value of the security

CF_t = the cash flow for period t

y   = the discount rate per period—yield to call

t   = the number of periods until the call date

Arithmetic mean

$$\text{AM} = \frac{\sum_{t=1}^{n} \text{HPR}_t}{n}$$

Time-weighted return

$$PV = \frac{CF_1}{(1+y)^1} + \frac{CF_2}{(1+y)^2} + \ldots + \frac{CF_t}{(1+y)^t}$$

PV	= the value of the security today
CF_t	= the cash flow for period t
y	= the discount rate based on the security type
t	= the number of cash flows to be evaluated

Note: Time-weighted return considers cash flows of investment only and does not consider cash flows of the investor.

Geometric mean

$$\sqrt[n]{(1+r_1)(1+r_2)(1+r_3)\ldots(1+r_n)} - 1$$

r_n	= return for each period
n	= number of periods

Real return (inflation adjusted)

$$\left[\frac{(1+R_n)}{(1+I)} - 1\right] \times 100$$

R_n = the absolute return

I = the rate of inflation for the period

Weighted-average return

$$\overline{X_w} = \sum_{i=1}^{N} [(R_i)(\%_i)]$$

$\overline{X_w}$	= weighted average
R_i	= return for security i
$\%_i$	= portion of security i to total portfolio
N	= number of securities

Valuation Models

The basic present value (valuation) model

$$PV = \frac{CF_1}{(1+y)^1} + \frac{CF_2}{(1+y)^2} + \ldots + \frac{CF_t}{(1+y)^t}$$

PV   = the present value of the security

CF_t = the cash flow for a particular period

y   = the discount rate based on the type of security and risk level of the investment

t   = the number of cash flows to be evaluated

Discounted Free Cash Flow Model

$$V = \frac{FCFE_1}{r-g} = \frac{FCFE_0 \times (1+g)}{r-g}$$

V   = intrinsic value

$FCFE_0$ = free cash flow to equity in current year

$FCFE_1$ = free cash flow to equity in period 1

r   = required rate of return

g   = growth rate

Capitalized earnings

$$V = \frac{E}{R_D}$$

V   = the estimated value of the company or firm

E   = the earnings for the company or firm

R_D = the discount (capitalization) rate

Perpetuity

$$V = \frac{D_1}{r}$$

V   = intrinsic value of the stock

D_1 = dividend paid at the end of period 1

r   = investor's required rate of return

* Conversion Value

$$CV = \frac{Par}{CP} \times P_s$$

CV   = conversion value

CP   = conversion price of the security

P_s = current market price of the security

Notes: Par = $1,000, CV is also used to denote Coefficient of Variation.

Notes

Notes

Notes

Notes

Notes

Notes

Notes

Notes